AMERICAN SCHOOL OF NEEDLEWORK

PRESENTS

The Great CROCHET Bazaar Book

President: Jean Leinhauser
Director of Marketing and Book Coordinator: Rita Weiss
Editorial Director: Mary Thomas
Art Director: Carol Wilson Mansfield
Operations Vice President: Irmgard Barnes

Photography by Stemo Photography, Inc., Northbrook, Illinois
Roderick A. Stemo, President
James E. Zorn, Photographer

Book design by CBG Graphics
Carol Belanger Grafton, Designer

STERLING PUBLISHING CO., INC. NEW YORK

We have made every effort to ensure the accuracy and completeness of the instructions in this book.
We cannot, however, be responsible for human error, typographical mistakes or variations in individual work.

Copyright © 1982 by the American School of Needlework, Inc.
Published by Sterling Publishing Co., Inc.
Two Park Avenue, New York, N. Y. 10016
Available in Canada from Oak Tree Press, Ltd.
c/o Canadian Manda Group, 215 Lakeshore Boulevard East
Toronto, Ontario M5A 3W9
Manufactured in the United States of America
Library of Congress Catalog Card No.: 81-85030
Sterling ISBN 0-8069-5456-6

Introduction

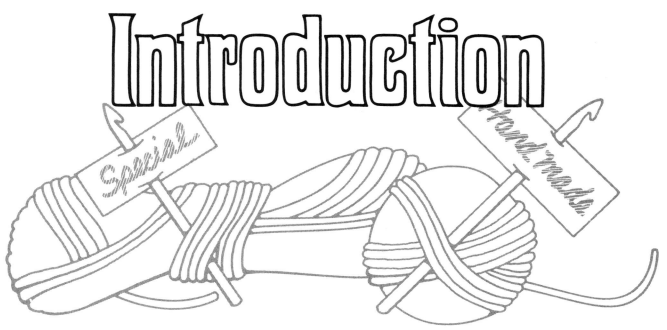

Come visit with us at our bazaar!

Stop at the colorful tables and see the fascinating items we have created for you. Whether you're making projects to sell at your church or school fair, or if you're just looking for enticing ideas, you are certain to find a crochet pattern in our bazaar to delight you.

Just inside the door, you'll find the "Basic Bazaar." Stop here if you need a review course in crochet basics. We've also included some simple instructions on working with crochet thread and a steel hook. Several of our patterns require this, and the technique is slightly different, but easy to learn. You'll also find a listing of the abbreviations and symbols used in the rest of our bazaar.

Our "Baby Bazaar" holds some wonderfully old-fashioned baby items—a complete layette, a baby's ribbon bonnet—and some more modern needs: a bottle holder, a pair of rattle toys.

Our "Fashion Bazaar" has some simple items of apparel. Anyone can wear them because most require no complicated sizing: elegant lace collars, warm slippers, a lacy shawl.

Stop at the "Home Sweet Home Bazaar" and find patterns for afghans, placemats, wall and window hangings, pillows and doilies—projects to decorate everyone's home.

Don't miss the "Kid's Bazaar" with its wonderful toys for all of the children on your list: two life-size dolls that can wear toddler two clothes, a cuddly baby doll, a funny frog—even a football player and cheerleader, wearing the school colors, for your teenagers.

Before you leave the bazaar, be sure to stop at our "Just For Fun" table. Here you'll find those zany items that bazaars are noted for: a cactus garden, a sunflower hand puppet, a turtle pincushion—and a complete mouse wedding party with charming little mouse figures costumed for the mouse nuptials.

We know you'll enjoy making our bazaar items, and we hope your bazaar will be a grand success.

Jean Leinhauser

Jean Leinhauser, *President*
American School of Needlework
3681 Commercial Drive
Northbrook, Illinois 60062

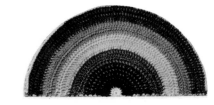

ACKNOWLEDGMENTS

Several designs in this book were originally created by us for the American Thread Company, Stamford, Connecticut, and were copyrighted by them. It is with their kind permission that we are able to include those designs in this book.

To ensure the accuracy and clarity of our instructions, all of the projects in this book were tested by a group of dedicated and hardworking women, who made the designs which we have photographed. We express our appreciation to the following group of pattern testers:

Irene Beitner, Berwyn, IL
Judy Demain, Highland Park, IL
Eleanor Denner, Pontiac, MO
Joan Kokaska, Wildwood, IL
Barbara Luoma, Largo, FL
Margaret Miller, Chicago, IL
Karen Moe, Buffalo Grove, IL
Wanda Parker, Mundelein, IL
Cindy Raymond, Vernon Hills, IL
Kathie Schroeder, Tucson, AZ
Mary Thomas, Libertyville, IL

We also acknowledge our thanks and appreciation to the following contributing designers:

Nannette M. Berkley, Antioch, IL
Judy Demain, Highland Park, IL
Eleanor Denner, Pontiac, MO
Nancy Dent, Des Plaines, IL
Ernestine H. Giesecke, Chicago, IL
Louise Kocka, Azuza, CA
Joan Kokaska, Wildwood, IL
Jean Leinhauser, Glenview, IL
Joyce Wallace Lerner, Riverwoods, IL
Carol Wilson Mansfield, Northbrook, IL
Sue Penrod, Loveland, CO
Kathie Schroeder, Tucson, AZ
Mary Thomas, Libertyville, IL

Contents

Basic Bazaar

CROCHETING

CHAIN (ch)

Crochet always starts with a basic chain. To begin, make a slip loop on hook (*Fig 1*), leaving a 4″ tail of yarn.

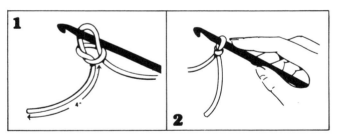

STEP 1: Take hook in right hand, holding it between thumb and third finger (*Fig 2*), and rest index finger near tip of hook.

STEP 2: Take slip loop in thumb and index finger of left hand (*Fig 3*) and bring yarn over third finger of left hand, catching it loosely at left palm with remaining two fingers.

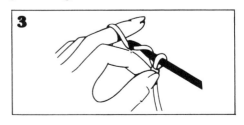

STEP 3: Bring yarn over hook from back to front (*Fig 4*), and draw through loop on hook.

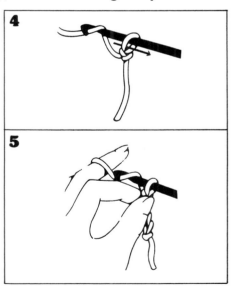

One chain made. Repeat Step 3 for each additional chain desired, moving your left thumb and index finger up close to the hook after each stitch or two (*Fig 5*).

When counting number of chains, do not count the loop on the hook or the starting slip knot.

SINGLE CROCHET (sc)

First, make a chain to desired length.

STEP 1: Insert hook in top loop of 2nd chain from hook (*Fig 6*); hook yarn (bring yarn over hook from back to front) and draw through (*Fig 7*).

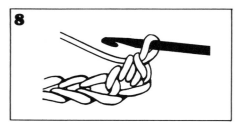

STEP 2: Hook yarn and draw through 2 loops on hook (*Fig 8*).

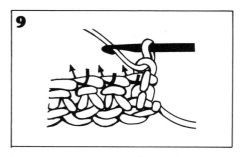

One single crochet made. Work a single crochet (repeat Steps 1 and 2) in each remaining chain.

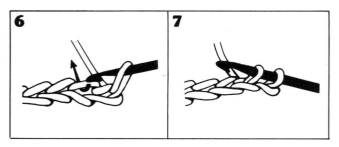

To work additional rows, chain 1 and turn work counterclockwise. Inserting hook under 2 loops of the stitch (*Fig 9*), work a single crochet (as before) in each stitch across.

DOUBLE CROCHET (dc)

Double crochet is a taller stitch than single crochet. Begin by making a chain to desired length.

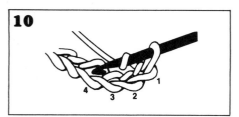

STEP 1: Bring yarn once over the hook; insert hook in the top loop of the 4th chain from hook (*Fig 10*). Hook yarn and draw through (*Fig 11*).

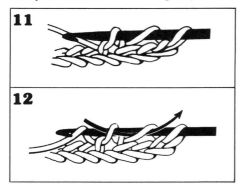

STEP 2: Hook yarn and draw through first 2 loops on hook (*Fig 12*).

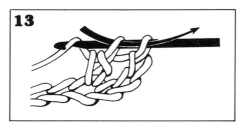

STEP 3: Hook yarn and draw through last 2 loops on hook (*Fig 13*).

One double crochet made. Work a double crochet (repeat Steps 1 through 3) in each remaining chain.

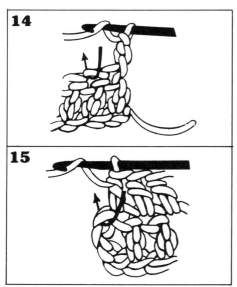

To work additional rows, make 3 chains and turn work counterclockwise. Beginning in 2nd stitch (*Fig 14*—3 chains count as first double crochet), work a double crochet (as before) in each stitch across (remember to insert hook under 2 top loops of stitch). At end of row, work last double crochet in the top chain of chain-3 (**Fig 15**).

HALF DOUBLE CROCHET (hdc)

This stitch eliminates one step of double crochet—hence its name. It is taller than single crochet, but shorter than double crochet. Begin by making a chain to desired length.

STEP 1: Bring yarn over hook; insert hook in top loop of 3rd chain from hook, hook yarn and draw through (3 loops now on hook).

STEP 2: Hook yarn and draw through all 3 loops on hook (**Fig 16**).

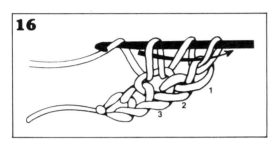

One half double crochet made. Work a half double crochet (repeat Steps 1 and 2) in each remaining chain.

To work additional rows, make 2 chains and turn work counterclockwise. Beginning in 2nd stitch (2 chains count as first half double crochet), work a half double crochet (as before) in each stitch across. At end of row, work last half double crochet in the top chain of chain-2.

TRIPLE CROCHET (trc)

Triple crochet is a tall stitch that works up quickly. First, make a chain to desired length.

STEP 1: Bring yarn twice over the hook, insert hook in 5th chain from hook (**Fig 17**); hook yarn and draw through (**Fig 18**).

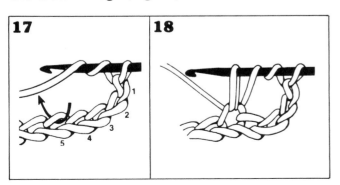

STEP 2: Hook yarn and draw through first 2 loops on hook (**Fig 19**).

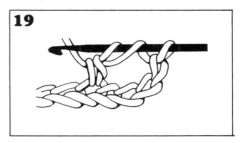

STEP 3: Hook yarn and draw through next 2 loops on hook (**Fig 20**).

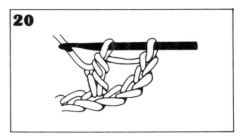

STEP 4: Hook yarn and draw through remaining 2 loops on hook (**Fig 21**).

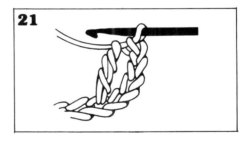

One triple crochet made. Work a triple crochet (repeat Steps 1 through 4) in each remaining chain.

To work additional rows, make 4 chains and turn work counterclockwise. Beginning in 2nd stitch (4 chains count as first triple crochet), work a triple crochet (as before) in each stitch across. At end of row, work last triple crochet in the top chain of chain-4.

SLIP STITCH (sl st)

This is the shortest of all crochet stitches, and usually is used to join work, or to move yarn across a group of stitches without adding height. To practice, make a chain to desired length; then work one row of double crochets.

STEP 1: Insert hook in first st; hook yarn and draw through both stitch and loop on hook in one motion. (**Fig 22**).

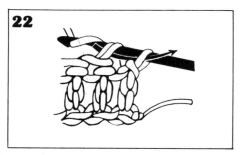

22

One slip stitch made. Work a slip stitch (repeat Step 1) in each stitch across.

DECREASING (dec)

To dec in single crochet: (pull up loop in next st) twice; YO and through all 3 loops = 1 sc decreased. To dec in double crochet: YO hook, pull up loop in next st, YO and through 2 loops; YO, pull up loop in next st, YO and through 2 loops; YO and through all 3 loops = 1 dc decreased.

INCREASING (inc)

In either single or double crochet, work 2 sts in same st = 1 st increased.

ABBREVIATIONS

beg	begin(ning)
ch(s)	chain(s)
dc	double crochet(s)
dec	decrease (-ing)
EOR	every other row
fig	figure
hdc	half double crochet(s)
inc	increase (-ing)
lp(s)	loop(s)
patt	pattern
prev	previous
rem	remain(ing)
rep	repeat(ing)
rnd(s)	round(s)
sc	single crochet(s)
sk	skip
sl	slip
sl st(s)	slip stitch(es)
sp(s)	space(s)
st(s)	stitch(es)
tch	turning chain
tog	together
trc	triple crochet(s)
YO	yarn over

work even: This term in instructions means to continue working in the pattern as established, without increasing or decreasing.

SYMBOLS

* An asterisk is used to mark the beginning of a portion of instructions which will be worked more than once; thus, "rep from * twice" means after working the instructions once, repeat the instructions following the asterisk twice more (3 times in all).

† The dagger identifies a portion of instructions that will be repeated again later in the pattern.

= The number after an equal sign at the end of a row/rnd indicates the number of stitches you should have when the row/rnd has been completed.

( ) Parentheses are used to enclose instructions which should be worked the exact number of times specified immediately following the parentheses, such as: (ch 3, dc) twice. They are also used to set off and clarify a group of sts that are to be worked all into the same sp or st, such as: (2 dc, ch 1, 2 dc) in corner sp.

[ ] Brackets and ( ) parentheses are used to provide additional information to clarify instructions.

GAUGE

It is essential to achieve the gauge—number of stitches and rows per inch—given in patt in order to make the correct size.

Before beginning your project, refer to the Gauge Note and make a gauge swatch using the hook and yarn specified. Work several rows; finish off. Place work on a flat surface and measure sts in center of piece. If you have more sts to the inch than specified, use a larger size hook. If you have less sts to the inch than specified, use a smaller size hook. Then make another gauge swatch and check your gauge once again. **Do not hesitate to change hook size to obtain the specified gauge.** Often you will not be able to achieve gauge with the size hook recommended.

While working, continue to check your gauge. Select sts/rnds near the center of your work, using small safety pins or straight pins to identify the sts to be measured and always measure over two or more inches.

POMPON

Cut 2 cardboard circles, each the diameter of finished pompon measurement, plus ½". Cut a hole in the center of each circle, approx ½" diameter. Thread a tapestry needle with 72" length of yarn, doubled. Holding both circles tog, insert needle through center hole, over outside edge, through center again until entire circle is covered. Thread more lengths of yarn as needed. (*Fig 23*)

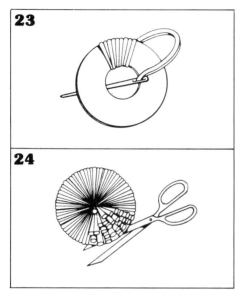

With very sharp scissors, cut yarn between the 2 circles all around the circumference (*Fig 24*). Using 12" strand of yarn doubled, slip yarn between circles, pull up tightly and tie very firmly. Remove cardboards and fluff out pompon by rolling it between your hands. Trim evenly with scissors.

NOTE: If diameter of pompon is less than 1", wrap yarn around tines of a dinner fork; then tie wrapped yarn securely between the center of the tines. Fluff and trim as for normal size pompon.

TWISTED CORD

STEP 1: Cut specified number of strands of yarn, each 4 times the finished specified cord length.

STEP 2: Make a single loop at each end of strands, sufficient in size to slip over a door knob or onto a hook for anchoring.

STEP 3: Place one loop on knob or hook.

STEP 4: Slip other loop at opposite end on index finger (or several fingers depending on loop size), or onto a pencil.

STEP 5: Holding strands taut, twist strands to your right until there is a firm even twist (slightly kinky) along the entire length.

STEP 6: Keeping strands taut, fold twisted strands in half lengthwise, slipping loop off index finger or pencil and onto knob or hook with other looped end.

STEP 7: Form cord by smoothing the twisted strands doubled in a downward direction from knob or hook between the thumb and finger.

STEP 8: Cut off looped ends. Knot each end of cord; trim ends evenly.

USING A STEEL CROCHET HOOK

A number of projects in this book are made with crochet cotton and steel hooks. Here are some special hints on working with these materials, in case they are new to you.

GETTING STARTED

Rule number 1 is—don't be afraid! You will be using exactly the same stitches you're familiar with, but if you've not worked with smaller hooks and finer thread before, you are going to feel clumsy and awkward at first. For an experienced crocheter, this is a bit of a surprise—suddenly feeling all thumbs again just as when you first learned to crochet. But this will pass in a few hours of crocheting, as you adjust your tension and working method to the new tools. Soon you will work much more by feel than when working with the heavier yarns. So be patient with any initial clumsiness and confusion—they won't be with you long.

STEEL HOOKS

Steel hooks are 5" long—shorter than the aluminum or plastic hooks—and range in size from 00 (large) to 14 (very fine). They are shaped as shown in *Fig 25*. There is the throat, then the shank, and after the shank the steel begins to widen again before it reaches the finger grip. When crocheting, it is important that the stitches do not slide beyond the shank

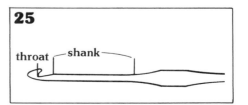

as this will cause a loose tension and alter the gauge. If you find you have difficulty at first, put a piece of cellophane tape around the hook to keep the stitches from sliding past the correct area. With practice, you will work in the right place automatically.

GAUGE

As in all crochet, it is essential that you achieve the gauge specified for each project—that is, the exact number of stitches and rows per inch specified in the instructions; or, if the project is made up of motifs, that your finished square, circle, or whatever, has the exact measurements given. If you do not achieve the exact gauge, your project will not be the correct size and you may not have sufficient thread to complete your project. **Do not hesitate to change hook size to obtain the gauge specified.**

FINISHING TECHNIQUES

When your project is completed, special care and treatment may be needed to add that finished "professional" look. Most often, pressing or a light starching is all that is required. To do this, spread the finished piece out on a flat padded surface (covered with terry toweling), having wrong side facing up. Use a warm iron and press through a damp pressing cloth, or use a commercial spray starch and spray until damp. Let dry thoroughly before removing.

If further blocking is required because of shape and texture, insert rust-proof pins along outside edges or as needed to hold in shape. Then thoroughly dampen project with sponge or cloth dipped in water. Let dry completely before removing pins.

For a stiffer finish, use a solution of a commercial boilable starch (spray starches won't do the job) or a sugar-and-water starch that was traditionally used for old-fashioned doilies as follows: Mix ½ cup each of granulated sugar and water in a small pan; heat to boiling. Immediately remove from heat; cool to room temperature. First dip in warm water, then immerse in starch. Remove from starch (very wet—don't wring out the starch). Smooth out into shape on a padded surface (pin with rust-proof pins, if necessary) and let dry completely.

If your finished project should need washing, use warm water and a mild soap. Wash gently; do not rub, twist or wring. Rinse thoroughly in warm water. Pin out and let dry as previously explained.

Baby Bazaar

RIBBON BABY BONNET

designed by Nancy Dent

Crochet this tiny bonnet, then weave colorful ribbon through the spaces—to create a lovely gift to charm any new mother.

Size

Bonnet is designed for ages 3 to 9 months, weight approx 11 to 18 pounds

Materials

Bedspread-weight crochet cotton in 250-yd ball:
    1 white
Steel crochet hooks sizes 5 and 8 (or size required for gauge)
¼" wide satin ribbon:
    2½ yds each of blue, green, lilac, pink and yellow
1" wide satin ribbon:
    1½ yds white
sewing thread:
    1½ yds white

Gauge

With size 5 hook, in mesh patt, (dc, ch 2) 4 times plus 1 dc = 1"; in dc, 9 sts = 1"; 4 rows = 1"
(NOTE: It is important that you achieve both st and row gauge; if rows are not the proper height, the ribbons will not lie flat after weaving. To check

gauge, use size 5 hook and ch 25; dc in 4th ch from hook, dc in each rem ch across. Work 10 rows even (23 dc each row). Your gauge swatch should measure 2½" square.)

Instructions

Beg at back of bonnet with size 5 hook, ch 8; join with a sl st to form a ring.

Rnd 1: Ch 3, 23 dc in ring; join with a sl st in top of beg ch-3. You should have 24 dc, counting beg ch-3 as 1 dc here and throughout.

Rnd 2: Ch 5, do not turn; mark for right side of work. * Dc in next dc, ch 2; rep from * around, join with a sl st in 3rd ch of beg ch-5 = 24 dc.

Rnd 3: Sl st in next sp, ch 5, do not turn; * dc in next sp, ch 2; rep from around, join as before = 24 sps.

Rnd 4: Sl st in next sp, ch 5, do not turn; work (dc, ch 2, dc) all in next sp [inc made]; ch 2, * dc in next sp, ch 2; work inc of (dc, ch 2, dc) in next sp, ch 2; rep from * 10 times more, join with a sl st in 3rd ch of beg ch-5 = 36 sps.

Rnd 5: Sl st in next sp, ch 5, do not turn; * dc in next sp, ch 2; rep from * around, join as before.

Rnd 6: Sl st in next sp, ch 5, do not turn; dc in same sp, ch 2; * (dc in next sp, ch 2) twice; inc as before in next sp, ch 2; rep from * 10 times more, work (dc, ch 2) in each of last 2 sps, join as before = 48 sps.

Rnd 7: Rep Rnd 5.

Rnd 8: Sl st in next sp, ch 5, do not turn; dc in same sp, ch 2; * (dc in next sp, ch 2) 3 times, inc in next sp, ch 2; rep from * 10 times more, work (dc, ch 2) in each of last 3 sps, join as before = 60 sps.

Rnd 9: Sl st in next sp, ch 5, do not turn; * dc in next sp, ch 2; rep from * 50 times more, dc in next sp. You will now work in rows, turning at beg of each row. [Rem 7 sps are left unworked for back of neck.]

CROWN: Row 1: Ch 3, turn; dc in first sp, ch 2; * dc in next sp, ch 2; rep from * 49 times more, dc in last sp (under Tch), dc in 3rd ch of ch-5 (Tch) = 51 sps.

Row 2: Ch 5, turn; sk first dc, * dc in next sp, ch 2; rep from * across, ending dc in last sp, ch 2, sk last dc, dc in top of Tch = 52 sps.

Rows 3 through 13: Rep Rows 1 and 2 five times, then rep Row 1 once more.

Rows 14 through 17: Change to size 8 hook; rep Rows 2 and 1 twice. Do not finish off; you will now be working into sps along neck edge.

NECK EDGE AND FRONT TRIM: Row 1: Ch 3, turn work slightly and work 2 dc in sp at end of each row of Crown [37 dc]; 2 dc in each of 7 sps left unworked for back neck edge [14 dc]; 2 dc in sp at end of each row of Crown to last row, 3 dc in last sp [37 dc]; use a small safety pin and mark last dc just made. You should have 88 dc.

Row 2: Ch 3, turn; dc in each dc across, ending dc in top of Tch. You will work in rnds along neck and front edge.

Rnd 1: Ch 3, turn; dc in each dc across neck edge, dc in top of Tch; ch 3, work a shell of (3 dc, ch 2, 3 dc) in marked st; sk the first sp on Crown, work a shell in next dc of Crown; * sk 1 dc, shell in next dc; rep from * 23 times more, work a shell in last sp on Crown; shell in dc at end of first row of Neck Edge Trim; join with a sl st in top of beg ch-3 = 28 shells.

Rnd 2: Ch 1, do not turn; sc in same sp as joining and in every dc along neck edge; across shells, sc in each dc and in each ch-2 sp; join with a sl st in beg sc. Finish off.

Finishing

Steam lightly on wrong side. Beg at center back and weave ribbons through each rnd and row, repeating this sequence: lilac, green, blue, yellow, pink. To weave, place a small safety pin in the end of ribbon and weave in and out of sps, leaving a 1" hem allowance on each end of ribbon. **Do not cut ribbon until finished weaving.** Fit ribbon as desired, remembering it will not stretch after tacking. Cut ribbon, turning under twice for hem, and pin each end to bottom edge of bonnet on inside. After all ribbons are in place, tack on inside with white sewing thread, stretching slightly as you stitch.

TIES (*make 2*): Cut white ribbon in half, cut a V-shaped notch into one end of each piece. At other end of each piece, make a half bow as shown in **Fig 1**; sew firmly to each corner of bonnet.

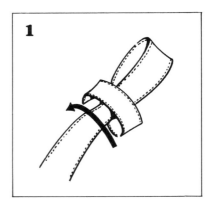

BABY'S BOTTLE HOLDER

designed by Sue Penrod

This crib favorite is just the right thing for the new baby. Our charming clown cradles baby's bottle while delighting him with his bright colors and sunny smile.

Size

Approx 11″ tall with hat

Materials

American Thread Dawn Sayelle Knitting Worsted Size Yarn:
  ½ oz each of baby blue and nile green
  ¼ oz each of white, black, lemon and flame
Size J aluminum crochet hook (or size required for gauge)
Polyester fiber (*for stuffing*)
Small felt pieces in red and black
Tracing paper and pencil
White craft glue

Gauge

In sc, in back lp of sts, 7 sts = 2″; 8 rnds = 2½″

Instructions

BODY RING: With baby blue, ch 20, join with a sl st to form a ring.

Rnd 1: Sc in each ch around = 20 sc. [*NOTE: Do not join; work continuous rnds. Mark first st of rnd (use small safety pin or piece of yarn in contrasting color); move marker at beg of each rnd.*]

Rnd 2: Sc **in back lp** (*lp away from you*) in each sc around.

Rnds 3 through 16: Rep Rnd 2, 14 times. At end of Rnd 16, change to nile green in last sc. [**To change color: Work last sc until 2 lps rem on hook; finish off baby blue, tie in nile green (leave ends on inside of ring); with nile green, YO and draw through 2 lps on hook = color changed.**]

Rnds 17 through 32: With nile green, rep Rnd 2, 16 times.

At end of Rnd 32, finish off, leaving approx 18″ sewing length. Stuff and shape body into a ring. Thread sewing length into tapestry or yarn needle and sew ends of ring tog.

HEAD AND COLLAR: With white, ch 4, join with a sl st to form a ring.

Rnd 1: Work 3 sc in each ch around = 12 sc. [*NOTE: Do not join; mark first st of rnd (as before).*]

Rnd 2: Work 2 sc **in both lps** in each sc around = 24 sc. (*NOTE: Continue by working in both lps of sts.*)

Rnd 3: Sc in each sc around.

Rnds 4 through 8: Rep Rnd 3, 5 times.

Rnd 9: * Sc in each of next 2 sc, sk one sc, sc in next sc; rep from * around = 18 sc.

Rnd 10: * Sc in next sc, sk one sc, sc in next sc; rep from * around = 12 sc. Stuff and shape head.

Rnd 11: * Sk next sc, sc in next sc; rep from * around, changing to nile green in last sc (leave approx 18″ end of nile green for sewing head to body later). Continue with collar as follows.

COLLAR: Rnd 1: With nile green, sl st in next sc, ch 3 (counts as first dc), 2 dc in same st; 3 dc in each of rem 5 sc, join with a sl st in top of beg ch-3 = 18 dc.

Rnd 2: Ch 3, do not turn; 2 dc in same st as joining, 3 dc **in back lp** in each rem dc around; join with a sl st in top of beg ch-3 = 54 dc.

Finish off; weave in end. Thread beg length of nile green into tapestry or yarn needle. Position head with attached collar on top of body ring (opposite end from where ends were sewn tog to form the ring). Working under collar, sew head in place.

HAT: With nile green, leave approx 16″ end for sewing hat to head later, ch 24, join with a sl st to form a ring (be careful not to twist chain).

Rnd 1: Sc in each ch around = 24 sc. [NOTE: Do not join; mark first st of rnd (as before).] Continue by working **in back lp** of sts.

Rnd 2: * Sc in each of next 2 sc, sk one sc, sc in next sc; rep from * around = 18 sc.

Rnd 3: Sc in each sc around.

Rnd 4: * Sc in next sc, sk one sc, sc in next sc, rep from * around = 12 sc.

Rnds 5 and 6: Rep Rnds 3 and 4. At end of Rnd 6, you should have 8 sc.

Rnd 7: Rep Rnd 3.

Rnd 8: * Sk next sc, sc in next sc; rep from * around = 4 sc.

Finish off; weave in this end. Then continue with edging as follows.

RUFFLED EDGING: Hold hat with foundation chain edge across top. With baby blue, make a slip knot on hook; join with a sc in any st around edge. Ch 3, * sc in next st, ch 3; rep from * around, join with a sl st in beg sc. Finish off; weave in baby blue ends. Thread beg length of nile green into tapestry or yarn needle. Working under ruffled edging, sew hat to top of head.

FEET (make 2): Beg at center bottom, with black, ch 4, join with a sl st to form a ring.

Rnd 1: Ch 3, work 4 dc in each ch around, join with a sl st in top of beg ch-3. Continue by working **in both lps** of sts.

Rnd 2: Ch 3, do not turn; * work dc dec. **[To work dc dec: Yo and draw up a lp in next dc, YO and draw through 2 lps on hook (2 lps now on hook); YO and draw up a lp in next dc. YO and draw through 2 lps on hook (3 lps now on hook); YO and draw through all 3 lps on hook = dc dec made.]** Rep from * 7 times more, join with a sl st in top of beg ch-3.

Finish off, leaving approx 12″ end. Thread into tapestry or yarn needle; weave through sts of last rnd and draw up tightly. Then sew center of foot to bottom of body ring on one side of color change.

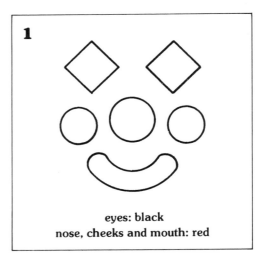

1

eyes: black
nose, cheeks and mouth: red

FACIAL FEATURES: Trace outlines in *Fig 1* on paper. Cut outlines and use as patterns on felt as indicated. (NOTE: To prevent pattern pieces from slipping on felt, tape pieces in place with cellophane tape; then cut felt through tape and discard tape.) With glue, attach felt pieces as shown in photo. If desired, use matching sewing thread and sew with overcast st around outside edges of felt pieces to secure.

POMPONS: Following instructions on page 11, use flame and make two 1″ diameter pompons. Attach one pompon on each side of head, just below hat. Then with lemon, make three ½″ diameter pompons. Attach one pompon to top of hat, and then attach one pompon to center of body at each color change.

BABY'S RATTLE TOYS

designed by Sue Penrod

Two adorable toys—a charming pig and a circus bear—have bases of plastic tubs with popcorn kernels inside. Just the right size for little hands to hold and shake. Made with worsted weight yarn.

CIRCUS BEAR

Size

Approx 11″ tall (with hat)

Materials

Worsted weight yarn:
    2 oz brown
    2 oz orange
    ½ oz yellow
    4 yds black

Size H aluminum crochet hook (or size required for gauge)
White plastic bowl with lid (4 oz non-dairy whipped topping size) filled with ½ cup of popcorn kernels (*for rattle*)
Polyester fiber (*for stuffing*)
Small felt pieces in black and white
Tracing paper and pencil
White craft glue
Size 16 tapestry needle or yarn needle

Gauge

In sc, 7 sts = 2″

Instructions

(*NOTE: Body, tutu, collar and head are made in one piece.*)

17

BODY: Beg at bottom, with brown, ch 4; join with sl st to form a ring.

Rnd 1: Work 2 sc in each ch around = 8 sc. [NOTE: Do not join; work continuous rnds (without joining). Use a small safety pin or piece of yarn in contrasting color and mark first st of rnd. Move marker at beg of each rnd.]

Rnd 2: Working **in back lp** (lp away from you— **Fig 1**) of each sc (now and on each following rnd, unless otherwise specified), work 2 sc in each sc around = 16 sc.

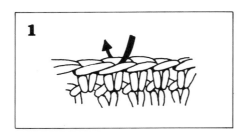

Rnd 3: Work 2 sc in each sc around = 32 sc.

Rnd 4: * Sc in next sc, 2 sc in next sc; rep from * around = 48 sc.

Rnds 5 through 16: Work 12 rnds even in sc on 48 sts. At end of Rnd 16, pull up lp on hook to approx 4"; remove hook from lp (do not cut yarn) and work tutu as follows.

TUTU: Rnd 1: Working **in front lp** (lp toward you) of each sc, join orange with a sl st in next sc, ch 1, sc in same st as joining; sc in each rem sc around, join with a sl st **in both lps** of beg sc.

Rnd 2: Turn. Working **in back lp** of each sc, work (sl st, ch 3, 2 dc) in next sc, 3 dc in each rem sc around; join with a sl st in top of beg ch-3.

Rnd 3: Do not turn. Working **in back lp** of each dc, ch 3, dc in next dc and in each rem dc around; join with a sl st in top of beg ch-3.

Rnd 4: Do not turn. Working **in back lp** of each dc, ch 1, sc in same st as joining; sc in each rem dc around, join with a sl st **in both lps** of beg sc. Finish off; weave in orange yarn ends. Return to last rnd of body; insert hook in dropped brown lp and pull lp taut on hook. Then work as follows.

BODY CONTINUED: Rnd 17: Working **in back lp** of each sc (front lps were used for tutu), sc in each sc around = 48 sc. (Remember to mark first st of rnd; do not join rnds.) Continue to work **in back lp** of sts, unless otherwise specified.

Rnds 18 through 24: Work 7 rnds even in sc on 48 sts. At end of Rnd 24, insert bowl filled with popcorn kernels into body, having lid at top.

Rnd 25 (marking rnd): (NOTE: In this rnd, 2 sts

are marked for sewing arms to body later.) Work (sc in each of next 3 sc, sk one sc) 3 times. In next sc, work sc in back lp and mark front lp (use marker different from beg of rnd). Sc in each of next 2 sc, sk one sc; work (sc in each of next 3 sc, sk one sc) 4 times; sc in each of next 2 sc, sk one sc. In next sc, work sc in back lp and mark front lp. Work (sc in each of next 3 sc, sk one sc) 3 times = 36 sc.

Rnd 26: * Sc in each of next 2 sc, sk one sc; rep from * around = 24 sc. Before working next rnd, lightly stuff and shape body. (NOTE: Stuffing should not be visible through the sts.)

Rnd 27 (neck shaping): * Sc in next sc, sk one sc; rep from * around = 12 sc.

Rnd 28 (neck shaping): Work 2 sc in each sc around = 24 sc. Pull up lp on hook to approx 4"; remove hook from lp (do not cut yarn) and work collar as follows.

COLLAR: Rnds 1 and 2: With yellow, rep Rnds 1 and 2 of Tutu instructions.

Rnd 3: Do not turn. Working **in back lp** of each dc, ch 1, sl st in next dc and in each rem dc around; join with a sl st in beg ch-1. Finish off; weave in yellow yarn ends. Return to last rnd of body; insert hook in dropped brown lp and pull taut on hook. Then work head as follows.

HEAD: Rnd 1: Working **in back lp** of each sc (front lps were used for collar), * sc in next sc, 2 sc in next sc; rep from * around = 36 sc. (Remember to mark first st of rnd; do not join rnds.) Continue to work **in back lp** of sts, unless otherwise specified.

Rnds 2 through 9: Work 8 rnds even in sc on 36 sts.

Rnd 10: * Sc in each of next 3 sc, sk one sc; rep from * around = 27 sc.

Rnd 11: * Sc in each of next 2 sc, sk one sc; rep from * around = 18 sc. Before working next rnd, lightly stuff and shape head.

Rnd 12: * Sc in next sc, sk one sc; rep from * around = 9 sc. Finish off, leaving approx 6" sewing length. Thread into tapestry or yarn needle; weave through sts of last rnd. Draw up tightly and fasten securely.

ARMS (make 2): With brown, leave approx 12" end for sewing arm to body later, ch 14; join with a sl st to form a ring, being careful not to twist chain.

Rnd 1: Sc in each ch around = 14 sc. (NOTE: Do not join; mark first st of rnd and move marker on each following rnd.)

Rnd 2: Sc **in both lps** of each sc around.

Rnds 3 through 10: Rep Rnd 2, 8 times.

Rnd 11: * Sc **in both lps** of next sc, sk one sc; rep from * around = 7 sc.

Rnd 12: * Sl st **in both lps** of next sc, sk one sc; rep from * twice more, sl st **in both lps** of last sc = 4 sl sts. Finish off, leaving approx 6" end. Thread into tapestry or yarn needle; weave through sts of last rnd. Draw up tightly and fasten securely. Lightly stuff and shape arm. Thread beg sewing length into tapestry or yarn needle. Sew opening closed, carefully matching 7 corresponding sts across. Then sew this edge to side of body below marker. (*NOTE: Between arms, there should be 24 sc across the back and 22 sc across the front of the bear.*)

HAT: Beg at top, with orange, ch 4; join with a sl st to form a ring.

Rnd 1: Work 2 sc in each ch around = 8 sc. (*NOTE: Do not join; mark first st of rnd and move marker on each following rnd.*)

Rnd 2: Working **in back lp** of each sc (*now and on each following rnd*), * sc in next sc, 2 sc in next sc; rep from * around = 12 sc.

Rnd 3: Sc in each sc around.

Rnd 4: * Sc in next sc, 2 sc in next sc; rep from * around = 18 sc.

Rnds 5 and 6: Work 2 rnds even in sc on 18 sts.

Rnds 7 (edging): Work (ch 4, sc) in each sc around to last sc, join with a sl st in last sc. Finish off, leaving approx 12" sewing length. Thread into tapestry or yarn needle; sew hat to top of head in 2nd rnd from top. Make ¾" diameter yellow pompon (see page 11) and attach securely to top of hat.

EARS (*make 2*): With brown, ch 4. Working under 2 top threads of each ch, work (sc, hdc, dc) in 2nd ch from hook; work 5 tr in next ch, work (dc, hdc, sc) in last ch. Join with a sl st in beg sc, pushing wrong side of sts toward outside of ear. Finish off, leaving approx 8" sewing length. Thread into tapestry or yarn needle; sew ear to side of head, slightly under hat edging.

MUZZLE: With brown, make two 1" diameter pompons. Attach pompons side by side to lower center front of head. For nose, make ½" diameter

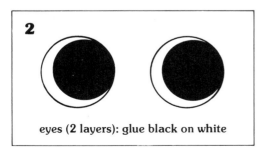

2

eyes (2 layers): glue black on white

black pompon and attach to head between and at top of other pompons.

EYES: Trace outlines in *Fig 2* on paper. Cut outlines and use as patterns on felt as indicated. (*NOTE: To prevent pattern piece from slipping on felt, tape piece on felt with scotch tape. Cut felt piece through tape; then discard tape.*) With glue, attach felt pieces as shown in photo.

BUTTONS: Make two ¾" diameter yellow pompons and attach to center front of body evenly spaced between collar and tutu.

DANCING PIG

Size
Approx 10" tall

Materials
Worsted weight yarn:
    2 oz pink
    2 oz ombre in shades of greens
Size H aluminum crochet hook (or size required for gauge)
White plastic bowl with lid (4-oz non-dairy whipped topping size) filled with ½ cup of popcorn kernels (*for rattle*)
Polyester fiber (*for stuffing*)
Small felt pieces in black and pink
Tracing paper and pencil
White craft glue
Size 16 tapestry needle or yarn needle

Gauge
In sc, 7 sts = 2"

Instructions
(*NOTE: Body, skirt and head are made in one piece.*)

BODY: Beg at bottom, with pink, ch 4; join with a sl st to form a ring.

Rnds 1 through 16: Work same as Circus Bear. At end of Rnd 16, pull up lp on hook to approx 4"; remove hook from lp (*do not cut yarn*) and work skirt as follows.

SKIRT: Rnds 1 through 4: With ombre, rep Rnds 1 through 4 of Tutu instructions for Circus Bear. At end of Rnd 16, pull up lp on hook to approx 4"; ends. Return to last rnd of body; insert hook in dropped pink lp and pull lp taut on hook. Then work as follows.

BODY CONTINUED: Rnds 17 through 28: Work same as Circus Bear. At end of Rnd 28, continue with same yarn and work head as follows.

HEAD: Work same as Circus Bear.

ARMS *(make 2)*: With pink, work same as Circus Bear.

SNOUT: With pink, leave approx 12" sewing length, ch 16; join with a sl st to form a ring, being careful not to twist chain.

Rnd 1: Sc in each ch around = 16 sc. (NOTE: Do not join; mark first st of rnd and move marker on each following rnd.)

Rnd 2: Sc **in both lps** of each sc around.

Rnds 3 and 4: Rep Rnd 2, twice.

Rnd 5: * Sc **in both lps** of next sc, sk one sc; rep from * around = 8 sc.

Rnd 6: * Sl st **in both lps** of next sc, sk one sc; rep from * around = 4 sl sts. Finish off, leaving approx 6" end. Thread into tapestry or yarn needle; weave through sts of last rnd. Draw up tightly and fasten securely. Lightly stuff and shape snout. Then thread beg sewing length into tapestry or yarn needle and sew snout to center front of head, approx 1 rnd above neck.

EARS *(worked in one piece)*: With pink, ch 11. Work (sc, hdc) in 2nd ch from hook; 2 dc in next ch, 2 tr in next ch [**To work tr: YO (yarn over) hook twice; insert hook in st and draw up a lp (4 lps now on hook); * YO and draw through 2 lps on hook; rep from * twice more = tr made**]. Work (2 dtr, ch 4, sl st) all in next ch (**To work dtr: YO hook 3 times; insert hook in st and draw up a lp—5 lps now on hook; * YO and draw through 2 lps on hook; rep from * 3 times more = dtr made**). One ear is now completed; sl st in each of next 2 chs, then continue with other ear as follows. Work (sl st, ch 4, 2 dtr) in next ch, 2 tr in next ch; 2 dc in next ch, work (hdc, sc) in last ch. Finish off, leaving approx 12" sewing length. Thread into tapestry or yarn needle and sew ears across top of head as shown in photo, keeping right side of sts to front of pig.

BOW: With ombre, make a chain to measure approx 10" long. Finish off; knot and trim each end of chain. With crochet hook, pull chain through st at top of head, between and in front of ears. Tie chain into a bow.

SHOULDER STRAPS *(make 2)*: With ombre, ch 34. Sc in 2nd ch from hook; * sk one ch, work (sc, hdc, dc, hdc, sc) all in next ch; sk one sc, sc in next ch; rep from * across. Finish off, leaving approx 16" sewing length. Sew foundation chain edge of each strap to body, having one strap over each shoulder (ease in sts of strap, if necessary). (Be sure to have right side of sts of each strap facing center of pig.) Sew ends of each strap to front and back of skirt.

TAIL: With pink, ch 8. Work 2 hdc in 3rd ch from hook, 3 hdc in each of next 4 chs; work (hdc, sc) in last ch. Finish off, leaving approx 6" sewing length. Thread into tapestry or yarn needle and sew this end to center back of pig, approx 2 rnds below skirt, having wrong side of sts facing you.

FACIAL FEATURES: Trace outlines in *Fig 3* on paper. Cut outlines and use as patterns on felt as indicated. With glue, attach felt pieces as shown in photo.

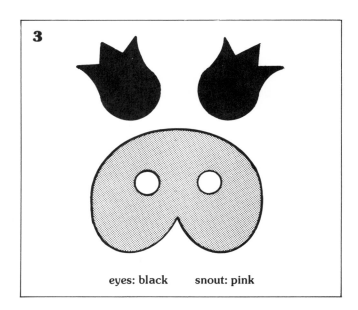

3

eyes: black   snout: pink

TRADITIONAL BABY LAYETTE

What better way to welcome a new arrival than with a lovingly handmade layette? This set, which includes jacket, bonnet, booties, mittens and afghan, is a classic design, featuring the easy shell stitch. You will enjoy making these tiny garments, and giving them with pride.

Size

Garments are designed to fit newborn to 3 months; afghan measures approx 30″ × 38″ with edging.

Materials

American Thread Dawn Wintuk Pompadour Baby Yarn:
> 7 oz buttercup (*for jacket, bonnet, booties & mittens*)
> 14 oz buttercup (*for afghan*)

Size E aluminum crochet hook (or size required for gauge)

Gauge

In dc, 11 sts = 2″

JACKET

Instructions

YOKE: Beg at neck edge, ch 67.

Row 1 (right side): Dc in 4th ch from hook and in each rem ch across = 65 dc (counting beg ch-3). (*NOTE: Ch-3 counts as one dc throughout patt.*)

Row 2: Ch 3, turn; dc in next dc, * 2 dc in next dc, dc in each of next 2 dc; rep from * across = 86 dc. (*NOTE: Last dc of each row is worked in top of ch-3 of prev row.*)

Row 3: Ch 3, turn; dc in next dc and in each rem dc across.

Row 4: Ch 3, turn; dc in each of next 2 dc, * 2 dc in next dc, dc in each of next 2 dc; rep from * to last 2 dc, dc in each of rem 2 dc = 113 dc.

Row 5: Rep Row 3.

Row 6: Ch 3, turn; dc in each of next 7 dc, dc **in front lp** (*lp toward you*) of next dc; * sk one dc, work (2 dc, ch 1, 2 dc) **in front lp** of next dc; sk one dc, dc **in front lp** of next dc; rep from * to last 8 dc, dc **in both lps** of rem 8 dc. Now continue by working **in both lps of sts.**

Row 7: Ch 3, turn; dc in each of next 8 dc, * sk 2 dc, work (2 dc, ch 1, 2 dc) in ch-1 sp; sk 2 dc, dc in next dc; rep from * to last 8 dc, dc in each of rem 8 dc.

Row 8: Ch 3, turn; dc in each of next 8 dc, * sk 2 dc, work (dc, ch 1, dc, ch 1, dc, ch 1, dc) all in ch-1 sp (**shell made**); sk 2 dc, dc in next dc; rep from * to last 8 dc, dc in each of rem 8 dc.

Row 9: Ch 3, turn; dc in each of next 8 dc, * work a shell in center sp of next shell, dc in dc between shells; rep from * to last shell; work a shell in center sp of last shell, dc in each of rem 9 dc.

Row 10: Rep Row 9.

Row 11 (dividing row): Ch 3, turn. **Across left front**, work dc in each of next 8 dc, * work a shell in center sp of next shell, dc in dc between shells; rep from * once more, work a shell in center sp of next shell. Ch 7 for underarm, sk next 4 shells for left sleeve. **Continuing across back**, work a shell in center sp of next shell, * dc in dc between shells, work a shell in center sp of next shell; rep from * 8 times more. Ch 7 for underarm, sk next 4 shells for right sleeve. **Continuing across right front**, work a shell in center sp of next shell, * dc in dc between shells, work a shell in center sp of next shell; rep from * once more, dc in each of rem 9 dc. Now continue with body as follows.

BODY: Row 1: Ch 3, turn; dc in each of next 8 dc, work a shell in center sp of next shell; work (dc in dc between shells, shell in center sp of next shell) twice; dc in first ch, sk 2 chs, work a shell in next ch; sk 2 chs, dc in last ch; work a shell in center sp of next shell; work (dc in dc between shells, shell in center sp of next shell) 9 times; dc in first ch, sk 2 chs, work a shell in next ch; sk 2 chs, dc in last ch; work a shell in center sp of next shell; work (dc in dc between shells, shell in center sp of next shell) twice; dc in each of rem 9 dc.

Row 2: Ch 3, turn; dc in each of next 8 dc, * work a shell in center sp of next shell, dc in dc between shells; rep from * to last shell; work a shell in center sp of last shell, dc in each of rem 9 dc.

Rows 3 through 16: Rep Row 2, 14 times. At end of last row, do not finish off; continue with edging as follows.

EDGING: In same st where last dc was just made, work (dc, hdc, sc) for corner. **Working across right front center edge**, * 2 sc in top of dc of next row, 2 sc in top of ch-3 of next row; rep from * to last row, work 2 sc in top of dc of last row. **Working across neck edge**, work (sc, hdc, 2 dc) in first st (*unused lp of foundation ch*) for corner, dc in each rem st across to last st; work (2 dc, hdc, sc) in last st for corner. **Working across left front center edge**, 2 sc in top of ch-3 of next row, * 2 sc in top of dc of next row, 2 sc in top of ch-3 of next row; rep from * to last 2 rows from bottom edge; work (sc, hdc, dc) in top of dc of next row, join with a sl st in top of ch-3 of last row. Finish off; weave in ends.

SLEEVE (*make 2*): Hold jacket with right side facing and underarm edge across top. Join with a sl st in st (unused lp of ch) above shell at center of underarm.

Rnd 1: Ch 4, work (dc, ch 1, dc, ch 1, dc) all in same st as joining; dc in st above next dc (at left of shell), work a shell in st at base of next dc (*corner of underarm*), dc in dc before next shell; * work a shell in center sp of next shell, dc in dc between shells; rep from * 3 times more; work a shell in st at corner of underarm, dc in st above next dc; join with a sl st in 3rd ch of beg ch-4.

Rnd 2: Turn; sl st in first dc, ch 3, work a shell in center sp of next shell; * dc in dc between shells, work a shell in center sp of next shell; rep from * around, join with a sl st in top of beg ch-3.

Rnd 3: Ch 3, turn; work a shell in center sp of next shell; * dc in dc between shells, work a shell in center sp of next shell; rep from * around, join with a sl st in top of beg ch-3.

Rnds 4 through 12: Rep Rnd 3, 9 times.

Rnd 13: Ch 3, turn; work (2 dc, ch 1, 2 dc) in center sp of next shell; * dc in dc between shells, work (2 dc, ch 1, 2 dc) in center sp of next shell; rep from * around, join with a sl st in top of beg ch-3.

Rnd 14: Ch 3, turn; sk next 2 dc, work (2 dc, ch 1, 2 dc) in ch-1 sp, sk next 2 dc; * dc in next dc, sk next 2 dc; work (2 dc, ch 1, 2 dc) in ch-1 sp, sk next 2 dc; rep from * around, join with a sl st in top of beg ch-3.

Rnd 15: Ch 5, turn; sk next 2 dc, sl st in ch-1 sp; ch 2, sk next 2 dc; * dc in next dc, ch 2, sk next 2 dc, sl st in ch-1 sp; ch 2, sk next 2 dc; rep from * around, join with a sl st in 3rd ch of beg ch-5.

Rnd 16: Ch 3, **Do not turn;** 2 dc in first ch-2 sp, sk sl st, 2 dc in next ch-2 sp; * dc in dc, 2 dc in ch-2 sp; sk sl st, 2 dc in next ch-2 sp; rep from * around, join with a sl st in top of beg ch-3. Finish off; weave in ends.

Finishing

Lightly steam press on wrong side.

NECKLINE TIE: Use 4 strands of yarn and make a 32″ tie. For a twisted cord tie, see instructions on page 11; or for a crocheted tie, make a chain to measure specified length. Weave tie through dcs around neck edge. Knot and trim each end of tie.

BONNET

Instructions

BACK SECTION: Beg at center, ch 4, join with a sl st to form a ring.

Rnd 1 (right side): Ch 3, work 15 dc in ring; join with a sl st in top of beg ch-3 = 16 dc (counting beg ch-3).

Rnd 2: Ch 3, do not turn; dc in same st as joining, work 2 dc in each rem dc around; join with a sl st in top of beg ch-3 = 32 dc.

Rnd 3: Ch 3, do not turn; dc in same st as joining, dc in next dc; * 2 dc in next dc, dc in next dc; rep from * around, join with a sl st in top of beg ch-3 = 48 dc.

Rnd 4: Ch 3, do not turn; dc in next dc and in each rem dc around; join with a sl st in top of beg ch-3.

Rnd 5: Ch 3, do not turn; dc in same st as joining, dc in each of next 3 dc; * 2 dc in next dc, dc in each of next 3 dc; rep from * around, join with a sl st in top of beg ch-3 = 60 dc.

Rnd 6: Rep Rnd 4.

Rnd 7: Rep Rnd 5 = 75 dc.

Rnd 8: Rep Rnd 4. [*NOTE: On following rnds, work shells in same manner as jacket (one shell = dc, ch 1, dc, ch 1, dc, ch 1, dc.)*]

Rnd 9: Ch 1, do not turn; sc in same st as joining, sc in each of next 5 dc, hdc in next dc; dc **in back lp** (*lp away from you*) of next dc; * sk 2 dc, work a shell **in back lp** of next dc; sk 2 dc, dc **in back lp** of next dc; sk one dc, work a shell **in back lp** of next dc; sk one dc, dc **in back lp** of next dc; rep from * to last 7 dc; hdc **in both lps** of next dc, sc **in both lps** in each of rem 6 dc; join with a sl st in beg sc. Finish off. Back section is now completed; continue with crown section, working back and forth in rows **in both lps** of sts.

CROWN: Row 1: Turn. With wrong side facing, sk first 7 sts from joining of prev rnd, join with a sl st in dc before first shell. Ch 3, * work a shell in center sp of next shell, dc in dc between shells; rep from * to last shell; work a shell in center sp of last shell, dc in dc after last shell (*leave rem sts unworked for back of neck*).

Row 2: Ch 3, turn; * work a shell in center sp of next shell, dc in dc between shells; rep from * to last shell; work a shell in center sp of last shell, dc in top of ch-3.

Rows 3 through 7: Rep Row 2, 5 times.

Row 8: Ch 3, turn; * work (2 dc, ch 1, 2 dc) in center sp of next shell, dc in dc between shells; rep from * to last shell, work (2 dc, ch 1, 2 dc) in center sp of last shell, dc in top of ch-3.

Row 9: Ch 3, turn; * sk 2 dc, work (2 dc, ch 1, 2 dc) in ch-1 sp; sk 2 dc, dc in next dc; rep from * across, ending last rep by working dc in top of ch-3.

Row 10: Rep Row 9. Do not finish off; continue with neck edging.

Finishing

NECK EDGING: Ch 3, do not turn. With right side facing and neck edge across top, work 2 dc in top of ch-3 (where last dc of prev row was worked), * 2 dc in top of dc of next row, 2 dc in top of ch-3 of next row; rep from * 3 times more; dc in dc of first shell row, dc in each of next 15 sts across back of neck; ** 2 dc in top of dc of next row, 2 dc in top of ch-3 of next row; rep from ** 3 times more; 2 dc in top of dc of next row, dc in top of ch-3 at beg of last row at front edge. Finish off; weave in all ends.

TIE: Make a tie same as for neckline of jacket. Weave tie through dcs around neck edge. Knot and trim each end of tie.

BOOTIES

Instructions (make 2)

SOLE: Ch 14. (*NOTE: All rnds are worked on right side.*)

Rnd 1: Work 3 sc in 2nd ch from hook; sc in each of next 11 chs, 3 sc in last ch. **Working on opposite side of starting chain,** sc in each of next 11 sts = 28 sc. Do not join rnds. Use a safety pin or piece of yarn in contrasting color and mark first st of rnd; move marker on each following rnd.

Rnd 2: Work 2 sc in each of next 3 sc, sc in each of next 11 sc; work 2 sc in each of next 3 sc, sc in each of rem 11 sc = 34 sc.

Rnd 3: Work (sc in next sc, 2 sc in next sc) 3 times, sc in each of next 11 sc; work (sc in next sc, 2 sc in next sc) 3 times, sc in each of rem 11 sc = 40 sc.

Rnd 4: Work (sc in each of next 2 sc, 2 sc in next sc) 3 times, sc in each of next 11 sc; work (sc in each of next 2 sc, 2 sc in next sc) 3 times, sc in each of rem 11 sc = 46 sc.

Rnd 5: Work (sc in each of next 3 sc, 2 sc in next sc) 3 times, sc in each of next 11 sc; work (sc in each of next 3 sc, 2 sc in next sc) 3 times, sc in each of rem 11 sc = 52 sc.

Rnd 6: Sl st loosely in each sc around. Finish off; weave in ends.

UPPER SECTION: Beg at center front, ch 7.

Rnd 1 (right side): Dc in 4th ch from hook; dc in next ch, 2 dc in next ch, 5 dc in last ch. **Working on opposite side of starting chain,** 2 dc in each of next 2 sts, work (dc, ch 1) 6 times in next st for shell; join with a sl st in top of beg ch-3.

Rnd 2: Ch 3, **do not turn;** dc in each of next 3 dc, work 2 dc in each of next 7 dc, dc in each of next 4 dc; ch 30, sk shell; join with a sl st in top of beg ch-3 = 52 dc (*counting beg ch-3*).

Rnd 3: Ch 3, turn; dc in each of 30 chs, dc in each of next 21 dc; join with a sl st in top of beg ch-3 = 52 dc (*counting beg ch-3*).

Rnd 4: Ch 3, turn; dc in next dc and in each rem dc around, join with a sl st in top of beg ch-3. Finish off, leaving approx 24″ sewing length.

Finishing

Fold sole in half lengthwise; mark each end for center of toe and heel. Mark center of toe and heel of top section in same manner. Now pin sole to top of bootie, having wrong sides tog and carefully matching center of toe and heel sections. Thread sewing length into tapestry or yarn needle. Working through both lps of sts in last dc rnd on sole (leave sl sts free) and last row of top section, sew sections tog with overcast sts.

TOP EDGING: Hold bootie with right side facing and front edge across top. Join with a sl st in ch-1 at left of shell. Work dc in unused lp in each of 30 chs around sides and back of bootie, join with a sl st in ch-1 at right of shell at center front. Finish off; weave in ends.

TIES: With 2 strands of yarn, make 2 ties (each 16″ long) in same manner as neckline tie of jacket. Weave one tie through dcs around top edge of each bootie, beg and ending at front of bootie below shell. Knot and trim each end of ties.

THUMBLESS MITTENS

Instructions (make 2)

Ch 4, join with a sl st in beg ch to form a ring.

Rnd 1 (right side): Ch 3, 2 dc in same ch as joining; work 3 dc in each of rem 3 chs, join with a sl st in top of beg ch-3 = 12 dc (counting beg ch-3).

Rnd 2: Ch 2, turn; dc in sl st, 2 dc in next dc; * dc in next dc, 2 dc in next dc; rep from * around, join with a sl st in beg dc = 18 dc. (NOTE: Do not count ch-2 as one st.)

Rnd 3: Ch 2, turn; * dc in next dc, 2 dc in next dc; rep from * 7 times more; dc in next dc, dc in next dc (where prev rnd was joined); join with a sl st in beg dc = 26 dc.

Rnd 4: Ch 2, turn; dc in next dc and in each dc around, ending by working last dc in dc where prev rnd was joined; join with a sl st in beg dc = 26 dc.

Rnds 5 through 10: Rep Rnd 4, 6 times.

Rnd 11 (beading rnd): Ch 3 (counts as one dc), turn; dc in next dc and in each rem dc around (do not work last dc in st where prev rnd was joined); join with a sl st in top of beg ch-3 = 26 dc (counting beg ch-3).

Rnd 12: Ch 3, turn; * sk one dc, work a shell (one shell = dc, ch 1, dc, ch 1, dc, ch 1, dc) **in front lp** of next dc; sk one dc, dc **in front lp** of next dc; rep from * 3 times more; sk 2 dc, work a shell **in front lp** of next dc; sk one dc, dc **in front lp** of next dc; sk 2 dc, work a shell **in front lp** of next dc; sk last dc, join with a sl st in top of beg ch-3.

Rnd 13: Ch 3, turn; work a shell in center sp of next shell, * dc in dc between shells (work **in both lps** of st), work a shell in center space of next shell; rep from * around, join with a sl st in top of beg ch-3. Finish off; weave in ends.

TIES: Make 2 ties same as for booties. Weave one tie through sts of beading rnd of each mitten. Knot and trim each end of ties.

AFGHAN

Instructions

Ch 159 loosely.

Row 1: Dc in 4th ch from hook and in each rem ch across = 157 dc (counting beg ch-3). (NOTE: Ch-3 counts as one dc throughout patt.)

Row 2: Ch 3, turn; dc in next dc and in each rem dc across, ending by working last dc in top of ch-3.

Rows 3 and 4: Rep Row 2, twice.

Row 5 (foundation shell row): Ch 3, turn; dc in each of next 6 dc; * † sk 2 dc, work (dc, ch 1, dc, ch 1, dc, ch 1, dc) all in next dc (shell made); sk 2 dc, dc in next dc †; rep from † to † 3 times; dc in each of next 6 dc; rep from * across.

Row 6 (shell patt row): Ch 3, turn; dc in each of next 6 dc; * † work a shell in center sp of next shell, dc in dc between shells †; rep from † to † twice; work a shell in center sp of next shell, dc in each of next 7 dc; rep from * across.

Rows 7 through 12: Rep Row 6, six times. You should now have 8 shell rows.

Row 13: Ch 3, turn; dc in each of next 6 dc; * † ch 2, sc in center sp of next shell; ch 2, dc in dc between shells †; rep from † to † twice; ch 2, sc in center sp of next shell; ch 2, dc in each of next 7 dc; rep from * across.

Row 14: Ch 3, turn; dc in each of next 6 dc; * † 2 dc in ch-2 sp, dc in sc; 2 dc in next ch-2 sp, dc in dc †; rep from † to † 3 times; dc in each of next 6 dc; rep from * across = 157 dc.

Row 15: Ch 3, turn; dc in next dc and in each rem dc across.

Rep Rows 5 through 15, 8 times more; then rep Row 15 twice more. Do not finish off; continue with edging as follows.

EDGING: Rnd 1: Ch 4, turn. **Working across last row just worked:** In first dc, work (dc, ch 1, dc, ch 1, dc) for beg corner shell; sk 2 dc, shell in next dc; * sk 2 dc, dc in next dc; sk 2 dc, shell in next dc; rep from * to within 3 sts from next corner; sk 2 dc, shell in top of ch-3 (corner shell). **Working across side edge along end of rows:** Sk first row, shell in next row; * sk one row, dc in next row, shell in next row; rep from * to last row, sk last row. **Working across foundation chain edge:** Shell in first st (corner shell), sk 2 dc, shell in next st; * sk 2 sts, dc in next st; sk 2 sts, shell in next st; rep from * to within 3 sts from next corner; sk 2 sts, shell in last st (corner shell). **Working across last edge along end of rows:** Sk first row, shell in next row; * sk one row, dc in next row, shell in next row; rep from * to last row, sk last row; join with a sl st in 3rd ch of beg ch-4.

Rnd 2: Do not turn. Sl st in ch-1, sl st in next dc and then into center sp of beg corner shell; ch 4. In same sp, work 5 dc with ch 1 between each dc. * Shell in center sp of next shell; † dc in dc between shells, shell in center sp of next shell †; rep from † to † to next corner shell. In center sp of corner shell, work 6 dc with ch 1 between each dc. Rep from * 3 times more, ending last rep without working corner shell. Join with a sl st in 3rd ch of beg ch-4. Finish off; weave in all ends.

Fashion Bazaar

Special

Handmade

PURSE

designed by Mary Thomas

This elegant bag is very simple to make. Just crochet twenty-four simple granny squares from bedspread cotton. Join them, add a set of handles, and you have created a real fashion plus. Make one for yourself and several for gifts.

Size

Approx 13″ wide × 9¾″ deep (without handles)

Materials

American Thread Puritan Crochet Bedspread and Tablecloth Cotton:
Size D aluminum crochet hook (or size required for gauge)
Plastic handle set (10″ wide)
(*MATERIALS NOTE: Two strands of thread are used throughout patt.*)

Gauge

One square = 3¼″

Instructions

SQUARE (make 24): With 2 strands, ch 4, join with a sl st to form a ring.
(*NOTE: All rnds are worked on right side.*)

Rnd 1: Ch 3, work 15 dc in ring; join with a sl st in top of beg ch-3.

Rnd 2: Ch 1, sc in same st as joining; work (sc, hdc, sc) in next dc for corner; * sc in each of next 3 dc, work (sc, hdc, sc) in next dc for corner; rep from * twice more; sc in each of rem 2 dc, join with a sl st in beg sc.

In next rnd, cluster sts are worked at corners. [**To make cluster st (abbreviated CL): * YO hook, insert hook in st and draw up a lp; YO and draw through 2 lps on hook; rep from * twice more in same st (4 lps now on hook—see Fig 1); YO and draw through all 4 lps on hook = CL made.**]

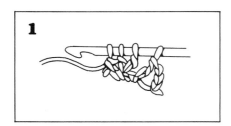

Rnd 3: Ch 3, dc in next sc, work (CL, ch 3, CL) in hdc at first corner; * dc in each of next 5 sc, work (CL, ch 3, CL) in hdc at next corner; rep from * twice more; dc in each of rem 3 sc, join with a sl st in top of beg ch-3.

Rnd 4: Ch 1, sc in same st as joining; sc in next dc, sc in CL; sc in first ch at corner, work (sc, hdc, sc) in center ch, sc in last ch; sc in CL, * sc in each of next 5 dc, sc in CL; sc in first ch at next corner, work (sc, hdc, sc) in center ch, sc in last ch, sc in CL; rep from * twice more; sc in each of rem 3 dc, join with a sl st in beg sc.

Rnd 5: Ch 3, dc in each of next 4 sc, work (CL, ch 3, CL) in hdc at first corner; * dc in each of next 11 sc, work (CL, ch 3, CL) in hdc at next corner; rep from * twice more; dc in each of rem 6 sc, join with a sl st in top of beg ch-3.

Rnd 6: Ch 1, sc in same st as joining; sc in each of next 4 dc, sc in CL; sc in first ch at corner, work (sc, hdc, sc) in center ch, sc in last ch; sc in CL, * sc in each of next 11 dc, sc in CL; sc in first ch at next corner, work (sc, hdc, sc) in center ch, sc in last ch, sc in CL; rep from * twice more; sc in each of rem 6 dc, join with a sl st in beg sc. Finish off, leaving approx 12″ sewing length.

ASSEMBLING: To join, hold two squares with right sides tog, positioned (when possible) with yarn end (left for sewing) in upper right-hand corner. Thread matching yarn in tapestry or yarn needle. Carefully matching sts on both squares, sew with overcast st **in outer lps** only (**Fig 2**) across side, beg and end with corner st. Continuing to join in this manner, join squares first into rows; then sew rows tog, being sure that all four-corner junctions are firmly joined. Weave in all yarn ends. Join 4 rows with 6 squares in each row.

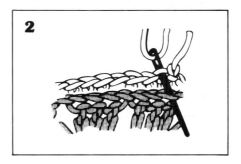

Finishing

Fold joined squares in half with right sides tog, having on each side of purse, 4 rows with 3 squares in each row. Beg at folded end and sew side edges closed across 2 squares to top square (*leave top squares free for side openings*). Sew one handle to each top edge of purse. Use double strand and overcast through slot of handle and through **both lps** of sts. Weave in all ends.

GRANNY SQUARE VEST

Designed by Carol Wilson Mansfield

Here's a fashion idea that never seems to go out of style: the crocheted vest. This easy-to-make version uses the old-favorite granny square to create a charming, timeless style. Quick and easy to make!

Sizes

	SMALL	MEDIUM	LARGE
Body Bust:	32"	35"	38"
Garment measurements:			
bust	36"	39"	42"
length (from bottom edge to shoulder)	17½"	18"	18½"

SIZE NOTE: Instructions are written for sizes as follows: Small, (Medium-Large).

Materials

American Thread Dawn Wintuk Sport Yarn:
    6(7-8) oz true blue
    2(3-4) oz nile green
    1(1½-2) oz baby blue
Sizes F and H aluminum crochet hooks (or size required for gauge)

MATERIALS NOTE: Smaller size hook is used for armhole edging only.

Gauge

With larger size hook, one square = 2¼"; 4 sc = 1"; 8 sc rows = 1½"

Instructions

SQUARE (make 28): With larger size hook and baby blue, ch 3, join with a sl st to form a ring.

Rnd 1 (right side): Ch 3, work 2 dc in ring; * ch 1, 3 dc in ring; rep from * twice more; ch 1, join with a sl st in top of beg ch-3. Finish off baby blue, leaving approx 4" end to weave in now or later.

Rnd 2: With right side facing you and larger size hook, join true blue with a sl st in any ch-1 sp; ch 6, 3 dc in same sp as joining; * work (3 dc, ch 3, 3 dc) in next ch-1 sp; rep from * twice more; 2 dc in next ch-1 sp (same sp as joining), join with a sl st in 3rd ch of beg ch-6. Finish off true blue, leaving approx 14" sewing length.

HALF SQUARE (make 50): With larger size hook and nile, ch 3, join with a sl st to form a ring.

Row 1 (wrong side): Ch 3, work (3 dc, ch 3, 4 dc) in ring.

Row 2: Ch 3 (counts as first dc), turn; 3 dc in first dc, sk next 3 dc, work (3 dc, ch 3, 3 dc) in ch-3 sp; sk next 3 dc, 4 dc in top of ch-3. Finish off nile, leaving approx 14" sewing length.

Assembling Squares

To join, hold two squares with right sides tog positioned (when possible) with yarn end (left for sewing) in upper right-hand corner. Thread matching yarn in tapestry or yarn needle. Carefully matching stitches on both squares, sew with overcast stitch **in outer loops only (Fig 1)** across side, beginning and ending with corner stitch. Be sure that all four-corner junctions are firmly joined. Weave in all yarn ends.

Join squares into 5 sections [*2 fronts, 2 sides (at underarms) and 1 back*] as shown in **Fig 2**. When joining half squares to squares, first and last dcs of half square are joined to 2 ch sts at corner of square.

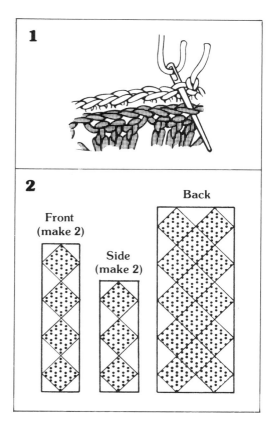

LEFT PANEL: Panel is worked lengthwise, beg at front lower edge and working up across edge of front section, then across left shoulder and down across edge of back section, ending at back lower edge.

Row 1: Hold one front section of joined squares with right side facing you and either long edge across top. With larger size hook, join true blue with a sl st in sp at upper right-hand corner. Ch 1, sc in same sp; sc in each of next 6 dc, sk last dc of first square. * On next square, 2 sc in each of first 2 rows (work sts in sp under end st), 2 sc in center ring, 2 sc in each of next 2 rows; rep from * twice more. On last square, sk first dc, sc in each of next 6 dc, sc in corner sp. You should now have 44 sc.

Continuing with same yarn, ch 40(44-48) for shoulder. (NOTE: *Any adjustment in length must be made now. Remember that 4 sc equals 1" ; then change number of chs accordingly.*) Now hold back section of joined squares with right side facing you and either long edge across top. Continuing with same yarn, sc in sp at upper right-hand corner, sc in each of next 6 dc, sk last dc of first square. * On next square, 2 sc in each of first 2 rows, 2 sc in center ring, 2 sc in each of next 2 rows; rep from * 3 times more. On last square, sk first dc, sc in each of next 6 dc, sc in corner sp. You should now have 54 sc across back section.

Row 2: Ch 1, turn; sc in each of 54 sc across back section, sc in each of 40(44-48) chs across shoulder, sc in each of rem 44 sc across front section = 138(142-146) sc.

Row 3: Ch 1, turn; sc in each sc across.

Rep Row 3, 12(14-16) times more. At end of last row, finish off.

RIGHT PANEL: Row 1: Hold work with right side facing and long edge of back section across top. With larger size hook, join true blue with a sl st in sp at upper right-hand corner. Ch 1, sc in same sp; work across back section in same manner as in left panel. You should now have 54 sc.

Continuing with same yarn, ch 40(44-48) for shoulder. Now hold rem front section of joined squares with right side facing and either long edge across top. Work across front section in same manner as in left panel. You should have 44 sc across front section.

Row 2: Ch 1, turn; sc in each of 44 sc across front section, sc in each of 40(44-48) chs across shoulder, sc in each of rem 54 sc across back section = 138(142-146) sc.

Row 3: Ch 1, turn; sc in each sc across.

Rep Row 3, 12(14-16) times more. At end of last row, finish off.

SIDE PANEL (make 2): Row 1: Hold one side section of joined squares with right side facing and either long edge across top. With larger size hook, join true blue with a sl st in sp at upper right-hand corner. Ch 1, sc in same sp as joining; sc in each of next 6 dc, sk last dc of first square. * On next square, 2 sc in each of first 2 rows, 2 sc in center ring, 2 sc in each of next 2 rows; rep from * once more. On last square, sk first dc, sc in each of next 6 dc, sc in corner sp. You should now have 34 sc.

Row 2: Ch 1, turn; sc in each sc across.

Rep Row 2, 5(7-9) times more. At end of last row, finish off. Rep these 7(9-11) rows on opposite edge of side section.

Finishing

Join side panels to left and right panels as follows. Hold panels with right sides tog. Carefully matching 34 sts of side panel with 34 sts from bottom edge of left/right panel, use larger size hook and true blue, and work sc **in both lps** of matching sts across.

ARMHOLE EDGING (make 2): With right side facing, use smaller size hook and join true blue with a sl st at underarm in right corner sp of joined squares.

Rnd 1: Ch 1, sc in same sp as joining; sc in each of next 6 dc, sk dc on each side of joining; sc in each of next 6 dc, sc in corner sp of square; sk next row, sc in each of next 3(5-7) rows; dec (decrease) over next 2 rows [**To dec: Draw up a lp in each of next 2 rows (or sts), YO and draw through all 3 lps on hook = dec made**], dec over next 2 rows (one on each side of seam); dec over next 2 sts, sc in each rem sc around armhole edge to within 3 sts of seam; dec over next 2 sts, dec over next st and row (one on each side of joining); dec over next 2 rows, sc in each of next 3(5-7) rows; sk last row, join with a sl st in beg sc.

Rnd 2: Ch 1, do not turn. Working from left to right in reverse sc (*see Fig 3*), work one st in each st around, skipping one st at each corner of underarm. Finish off; weave in ends.

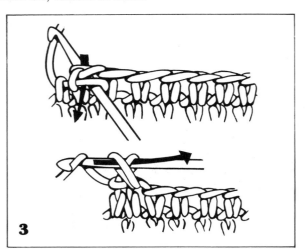

3

FRONT, NECK AND BOTTOM EDGING: Hold vest with right side facing and bottom edge across top. With larger size hook, join true blue with a sl st at seam to the right of back section.

Rnd 1: Ch 1, work in sc evenly spaced across bottom edge to lower right front corner. Work 3 sc in corner sp, then work in sc evenly spaced (work same as in Row 1 of right panel) across center front to next corner. Work 3 sc in corner sp, then work in sc evenly spaced to within 2 sts of first inside corner of neck edge. Dec over next 2 sts, dec over corner sp and first ch of shoulder, dec over next 2 chs; sc in each rem ch across shoulder to within 3 sts of next inside corner. Work 3 decreases as before; then complete edging around neck, left front and bottom edges in same manner as corresponding edges. Join with a sl st in beg sc.

Rnd 2: Ch 1, turn; sc in same sp as joining. Across each edge (including inside corners of neck edge), * ch 1, sk one sc, sc in next sc; rep from * across. At each corner at center front, work (ch 1, sc) in each st. At end of rnd, ch 1, join with a sl st in beg sc.

Rnd 3: Ch 1, turn. Working in reverse sc, work one st in each st and in each ch-1 sp around.

Finish off; weave in all ends. Lightly steam press vest on wrong side.

TIES (*make 2*): Cut 4-yd strand of true blue; fold strand in half. With larger size hook, pull folded end (lp) through st at center front neck edge. Now make a chain with doubled strand to measure approx 12" long. Finish off; knot and trim end.

Collar with Ribbon Tie (left)   Round Collar (right)

LACE COLLARS

designed by Mary Thomas

Three delightful collars, fashionably made with bedspread cotton or perle cotton. Easy to make even if you haven't worked with thread before. Add this current fashion accessory to your wardrobe today!

COLLAR WITH RIBBON TIE

Size

Approx 16″ around neck edge ×3″ deep (at points)

Materials

#5 Perle cotton:
    2 balls (53 yds each) ecru
Size 3 steel crochet hook (or size required for gauge)
1 yd, ¼″ Velvet ribbon in color of your choice

Gauge

In dc, 8 sts = 1″; 4 rows = 1″

Instructions

Beg at end of collar, ch 7.

Row 1: Work (dc, ch 3, dc) in 7th ch from hook.

Row 2 (right side): Ch 4, turn. In first sp, work (dc, ch 3, dc; ch 2, sc, ch 2; dc, ch 3, dc). Ch 2, sk next 2 chs, dc in next ch.

Row 3: Ch 5, turn. Sk first sp, work (dc, ch 3, dc) in next sp. Ch 2, sk next 2 sps *(on each side of sc)*, work (dc, ch 3, dc) in next sp *(leave rem sp unworked)*.

Row 4: Ch 4, turn. In first sp, work dc, then (ch 3, dc) twice. Sk next sp. In next sp, work (dc, ch 3, dc; ch 2, sc, ch 2; dc, ch 3, dc). Ch 2, dc in 3rd ch of ch-5.

Row 5: Ch 5, turn. Sk first sp, work (dc, ch 3, dc) in next sp. * Ch 2, sk next 2 sps, work (dc, ch 3, dc) in next sp. Rep from * once more *(leave rem sp unworked)*.

Row 6: Ch 4, turn. In first sp, work dc, then (ch 3, dc) twice. Sk next sp. In next sp, work dc, then (ch 3, dc) 3 times. Sk next sp. In next sp, work (dc, ch 3, dc; ch 2, sc, ch 2; dc, ch 3, dc). Ch 2, dc in 3rd ch of ch-5.

Row 7: Ch 5, turn. Sk first sp, work (dc, ch 3, dc) in next sp. * Ch 2, sk next 2 sps, work (dc, ch 3, dc) in next sp. Rep from * once more. Ch 2, sk next 3 sps, work (dc, ch 3, dc) in next sp (*leave rem sp unworked*).

Row 8: Ch 4, turn. In first sp, work dc, then (ch 3, dc) twice. * Sk next sp. In next sp, work dc, then (ch 3, dc) 3 times. Rep from * once more. Sk next sp. In next sp, work (dc, ch 3, dc; ch 2, sc, ch 2; dc, ch 3, dc). Ch 2, dc in 3rd ch of ch-5.

Row 9: Ch 5, turn. Sk first sp, work (dc, ch 3, dc) in next sp. * Ch 2, sk next 2 sps, work (dc, ch 3, dc) in next sp. Rep from * once more. ** Ch 2, sk next 3 sps, work (dc, ch 3, dc) in next sp. Rep from ** once more (*leave rem sp unworked*).

Row 10: Ch 4, turn. In first sp, work dc, then (ch 3, dc) twice. * Sk next sp. In next sp, work dc, then (ch 3, dc) 3 times. Rep from * twice more. Sk next sp. In next sp, work (dc, ch 3, dc; ch 2, sc, ch 2; dc, ch 3, dc). Ch 2, dc in 3rd ch of ch-5.

Row 11: Ch 5, turn. Sk first sp, work (dc, ch 3, dc) in next sp. * Ch 2, sk next 2 sps, work (dc, ch 3, dc) in next sp. Rep from * once more. ** Ch 2, sk next 3 sps, work (dc, ch 3, dc) in next sp. Rep from ** twice more (*leave rem sp unworked*).

Row 12: Ch 5, turn. Sc in each of first 2 sps. * Work (sc, ch 4, sc) in next sp, sc in next sp. Rep from * once more. In next sp, work sc, then (ch 3, dc) 3 times. Sk next sp. In next sp, work dc, then (ch 3, dc) 3 times. Sk next sp. In next sp, work (dc, ch 3, dc; ch 2, sc, ch 2; dc, ch 3, dc). Ch 2, dc in 3rd ch of ch-5.

Rep Rows 7 through 12, five times more. Then rep Rows 7 through 10 once.

Next Row: Ch 3, turn. Sk first sp, work (dc, ch 3, dc) in next sp. * Ch 2, sk next 2 sps, work (dc, ch 3, dc) in next sp. Rep from * once more. ** Ch 2, sk next 3 sps, work (dc, ch 3, dc) in next sp. Rep from ** twice more (*leave rem sp unworked*).

Last Row: Ch 5, turn. Sc in each of first 2 sps. * Work (sc, ch 4, sc) in next sp, sc in next sp. Rep from * 3 times more. Work (sc, ch 4, sc) in next sp, 2 sc in sp under turning ch. Finish off; weave in ends securely.

Lightly steam press on wrong side. If necessary, lightly spray with commercial spray starch on wrong side. Weave ribbon through sps around neck edge.

ROUND COLLAR

Size
Approx 16″ around neck edge × 2½″ deep

Materials
Bedspread weight crochet cotton:
    100 yds ecru
Size 5 steel crochet hook (or size required for gauge)
Pearl button (⅜″ diameter)

Gauge
In sc, 15 sts = 2″

Instructions
Beg at neck edge, ch 116.

Row 1: Sc in 2nd ch from hook and in each rem ch across = 115 sc.

Row 2: Ch 1, turn; sc in first sc, * ch 3, sk 2 sc, sc in next sc; rep from * across = 38 ch-lps.

Row 3: Ch 4, turn; sc in first ch-lp, * ch 3, sc in next ch-lp; rep from * across = 38 ch-lps.

Row 4: Rep Row 3.

Row 5: Ch 5, turn; sc in first ch-lp, * ch 4, sc in next ch-lp; rep from * across = 38 ch-lps.

Rows 6 and 7: Rep Row 5, twice.

Row 8: Ch 6, turn; sc in first ch-lp, * ch 5, sc in next ch-lp; rep from * across = 38 ch-lps.

Rows 9 and 10: Rep Row 8, twice.

Row 11: Ch 4, turn; sc in first ch-lp, * ch 5, sc in next ch-lp; rep from * to last ch-lp, ch 3, sc in last ch-lp = 38 ch-lps. Finish off.

EDGING: Turn; hold end of collar (*along end of rows*) across top with last st worked of prev row to your left and neck edge to your right. Join with a sl st in sc at upper right-hand corner (*at neck edge*).

Row 1: Sk first ch-lp, work (3 dc, ch 1) in each of next 4 ch-lps across end of collar (*along end of rows*); work (3 dc, ch 1) in next ch-lp at corner. Along outer edge of collar, work a shell of (3 dc, ch 1, 3 dc) in each of next 36 ch-lps. Work (ch 1, 3 dc) in next ch-lp at corner; work (ch 1, 3 dc) in each of next 4 ch-lps across end of collar (*along end of rows at opposite end*). Sl st in st at neck edge.

Row 2 (right side): Ch 1, turn; * sc in each of next 3 dc, work picot of (sc, ch 3, sc) in ch-1 sp; rep from * 4 times more. Then work as follows across each of next 36 shells. Dc in each of next 3 dc, picot in ch-1 sp, dc in each of next 3 dc. Across opposite end of collar, work (picot in ch-1 sp, sc in each of next 3 dc) 5 times. Ch 7 (*for button lp*), sl st in st at neck edge. Finish off; weave in all ends securely.

Sew on button. Lightly steam press on wrong side. If necessary, lightly spray with commercial spray starch on wrong side.

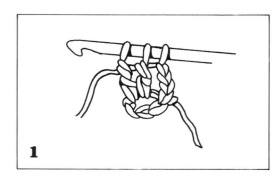

GRANNY-SQUARE COLLAR

Size

Approx 15″ around neck edge × 2¼″ deep

Materials

American Thread Puritan Crochet Bedspread and
    Tablecloth Cotton:
    175 yds white
Size 7 steel crochet hook (or size required for gauge)
½ yd, ¼″ wide satin ribbon in color of your choice

Gauge

One square = 1¾″

Instructions

SQUARE (make one): Ch 6, join with a sl st to form a ring.

Rnd 1 (right side): Work beg petal in ring. [**To work beg petal: Ch 4, † (YO hook) twice, insert hook in ring and draw up a lp (YO and draw**

through 2 lps on hook) twice †; rep from † to † once more (3 lps now on hook—see *Fig 1*); YO and draw through all 3 lps on hook = beg petal made.] * Ch 3, work petal in ring. [**To work petal: Rep from † to † 3 times (4 lps now on hook); YO and draw through all 4 lps on hook = petal made.**] Rep from * 6 times more; ch 3, join with a sl st in top of beg petal = 8 petals.

Rnd 2: Do not turn, sl st into next ch-3 sp; ch 3, work (2 dc, ch 3, 3 dc) in same sp for beg corner. * Work 3 dc in next ch-3 sp for side, work (3 dc, ch 3, 3 dc) in next ch-3 sp for corner; rep from * twice more; 3 dc in next ch-3 sp for last side, join with a sl st in top of beg ch-3. Finish off, leaving approx 12″ sewing length.

MOTIFS (make 10): Ch 6, join with a sl-st to form a ring.

Rnd 1: Work same as for Square.

Rnd 2: Do not turn, sl st into next ch-3 sp; ch 3, work (2 dc, ch 3, 3 dc) in same sp for beg corner. Work (3 dc, ch 3, 3 dc) in next ch-3 sp for next corner, 3 dc in next ch-3 sp for side edge. Work (3 dc, ch 3, 3 dc) in next ch-3 sp for corner, 3 dc in each of next two ch-3 sps for outer edge. Work (3 dc, ch 3, 3 dc) in next ch-3 sp for corner, 3 dc in next ch-3 sp for side edge. Join with a sl st in top of beg ch-3. Finish off, leaving approx 12″ sewing length.

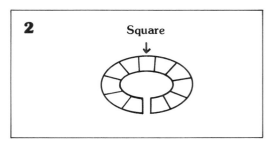

Assembling

Position square and motifs as shown in *Fig 2,* having square at center back. To join, hold two motifs with right sides tog positioned (when possible) with thread end (left for sewing) in upper right-hand corner. Carefully matching stitches on both motifs,

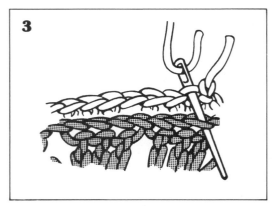

sew with overcast stitch in outer loops only (**Fig 3**) across side, beg and end with corner stitch. Be sure that all four-corner junctions are firmly joined. Weave in ends.

EDGING: Hold collar with right side facing and neck edge across top. Join with a sl st in ch-3 sp at upper right-hand corner.

Rnd 1: Ch 1, sc in same sp as joining. **Continuing across neck edge**, sc in each dc across first motif, * sc in ch-3 sp of same motif (*before joining*), sc in joining, sc in next ch-3 sp (*after joining*), sc in each dc across next motif; rep from * to ch-3 sp at upper left-hand corner; work (sc, hdc, 3 dc) in corner sp. **Continuing across left front center edge**, work (ch 1, 3 dc) in each of next 2 sps (*between 3-dc groups*), ch 1; work (3 dc, ch 3, 3 dc) in ch-3 corner sp. **Continuing across outer edge**, work (ch 1, 3 dc) in each of next 3 sps (*between 3-dc groups*) across first motif; * work (ch 1, 3 dc) in each of next 2 sps (*on each side of joining*), work (ch 1, 3 dc) in each of next 3 sps across next motif; rep from * to ch-3 sp at next corner; ch 1, work (3 dc, ch 3, 3 dc) in corner sp. **Continuing across right front center edge**, work (ch 1, 3 dc) in each of next 2 sps, ch 1; work (3 dc, hdc) in beg corner sp. (*NOTE: Do not join rnd.*)

Rnd 2: Do not turn. **Across neck edge**, work sc in each sc to group of sts at next corner; sc in next sc and in next hdc; 2 hdc in dc, work (dc, ch 3 for eyelet, dc) in next dc, hdc in last dc. **Continuing across left front center edge**, * sc in ch-1 sp, hdc in first dc of next 3-dc group, 2 dc in center dc, hdc in last dc; rep from * to ch-3 corner sp; work (sc, hdc, 2 dc, hdc, sc) in corner sp. **Continuing across outer edge**, hdc in first dc of first 3-dc group, 2 dc in center dc, hdc in last dc; * sc in ch-1 sp, hdc in first dc of next 3-dc group, 2 dc in center dc, hdc in last dc; rep from * to ch-3 corner sp; work (sc, hdc, 2 dc, hdc, sc) in corner sp. **Continuing across right front center edge**, * hdc in first dc of next 3-dc group, 2 dc in center dc, hdc in last dc, sc in ch-1 sp; rep from * to beg corner sts; hdc in first dc, work (dc, ch 3 for eyelet, hdc) in next dc, sc in next dc; sc in hdc, sl st in next sc. Finish off; weave in ends.

Lightly steam press collar on wrong side. Insert ribbon through eyelets at center front neck edge.

Hexagon Boot Slipper (left)   Ribbed Slipper (right)

COZY SLIPPERS

designed by Nannette M. Berkley

Two different pairs of slippers made in worsted weight yarn. One is boot style with granny hexagon motifs, the other is a ribbed slip-on. Easy to make, quick and ideal for gifts.

HEXAGON BOOT SLIPPER

Sizes

	SMALL	LARGE
Fits shoe sizes:	5–7	8–10

Materials

Worsted weight yarn:
  3 oz wine
  1½ oz cream
  ½ oz medium blue
  1 oz ombre in shades of blue, wine and beige

Aluminum crochet hooks; sizes F and I (for small size); or sizes H and J (for large size); (or size required for gauge)
Size 16 tapestry needle or yarn needle

Gauge

With size F hook (for small size), one motif = 5″
With size H hook (for large size), one motif = 5½″

(*GAUGE NOTE: Motif is measured from side to side.*)

Instructions

MOTIF (make 6): With blue, ch 6, join with a sl st to form a ring.

(NOTE: Throughout motif, use size F hook (or size required for gauge) for small size, or size H hook (or size required for gauge) for large size. All rnds of motif are worked on right side.)

Rnd 1: Make a beg PC (popcorn) in ring. [**To make beg PC: Ch 3, work 4 dc in ring; drop lp from hook, insert hook in top of ch-3; hook dropped lp (Fig 1) and pull through st = beg PC made.**] * Ch 3, make PC in ring. [**To make PC: Work 5 dc in ring; drop lp from hook, insert hook in top of first dc of 5-dc group just made; hook dropped lp and pull through st = PC made.**] Rep from * 4 times more. Ch 3, join with a sl st in top of beg PC = 6 PC. Finish off blue.

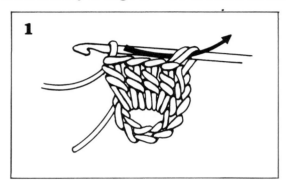

Rnd 2: Join cream with a sl st in any ch-3 sp. Ch 3 (counts as first dc), work (2 dc, ch 1, 3 dc) in same sp as joining (beg shell made). Work (3 dc, ch 2, 3 dc) in each rem ch-3 sp around. Join with a sl st in top of beg ch-3 = 6 shells. Finish off cream.

Rnd 3: Join ombre with a sl st in first dc of any shell. Work beg PC in same st as joining, ch 2; work (PC, ch 2) in ch-1 sp and in last dc of same shell (3 PCs made). * Work (PC, ch 2) in first dc, in ch-1 sp and in last dc of next shell; rep from * around. Join with a sl st in top of beg PC = 18 PC. Finish off ombre.

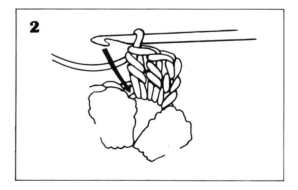

Rnd 4: Join cream with a sl st in first ch-2 sp (following beg PC). Ch 3 (counts as first dc), 2 dc in same sp. * Work tr in first dc of next PC (where dropped lp was pulled through—**Fig 2**) as follows. YO (yarn over) hook twice, insert hook in st and draw up a lp

(4 lps now on hook); work (YO and draw through 2 lps on hook) 3 times (tr made). Work 3 dc in each of next 3 ch-2 sps (for side). Rep from * 5 times more, ending last rep by working 3 dc in each of last 2 ch-2 sps (instead of next 3 ch-2 sps). Join with a sl st in top of beg ch-3 = 9 dc across each side and one tr at each corner. Finish off cream.

Rnd 5: Join wine with a sl st in tr at any corner. Ch 1, 3 sc in same st as joining. * Sc in each of next 9 dc (along side), 3 sc in tr (at next corner). Rep from * 5 times more, ending last rep without working corner. Join with a sl st in beg sc. Finish off wine, leaving approx 14″ sewing length.

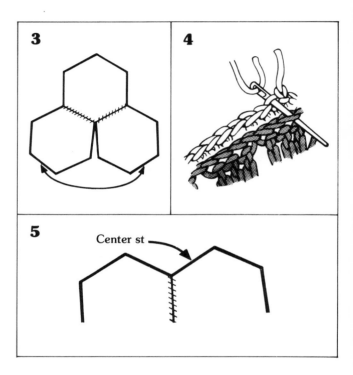

Center st

TOP SECTION (make 2): Join 3 motifs for top section of each slipper as shown in **Fig 3**. To join, hold 2 motifs with right sides tog. Thread wine yarn into tapestry or yarn needle. Carefully matching sts, beg in center corner st and sew with overcast st through **outer lps** only (**Fig 4**) across 13 sts of side, ending in center st at next corner. Weave in ends on wrong side. Work one rnd around bottom edge of joined motifs of each slipper (for joining to sole later) as follows. Hold joined motifs with bottom side edge across top, with toe to your right and heel to your left. With same size hook used for motifs, join wine with a sl st in 6th st to the right of joining (center st of side—see **Fig 5**). Ch 1, * sc in each of next 2 sts, hdc in each of next 2 sts; dc in next st, dc in joining, dc in next st (of next motif); hdc in each of next 2 sts; sc in each of next 2 sts; sl st in each st around to within 5 sts of next joining. Rep from * twice more, ending last rep at beg of rnd (instead of 5 sts before next joining). Join with a sl st in beg sc. Finish off, leaving approx 30″ sewing length.

SOLE *(make 2):* With 2 strands of wine, ch 21. (*NOTE: Use size I hook for small size; or size J hook for large size. All rnds of sole are worked on right side.*)

Rnd 1: Work 3 sc in 2nd ch from hook (heel); sc in each of next 9 chs, hdc in each of next 9 chs; work 5 hdc in last ch (toe). Continue working across opposite side of chain as follows. Hdc in each of next 9 sts, sc in each of rem 9 sts. Join with a sl st in beg sc.

Rnd 2: Ch 1, work 2 sc in same st as joining. Work 2 sc in each of next 2 sts, sc in each of next 7 sts. Decrease over next 2 sts as follows. Draw up a lp in each of next 2 sts, YO and draw through all 3 lps on hook (**Fig 6**—decrease made). Hdc in each of next 9 sts, 2 hdc in each of next 5 sts; hdc in each of next 8 sts, 2 hdc in next st; sc in each of rem 9 sts. Join with a sl st in beg sc.

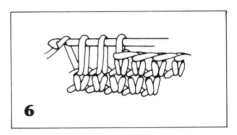

Rnd 3: Ch 1, sc in same st as joining. Work 2 sc in each of next 4 sc, sc in each of next 11 sts; hdc in each of next 9 sts, 2 hdc in next st, hdc in next st; work 2 hdc in each of next 5 sts, hdc in next st; work 2 hdc in next st, hdc in each of next 11 sts; sc in each of rem 7 sts. Join with a sl st in beg sc. Finish off; weave in ends.

Finishing

Pin sole to top of slipper, carefully matching center of toe and heel sections. Working from right side, sew sole to slipper, working through complete st on sole and outside (*back lp*) of st on top of slipper, easing in top of slipper as needed. Weave in all ends.

EDGING: With same size hook used for motifs, join wine with a sl st in joining at top back of slipper. Ch 1, work sc in each st and in each joining around top edge. Join with a sl st in beg sc. Finish off; weave in ends.

RIBBED SLIPPER

Size
Written in one size, with adjustable foot length

Materials
Worsted weight yarn:
    6 oz powder blue
Size H aluminum crochet hook (or size required for gauge)

Gauge
In patt st (3 BPdc, 3 FPdc), 6 sts = 1½″; 2 rows/rnds = 1″

Pattern Stitches
FRONT POST DC *(abbreviated FPdc):* YO hook, insert hook from **front to back to front** around post of dc in row below (**Fig 7**). Hook yarn and draw lp through (*3 lps now on hook*). Work (YO and draw through 2 lps on hook) twice.

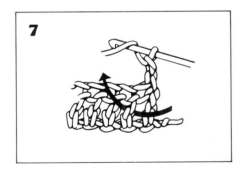

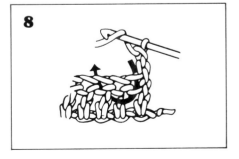

BACK POST DC *(abbreviated BPdc):* Same as FPdc, except insert hook from **back to front to back** around post of dc in row below (**Fig 8**).

Instructions (make 2)

Beg at toe, ch 4, join with a sl st to form a ring.

Rnd 1: Ch 3, work 24 dc in ring; join with a sl st in top of beg ch-3.

Rnd 2 (inc rnd): (*NOTE: Mark this rnd for wrong side of slipper.*) Ch 2, turn. * Work BPdc around each of next 3 dc; work 3 FPdc around next dc (2 sts increased). Rep from * 5 times more; join with a sl st in top of beg dc.

Rnd 3: Ch 2, turn. * Work BPdc around each of next 3 sts; work FPdc around each of next 3 sts. Rep from * 5 times more; join with a sl st in top of beg dc.

Rep Rnd 3 until work measures desired length from toe to ankle, measuring at top of foot. Then work back and forth in rows as follows.

Row 1: Ch 3, turn. * Work BPdc around each of next 3 sts, work FPdc around each of next 3 sts. Rep from * 4 times more; work BPdc around each of next 3 sts, dc in next st. (*Leave rem 2 sts unworked for front opening.*)

Row 2: Ch 3, turn. * Work FPdc around each of next 3 sts; work BPdc around each of next 3 sts. Rep from * 4 times more; work FPdc around each of last 3 sts, dc in top of ch-3.

Row 3: Ch 3, turn. * Work BPdc around each of next 3 sts; work FPdc around each of next 3 sts. Rep from * 4 times more; work BPdc around each of last 3 sts, dc in top of ch-3.

Rep Rows 2 and 3 until slipper measures desired length to heel, ending by working Row 3. Finish off, leaving approx 12" sewing length. Thread into tapestry needle. Fold work in half with right sides tog. Sew edges of last row tog, carefully matching sts across.

EDGING: With right side facing, join with a sl st in seam at top back edge of slipper. Ch 1, sc in same st as joining. * Ch 3, work 2 dc in 3rd ch from hook; sk next row (opening for weaving tie later), sc in next row. Rep from * around (counting each of the 3 sts at front of slipper as one row), ending last rep by joining with a sl st in beg sc (instead of sc in next row). Finish off; weave in all ends.

TIE (*make 2*): For weaving through openings in edging rnd, make a crocheted tie (use 2 strands of yarn and make a chain to measure approx 24" long, finish off; knot and fringe each end of chain); or make a twisted cord tie as follows.

Step 1: Cut 2 strands of yarn, each 96" long (4 times the finished cord length).

Step 2: Make a single loop at each end of strands, sufficient in size to slip over a door knob or onto a hook for anchoring.

Step 3: Place one loop on knob or hook.

Step 4: Slip other loop at opposite end on index finger (or several fingers depending on loop size), or onto a pencil.

Step 5: Holding strands taut, twist strands to your right until there is a firm even twist (slightly kinky) along the entire length. (*NOTE: This step can be accomplished rapidly by attaching strands to one beater of your electric mixer; then beat, keeping strands taut. Remember it is better to over beat than to under beat.*)

Step 6: Keeping strands taut, fold twisted strands in half lengthwise, slipping loop off index finger or pencil (or beater) and onto knob or hook with other looped end.

Step 7: Form cord by smoothing the twisted strands doubled in a downward direction from knob or hook between the thumb and finger.

Step 8: Cut off looped ends. Knot each end of cord; trim ends evenly.

SPIDER-WEB-LACE SHAWL

designed by Ernestine H. Giesecke

Made in bedspread cotton, the body and border of this lacy shawl are worked separately, then joined. The body of the shawl is worked first in a very easy shell pattern. Then the border is made which is an adaptation of a popular pattern of many years ago, called Spider Web Lace.

Sizes (including border)

Small size measures approx 68″ wide × 36″ deep
Large size measures approx 80″ wide × 42″ deep

Materials

American Thread Puritan Bedspread Cotton in
　　250-yd balls:
　　　　9 balls white
Steel crochet hook size 5 (for small size); or size 1
　　(for large size)—or size required for gauge

[*MATERIALS NOTE: Throughout body and border of shawl, use size 5 hook (or size required for gauge) for small size; or size 1 hook (or size required for gauge) for large size.*]

Gauge

With size 5 hook (for small size),
　　　3 shell units = 2¾″
　　　(one shell unit = sc, ch 2, shell, ch 2)
　　　4 shell rows = 2″
With size 1 hook (for large size),
　　　4 shell units = 4½″
　　　5 shell rows = 3″

(*GAUGE NOTE: To test gauge, ch 49. Work following Rows 1 through 3 once; then rep Rows 2 and 3, 5 times more. Finish off and measure sts and rows in center of piece. If you have more sts to the inch than specified, use a larger size hook. If you have fewer sts to the inch than specified, use a smaller size hook. Do not hesitate to change hook size to obtain the specified gauge.*)

BODY

Instructions

Beg at top edge, ch 367. (*NOTE: For ease in counting number of chains, mark every 20th or 30th chain as you are working. Use small safety pins or pieces of thread in contrasting color for markers.*)

Row 1 (foundation row): Sc in 7th ch from hook. * Ch 3, sk 2 chs, sc in next ch; ch 5, sk 2 chs, sc in next ch. Rep from * across = 60 ch-3 sps.

Row 2 (shell row): Turn; sl st in each of first 3 chs of ch-5, sc in first ch-5 sp. * Ch 2, work 4 tr (triple crochet) in next ch-3 sp (shell made). **[To work tr: YO (yarn over) hook twice; insert hook in sp and draw up a lp (4 lps now on hook); work (YO and draw through 2 lps on hook) 3 times = tr made.]** Ch 2, sc in next ch-5 sp. Rep from * across = 60 shells.

Row 3: Turn; sl st into first ch-2 sp, sc in first tr of first shell, ch 5, sc in last tr of same (first) shell. * Ch 3, sc in first tr of next shell, ch 5, sc in last tr of same shell. Rep from * across = 59 ch-3 sps.

Rep Rows 2 and 3 until 2 shells rem, ending by working Row 2 (shell row). (*NOTE: You will be decreasing one shell every patt repeat—every 2 rows.*) Finish off; weave in ends.

BORDER:

Instructions
Ch 52.

Row 1: Dc in 7th ch from hook, (*mark this sp for first joining point*), dc in each of next 3 chs. * Ch 8, sk 6 chs, sc in each of next 5 chs; ch 8, sk 6 chs, dc in each of next 4 chs. Rep from * once more.

Row 2: Ch 7, turn. Sk first 3 dc, dc in next dc, 3 dc in ch-8 sp; ch 7, sk one sc, sc in each of next 3 sc, sk one sc; ch 7, 3 dc in ch-8 sp; dc in next dc, ch 2, sk 2 dc, dc in next dc; 3 dc in ch-8 sp, ch 7, sk one sc, sc in each of next 3 sc, sk one sc; ch 7, 3 dc in ch-8 sp, dc in next dc (*leave rem 3 dc unworked*).

Row 3: Ch 7, turn. Sk first 3 dc, dc in next dc, 3 dc in ch-7 sp; ch 4, sk one sc, tr in next sc, sk one sc; ch 4, 3 dc in ch-7 sp; dc in next dc, ch 4, sk 3 dc, tr in next ch-2 sp; ch 4, sk 3 dc, dc in next dc; 3 dc in ch-7 sp, ch 4, sk one sc, tr in next sc, sk one sc; ch 4, 3 dc in ch-7 sp, dc in next dc (*leave rem 3 dc unworked*).

Row 4: Ch 7, turn. Sk first 3 dc, dc in next dc, 3 dc in ch-4 sp; ch 2, sk tr, 3 dc in next ch-4 sp, dc in next dc; ch 7, sk 3 dc, sc in ch-4 sp, sc in tr, sc in next ch-4 sp; ch 7, sk 3 dc, dc in next dc, 3 dc in ch-4 sp; ch 2, sk tr, 3 dc in next ch-4 sp, dc in next dc (*leave rem 3 dc unworked*).

Row 5: Ch 6, turn. Sk first 3 dc, dc in next dc, 2 dc in ch-2 sp, dc in next dc; ch 8, sk 3 dc, sc in ch-7 sp, sc in each of next 3 sc, sc in ch-7 sp; ch 8, sk 3 dc, dc in next dc, 2 dc in ch-2 sp, dc in next dc (*leave rem 3 dc unworked*).

Row 6: Ch 11, turn. Dc in 10th ch from hook, 2 dc in next ch, dc in first dc; ch 2, sk 2 dc, dc in next dc, 3 dc in ch-8 sp; ch 7, sk one sc, sc in each of next 3 sc, sk one sc; ch 7, 3 dc in ch-8 sp, dc in next dc; ch 2, sk 2 dc, dc in next dc, 3 dc in turning ch sp.

Row 7: Ch 11, turn. Dc in 10th ch from hook, 2 dc in next ch, dc in first dc; ch 4, sk 3 dc, tr in ch-2 sp; ch 4, sk 3 dc, dc in next dc, 3 dc in ch-7 sp; ch 4, sk one sc, tr in next sc, sk one sc; ch 4, 3 dc in ch-7 sp, dc in next dc; ch 4, sk 3 dc, tr in ch-2 sp; ch 4, sk 3 dc, dc in next dc, 3 dc in turning ch sp.

Row 8: Ch 11, turn. Dc in 10th ch from hook, 2 dc in next ch, dc in first dc; ch 7, sk 3 dc, sc in ch-4 sp, sc in tr, sc in next ch-4 sp; ch 7, sk 3 dc, dc in next dc, 3 dc in ch-4 sp; ch 2, sk tr, 3 dc in next ch-4 sp, dc in next dc; ch 7, sk 3 dc, sc in ch-4 sp, sc in tr, sc in next ch-4 sp; ch 7, sk 3 dc, dc in next dc, 3 dc in turning ch sp.

Row 9: Ch 9, turn. Dc in 8th ch from hook (*2nd joining point made*), 2 dc in next ch, dc in first dc; ch 8, sk 3 dc, sc in ch-7 sp, sc in each of next 3 sc, sc in next ch-7 sp; ch 8, sk 3 dc, dc in next dc, 2 dc in ch-2 sp, dc in next dc; ch 8, sk 3 dc, sc in ch-7 sp, sc in each of next 3 sc, sc in next ch-7 sp; ch 8, sk 3 dc, dc in next dc, 3 dc in turning ch sp.

Rep Rows 2 through 9 until 44 joining points have been completed, ending by working Row 9. Finish off; weave in ends.

Assembling
Lightly steam press shawl and border on wrong side. Then pin border to shawl as follows. With right sides facing you, beg at lower center back of shawl and pin center 2 joining points (22nd and 23rd points) of border to 2 bottom shells at point of shawl. Pin rem joining points to each side of shawl as follows. Work (sk one shell row, pin next joining point to next shell row) 5 times; then work (sk next 2 shell rows, pin next joining point to next shell row) 16 times.

Now join border to shawl as follows. Hold shawl with neck edge across top. With same size hook as used for shawl and border, make a slip knot on hook. Join with a sc in st at upper left-hand corner. Working along side edge (removing pins as you work), * sc in joining point, work in sc evenly spaced along edge of shawl to next point; rep from * until all points across both sides of shawl have been joined, ending at top edge of shawl. Finish off.

TOP EDGING: Hold shawl with right side facing you and neck edge across top. With same size hook as used for shawl and border, make a slip knot on hook. Join with a sc in st at upper right-hand corner at outer edge of border. Work in sc evenly spaced across top edge of shawl, ending at upper left-hand corner at outer edge of border at opposite end. Finish off; weave in all ends.

Lightly steam press on wrong side; use spray starch lightly if desired.

PICTURE WALL HANGINGS

designed by Joyce Wallace Lerner

These delightful wall hangings are fascinating to make and are great gifts. The pictorial design is simply created from 2¼″ granny squares, some worked in two colors. Details are added with chains and other shapes, appliqued to the finished hanging. We suggest that you work from the top to the bottom of the hanging, sewing the squares together every two or three rows. This makes it exciting as the picture gradually develops. These wall hangings will not only add to the decor of any room, but if you get cold, just take *these* pictures off the wall and use them as afghans!

Square Instructions

Our Picture Wall Hangings are made of 2-rnd granny squares: one-color, two-color (*different color used for each rnd*), and diagonal two-color (*resembles a pair of joined triangles*). To make squares, use size G aluminum crochet hook—or size required for gauge (one square = 2¼″). Colors or combination of colors for squares are listed with the individual pattern instructions.

ONE-COLOR SQUARE: Ch 4, join with a sl st to form a ring.

Rnd 1 (wrong side): Ch 3, 2 dc in ring (*Fig 1*); * ch 2, 3 dc in ring; rep from * twice more; ch 2, join with a sl st in top of beg ch-3 (*Fig 2*).

Rnd 2: Turn; sk joining st, sl st in next ch st and then into ch-2 sp; ch 3, 2 dc in same sp; * ch 1, work (3 dc, ch 2, 3 dc) all in next ch-2 sp for corner; rep from * twice more; ch 1, 3 dc in beg corner sp (*Fig 3*); ch 2, join with a sl st in top of beg ch-3. Finish off, leaving approx 14″ sewing length.

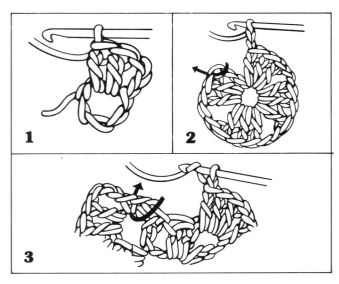

TWO-COLOR SQUARE: With first color listed for square (center color), ch 4, join with a sl st to form a ring.

Rnd 1 (wrong side): Ch 3, 2 dc in ring; * ch 2, 3 dc in ring; rep from * twice more; ch 2, join with a sl st in top of beg ch-3. Finish off center color, leaving approx 4″ end to weave in now or later.

Rnd 2: Turn; join second color listed for square with a sl st in any ch-2 sp; ch 3, 2 dc in same sp; * ch 1, work (3 dc, ch 2, 3 dc) all in next ch-2 sp for corner; rep from * twice more; ch 1, 3 dc in beg corner sp; ch 2, join with a sl st in top of beg ch-3. Finish off, leaving approx 14″ sewing length.

DIAGONAL TWO-COLOR SQUARE: With Color A, ch 4, join with a sl st to form a ring. (*NOTE: For "Color A", use either color listed for square; then for "Color B", use remaining color listed. When joining squares later, be sure to match colors with adjacent squares to form the picture.*)

Rnd 1 (wrong side): Ch 3, 2 dc in ring; ch 2, 3 dc in ring; drop Color A (*do not cut*); with Color B (*leave approx 4″ end to weave in now or later*), ch 2 (*Fig 4*); continuing with Color B, work (3 dc in ring, ch 2) twice; join with a sl st in top of beg ch-3.

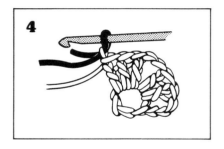

Rnd 2: Turn; sk joining st, sl st in next ch st and then into ch-2 sp; ch 3, 2 dc in same sp; ch 1, work (3 dc, ch 2, 3 dc) all in next ch-2 sp for corner; ch 1, 3 dc in next ch-2 sp, ch 2; finish off Color B, leaving approx 14″ sewing length. With Color A, work 3 dc in same sp (*corner completed*); ch 1, work (3 dc, ch 2, 3 dc) all in next ch-2 sp for corner; ch 1, 3 dc in beg corner sp (over sl sts of Color B); ch 2, join with a sl st in top of beg ch-3. Finish off, leaving approx 14″ sewing length.

Joining Squares

Arrange and join squares to form the "picture" following chart given with the individual wall hanging instructions.

To join, hold two squares with right sides tog, positioned (whenever possible) with sewing length in upper right-hand corner. Thread yarn (use matching

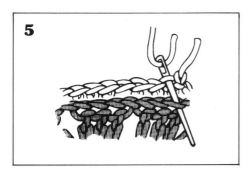

yarn when a sewing length is not available) into tapestry or yarn needle. Carefully matching sts on both squares, beg with one corner st and sew with overcast st **in outer lps only (Fig 5)** across side, ending with one st at next corner. Join squares in rows across and then sew these rows tog; or sew squares to form parts of the "picture", then sew these units tog. At each four-corner junction, either join all four corners securely, or if a small decorative opening is desired, do not join.

WINDOW VIEW

Size
Approx 47¼" × 60¾"

Materials
American Thread Dawn Sayelle Knitting Worsted
Size Yarn:
- 13 oz white
- 10 oz each of true blue and chocolate brown
- 6 oz each of sandstone, baby green, grass green and baby blue
- 4 oz each of shaded greens, watermelon and rust
- 3 oz each of honey beige and burnt orange
- 2 oz golf green
- 1 oz forest green

Size G aluminum crochet hook (or size required for gauge)
Metal macrame ring (1½" diameter) for shade pull

Gauge
One square = 2¼"

Instructions
Following One-Color Square and Diagonal Two-Color Square instructions, make the following number of squares:

ONE-COLOR SQUARES	DIAGONAL TWO-COLOR SQUARES
41 sandstone	10 white/baby blue
6 watermelon	5 baby blue/grass green
13 honey beige	1 honey beige/grass green
43 baby green	1 honey beige/sandstone
23 shaded greens	5 baby green/sandstone
95 chocolate brown	7 shaded greens/sandstone
19 rust	4 shaded green/baby green
20 burnt orange	3 shaded greens/burnt orange
30 grass green	2 shaded greens/burnt orange
121 white	
84 true blue	
34 baby blue	

When all squares have been made and joined, lightly steam press wall hanging on wrong side.

Applique Details
Make the following applique details and sew in place as indicated on Window Chart, (*Fig 6*) using matching sewing thread (*except for shade pull and flowers*).

SHADE PULL: With true blue, make a slip knot on hook, work scs over metal ring until ring is completely covered; join with a sl st in beg sc. Continue with same yarn and make a chain to measure 2½". Finish off, leaving approx 4" end; thread into tapestry or yarn needle and attach end of chain securely to center lower edge of shade. Weave in ends.

MULLIONS (make 2): With chocolate brown, make a chain to measure 13" long; then sl st in 2nd ch from hook and in each rem ch across. Finish off; weave in ends. Sew to upper window for strip dividing window panes, having right side of sts facing up.

HEM OUTLINE ON SHADE: With true blue, make a chain to measure approx 33" long. Finish off; weave in ends. Sew across top edge of hem, having wrong side of chain facing up.

FLOWERS (make 6): With watermelon, ch 4, join with a sl st to form a ring.

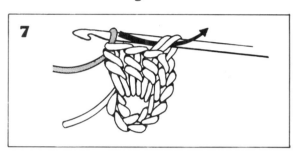

Rnd 1: Work beg PC (popcorn) in ring [**To make beg PC: Ch 3, work 3 dc in ring, drop lp from hook; insert hook in top of ch-3, hook dropped lp (*Fig 7*) and pull through st = beg PC made**]. * Ch 3, work PC in ring (**To make PC: Work 4 dc in ring, drop lp from hook; insert hook in top of first dc of 4-dc group just made, hook dropped lp and pull through st = PC made**); rep from * twice more; ch 3, join with a sl st in top of ch-3 of beg PC = 4 ch-3 sps.

Rnd 2: * Work (sc, hdc, 5 dc, hdc, sc) all in next ch-3 sp for petal; rep from * 3 times more = 4 petals. (*NOTE: Do not join at end of rnd.*)

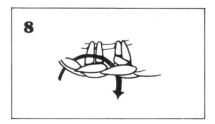

Rnd 3: * Work BP (back post) sl st around first sc of next petal [**To work BP sl st: Insert hook from back to front to back around post of st (*Fig 8*);**

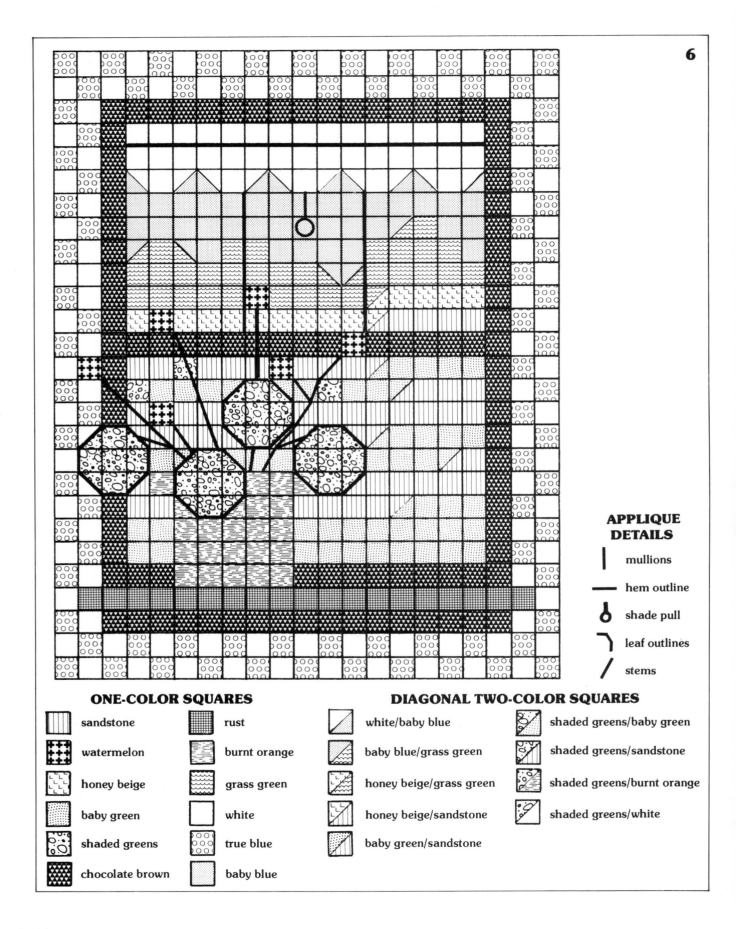

APPLIQUE DETAILS

	mullions
	hem outline
	shade pull
	leaf outlines
	stems

ONE-COLOR SQUARES

	sandstone		rust
	watermelon		burnt orange
	honey beige		grass green
	baby green		white
	shaded greens		true blue
	chocolate brown		baby blue

DIAGONAL TWO-COLOR SQUARES

	white/baby blue		shaded greens/baby green
	baby blue/grass green		shaded greens/sandstone
	honey beige/grass green		shaded greens/burnt orange
	honey beige/sandstone		shaded greens/white
	baby green/sandstone		

hook yarn and draw back around st and through lp on hook = **BP sl st made**]; ch 3, sk 3 sts, work BP sl st around next st (center st) of same petal; ch 3, sk last 4 sts of petal; rep from * 3 times more, join with a sl st in beg sl st = 8 ch-3 sps.

Rnd 4: * Work (sc, hdc, 3 dc, hdc, sc) in next ch-3 sp; rep from * 7 times more, join with a sl st in beg sc = 8 petals. Finish off, leaving approx 10″ sewing length. Sew flower to wall hanging over watermelon square.

LEAF OUTLINE (*make 4):* With forest green, make a chain to measure approx 21″ long. Finish off; weave in ends. Sew chain around edge of leaf, having wrong side of chain facing up.

FLOWER STEMS: With golf green, make one chain in each of following approx lengths: 2¾″, 3½″, 6¾″, 11″, 12″ and 13½″ (6 total). Weave in ends; then sew each chain to wall hanging, having wrong side of chain facing up.

LEAF STEMS: With golf green, make one chain in each of the following approx lengths: 2¼″, 2¾″ and 3″ (3 total). Weave in ends; then sew each chain to wall hanging, having wrong side of chain facing up.

ROCKET SHIP

Size

Approx 49½″ × 60¾″

Materials

American Thread Dawn Sayelle Knitting Worsted Size Yarn:
20 oz blue
12 oz steel gray
8 oz each of turquoise and white
7 oz shaded greens
4 oz flame
2 oz lemon
1 oz each of true blue and gray blue
½ oz each of hot orange and hot pink
Size G aluminum crochet hook (or size required for gauge)

Gauge

One square = 2¼″

Instructions

Following One-Color Square, Two-Color Square and Diagonal Two-Color Square instructions, make the following number of squares:

ONE-COLOR SQUARES

192 blue	55 steel gray
64 turquoise	1 hot orange
52 turquoise	2 hot pink
59 white	4 true blue

TWO/COLOR SQUARES

24 lemon/blue

DIAGONAL TWO-COLOR SQUARES

9 blue/steel gray	33 steel gray/gray blue
5 blue/white	6 steel gray/turquoise
1 blue/shaded greens	11 steel gray/shaded greens
1 lemon/flame	26 steel gray/white
3 lemon/hot orange	1 hot pink/turquoise
3 lemon/shaded greens	4 hot pink/hot orange
6 flame/hot orange	4 true blue/white
3 flame/turquoise	4 true blue/steel gray
5 flame/hot pink	1 shaded greens/hot orange
3 turquoise/lemon	4 shaded greens/flame
4 turquoise/shaded greens	
4 turquoise/blue	

When all squares have been made and joined, lightly steam press wall hanging on wrong side.

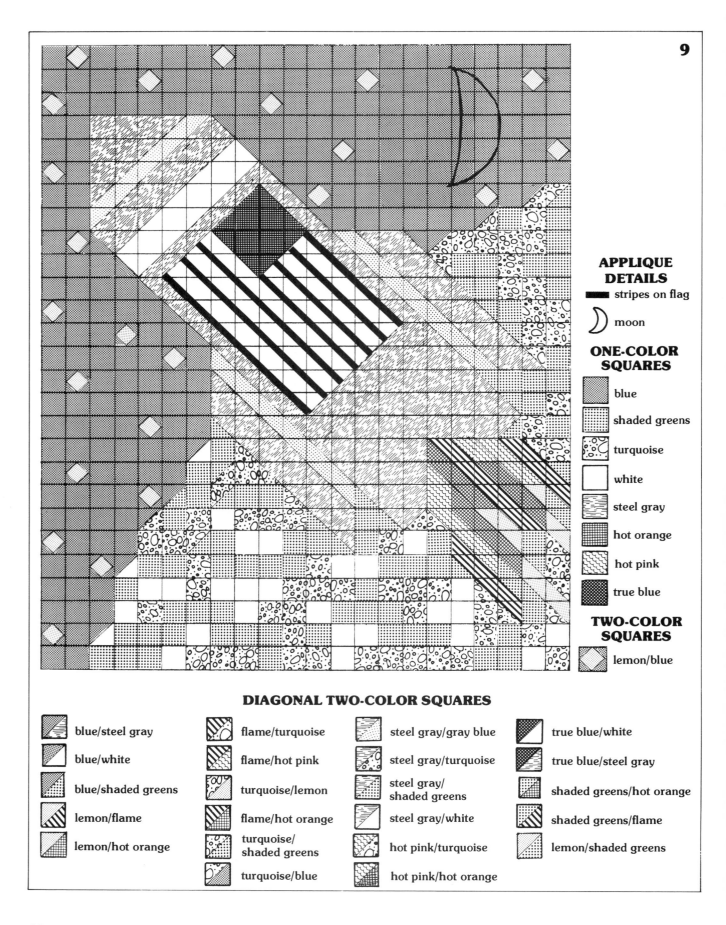

9

APPLIQUE DETAILS

▬ stripes on flag

☾ moon

ONE-COLOR SQUARES

blue

shaded greens

turquoise

white

steel gray

hot orange

hot pink

true blue

TWO-COLOR SQUARES

lemon/blue

DIAGONAL TWO-COLOR SQUARES

blue/steel gray

blue/white

blue/shaded greens

lemon/flame

lemon/hot orange

flame/turquoise

flame/hot pink

turquoise/lemon

flame/hot orange

turquoise/ shaded greens

turquoise/blue

steel gray/gray blue

steel gray/turquoise

steel gray/ shaded greens

steel gray/white

hot pink/turquoise

hot pink/hot orange

true blue/white

true blue/steel gray

shaded greens/hot orange

shaded greens/flame

lemon/shaded greens

Applique Details

Make the following applique details and sew in place as indicated on Rocket Ship Chart (**Fig 9**), using matching sewing thread.

STRIPES ON FLAG (*make three 18" long and four 12" long = 7 total*): With flame, make a chain to measure the specified length of stripe; then work sc in 2nd ch from hook and in each rem ch across. Finish off; weave in ends. Sew to wall hanging, having wrong side of sts facing up and foundation chain edge facing bottom edge of flag.

MOON: With White, ch 49.

Row 1 (right side): Sc in 2nd ch from hook and in each of next 31 chs = 32 sc (leave rem 16 chs unworked). (*NOTE: You will be working in "short" rows, leaving sts unworked at end of rows. Do not ch 1 at beg of rows.*)

Row 2: Turn; sc in each of first 18 sc.

Row 3: Turn; sc in first sc, 2 sc in next sc; * sc in each of next 3 sc, 2 sc in next sc; rep from * twice more; sc in each of next 4 sc, sc in each of next 4 chs = 26 sc.

Row 4: Turn; sc in each of first 26 sc, sc in each of next 3 sc = 29 sc.

Row 5: Turn; sc in each of first 29 sc, sc in each of next 3 chs = 32 sc.

Row 6: Turn; sc in each of first 32 sc, sc in each of next 2 sc = 34 sc.

Row 7: Turn; sc in each of first 2 sc, 2 sc in next sc; * sc in each of next 4 sc, 2 sc in next sc; rep from * 4 times more; work (sc in next sc, 2 sc in next sc) twice, sc in each of next 2 sc, sc in each of next 3 chs = 45 sc.

Row 8: Turn; sc in each of first 45 sc, sc in each of next 3 sc = 48 sc.

Row 9: Turn; sc in each of first 48 sc, sc in each of next 2 chs = 50 sc.

Row 10: Turn; sc in each of first 50 sc, sc in each of next 3 chs = 53 sc.

Row 11: Turn; sc in each of first 2 sc, 2 sc in next sc; * sc in each of next 5 sc, 2 sc in next sc; rep from * 7 times more; sc in each of next 2 sc, sc in each of next 2 chs = 64 sc.

Row 12: Turn; sc in each of first 64 sc, sc in each of next 2 sc, work 3 sc in last st = 69 sc.

Row 13: Turn; sc in each of first 69 sc, sc in next ch, sl st in last ch. Finish off; weave in ends. Sew to wall hanging, having right side of moon facing up.

FREEDOM RIPPLE AFGHAN

designed by Jean Leinhauser

Here's a great afghan classic, the ripple, in a new version. We call it our "Freedom Ripple" because it's crocheted in shades of red, white and blue. It's also our patriotic afghan because it is a great energy-saver. Wrap up in this charmer, and you can keep your thermostat turned way down.

Size

Approx 44″ × 60″

Materials

American Thread Dawn Sayelle Knitting Worsted
   Size Yarn in 4-oz skeins:
     4 skeins baby blue
     3 skeins true blue
     2 skeins each of flame and white
Size K aluminum crochet hook (or size required for
   gauge)

Gauge

In sc, 3 sts = 1″

Instructions

With true blue, ch 176 **loosely**.

Row 1 (foundation row—right side): Sc in 2nd ch from hook, sk one ch, sc in each of next 4 chs. * Work 3 sc in next ch (for point), sc in each of next 3 chs; sk 2 chs, sc in each of next 3 chs; rep from * to last 7 chs. Work 3 sc in next ch (for last point), sc in each of next 4 chs; sk one ch, sc in last ch.

Row 2 (patt row): Ch 1, turn; sc in first sc, sk one sc, sc in each of next 4 sc. * Work 3 sc in next sc (*center sc of 3-sc group at point*), sc in each of next 3 sc; sk 2 sc, sc in each of next 3 sc; rep from * to last 7 sc. Work 3 sc in next sc (*center sc of 3-sc group at last point*), sc in each of next 4 sc; sk one sc, sc in last sc.

Row 3: Rep Row 2, changing to white in last sc. [**To change colors: Work last st until 2 lps rem on hook; finish off, leaving approx 4″ end. With new color (leave 4″ end), complete st (YO and draw through both lps on hook) = color changed.**] (*NOTE: At beg of next row, work over yarn ends for several sts as shown in Fig 1.*)

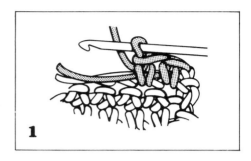

Row 4: With white, rep Row 2, changing to flame in last sc.

Row 5: With flame (remember to work over yarn ends), rep Row 2, changing to baby blue in last sc.

Row 6: With baby blue, rep Row 2.

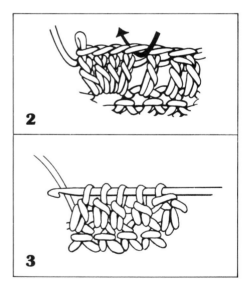

Row 7 (PC row): Continuing with baby blue, ch 2, turn; sk first sc, dc in each of next 3 sc, work PC (popcorn) in next sc [**To make PC: Work 4 dc in st; remove hook from lp and insert in first dc of 4-dc group just made (Fig 2); hook dropped lp and pull through lp on hook, ch 1 tightly = PC made**], dc in next sc. * Work 3 dc in next sc (center sc of 3-sc group at point), dc in next sc; PC in next sc, work CL (cluster) over next 4 sc [**To make CL: Work (YO, insert hook in next sc and draw up a lp, YO and draw through 2 lps on hook) 4 times (5 lps now on hook—see Fig 3); YO and draw through all 5 lps on hook = CL made**]; PC in next sc, dc in next sc; rep from * to last 7 sc. Work 3 dc in next sc (center sc of 3-sc group at last point), dc in next sc; PC in next sc, dc in each of next 2 sc; work dc dec (decrease) over last 2 sc. [**To make dec: Work (YO, insert hook in next sc and draw up a lp, YO and draw through 2 lps on hook) twice (3 lps now on hook); YO and draw through all 3 lps on hook = dc dec made.**]

Row 8: Continuing with baby blue, ch 1, turn; sc in first st (dc dec), sk next dc, sc in next dc; sc in PC (*work in dc where dropped lp was pulled through*), sc in each of next 2 dc. * Work 3 sc in next dc (*center dc of 3-dc group at point*), sc in each of next 2 dc, sc in PC, sk cluster, sc in next PC; sc in each of next 2 dc; rep from * to last point. Work 3 sc in next dc (*center dc of 3-dc group at last point*), sc in each of next 2 dc; sc in next PC, sc in next dc, sk next dc; sc in last dc, changing to flame. (*NOTE: Ch-2 at end of row is left unworked.*)

Row 9: With flame, rep Row 2, changing to white in last sc.

Row 10: With white, rep Row 2, changing to true blue in last sc.

Rep Rows 1 through 10, 12 times more; then rep Rows 1 through 3 once more. At end of last row, do not change to white. Finish off; weave in ends. Lightly steam press edges on wrong side to prevent curling.

GRANNY RAINBOW AFGHAN

designed by Joan Kokaska

Combine two favorite afghan techniques: the granny square and the ripple. You create this colorful "Granny Rainbow." What a delightful way to add plenty of color to your life while keeping warm!

Size

Approx 46″ × 72″

Materials

American Thread Dawn Sayelle Knitting Worsted Size Yarn in 4-oz skeins:
  5 skeins white
  2 skeins each of flame, hot orange, lemon, nile green, blue, and lilac
Size I aluminum crochet hook (or size required for gauge)

Gauge

In dc, 13 sts = 4″

Instructions

With flame, ch 210 **loosely.**

Row 1: Sc in 2nd ch from hook and in each rem ch across = 209 sc.

Row 2: Ch 3, turn; sk first 3 sc, work (3 dc in next sc, sk 2 sc) 3 times; work (3 dc, ch 3, 3 dc) in next sc for point. * Sk 2 sc, work (3 dc in next sc, sk 2 sc) twice; work cluster st (abbreviated CL) in next sc **[To make CL: Work (YO, insert hook in st and draw up a lp; YO and draw through 2 lps on hook) 3 times (4 lps now on hook—see *Fig 1*); YO and draw through all 4 lps on hook = CL made]**; sk 4 sc, CL in next sc; sk 2 sc, work (3 dc in

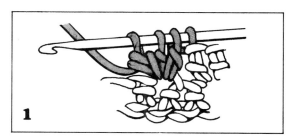

next sc, sk 2 sc) twice; work (3 dc, ch 3, 3 dc) in next sc for point; rep from * 7 times more. Sk 2 sc, work (3 dc in next sc, sk 2 sc) 3 times, dc in last sc.

Row 3 (patt row): Ch 3, turn; sk first sp (*between first dc and 3-dc group*); work 3 dc in each of next 3 sps (*between 3-dc groups*); work (3 dc, ch 3, 3 dc) in ch-3 sp at point. * Work 3 dc in each of next 2 sps, CL in next sp; sk next sp (*between CL*), CL in next sp; work 3 dc in each of next 2 sps, work (3 dc, ch 3, 3 dc) in ch-3 sp at next point; rep from * 7 times more. Work 3 dc in each of next 3 sps; dc in last sp (between last 3-dc group and ch-3). Finish off flame; join white.

Rep Row 3 in the following 18-row color sequence:

  1 row white/2 rows hot orange
  1 row white/2 rows lemon
  1 row white/2 rows nile green
  1 row white/2 rows blue
  1 row white/2 rows lilac
  1 row white/2 rows flame

Rep prev 18-row color sequence, 4 times more. Then rep first 15 rows of color sequence once more, ending by working 2 rows lilac. Finish off; weave in all ends.

PINK PINEAPPLE DOILY

Here is a favorite reworked and rewritten old-time doily pattern. We've updated it for today's lifestyle, still keeping the old-fashioned charm of one of America's all-time favorite crochet motifs, the pineapple.

Size

Approx 17½″ diameter

Materials

American Thread Puritan or Giant Crochet Thread: 350 yds pink
Size 7 steel crochet hook (or size required for gauge)

Gauge

First 7 rnds = 5″ diameter

Instructions

Ch 11, join with a sl st to form a ring. (*NOTE: All rnds are worked on right side.*)

Rnd 1: Ch 3, work 24 dc in ring; join with a sl st in top of beg ch-3.

Rnd 2: Ch 6, trc (*triple crochet*) in next dc; * ch 2, trc in next dc; rep from * around, ch 2, join with a sl st in 4th ch of beg ch-6 = 25 ch-2 sps.

Rnd 3: Sl st into first ch-2 sp, ch 5, dc in same sp;

* work (dc, ch 2, dc) in next ch-2 sp; rep from * around, join with a sl st in 3rd ch of beg ch-5 = 25 ch-2 sps.

Rnd 4: Sl st into first ch-2 sp, ch 6, trc in same sp; * work (trc, ch 2, trc) in next ch-2 sp; rep from * around, join with a sl st in 4th ch of beg ch-6 = 25 ch-2 sps.

Rnd 5: Sl st into first ch-2 sp, ch 6, dc in same sp; * work (dc, ch 3, dc) in next ch-2 sp; rep from * around, join with a sl st in 3rd ch of beg ch-6 = 25 ch-3 sps.

Rnd 6: St st into first ch-3 sp; ch 8, trc in same sp; * work (trc, ch 4, trc) in next ch-3 sp; rep from * around, join with a sl st in 4th ch of beg ch-8 = 25 ch-4 sps.

Rnd 7: Sl st into first ch-4 sp, ch 5, dc in same sp; * work (dc, ch 2, dc) in sp between next 2 trcs (before next ch-4 sp), work (dc, ch 2, dc) in next ch-4 sp; rep from * around, work (dc, ch 2, dc) in sp between last trc and ch-4; join with a sl st in 3rd ch of beg ch-5 = 50 ch-2 sps.

Rnd 8: Rep Rnd 4 = 50 ch-2 sps.

Rnd 9: Rep Rnd 5 = 50 ch-3 sps.

Rnd 10: Sl st into first ch-3 sp, work (ch 3, dc, ch 2, 2 dc) in same sp (**for beg shell**); * ch 4, sc in next ch-3 sp, ch 4, work (trc, ch 4, trc) in next ch-3 sp; ch 4, sc in next ch-3 sp, ch 4, work (2 dc, ch 2, 2 dc) in next ch-3 sp (**for shell**); work a shell in next ch-3 sp; rep from * around, *ending last rep without working last shell*; join with a sl st in top of ch-3 of beg shell. (*NOTE: Join each following rnd in this manner, unless otherwise specified.*)

Rnd 11: Sl st in next dc and then into sp of beg shell, work beg shell in same sp; * ch 2, sk next two ch-4 sps, work 10 trc in next ch-4 sp (between trcs) for base of pineapple; ch 2, sk next two ch-4 sps, work a shell in sp of next shell, ch 1, work a shell in sp of next shell; rep from * around, *ending last rep without working shell*; join (as before).

Rnd 12: Sl st into sp of beg shell (as before), work beg shell in same sp; * trc in first trc of pineapple, (ch 1, trc in next trc of pineapple) 9 times; work a shell in sp of next shell, ch 1, work a shell in sp of next shell; rep from * around, *ending last rep without working shell*; join.

Rnd 13: Sl st into sp of beg shell, work beg shell in same sp; * sc in first ch-1 sp of pineapple, (ch 3, sc in next ch-1 sp of pineapple) 8 times; work a shell in sp of next shell, ch 1, work a shell in sp of next shell; rep from * around, *ending last rep without working shell*; join.

Rnd 14: Sl st into sp of beg shell, work beg shell in same sp; * ch 1, sc in first ch-3 sp of pineapple, (ch 3, sc in next ch-3 sp of pineapple) 7 times; (ch 1, work a shell in sp of next shell) twice; rep from * around, *ending last rep without working shell*; join.

Rnd 15: Sl st into sp of beg shell, work beg shell in same sp; * ch 1, sk next ch-1 sp, sc in first ch-3 sp of pineapple, (ch 3, sc in next ch-3 sp of pineapple) 6 times; (ch 1, work a shell in sp of next shell) twice; rep from * around, *ending last rep without working shell*; join.

Rnd 16: Sl st into sp of beg shell, work beg shell in same sp; * ch 1, sk next ch-1 sp, sc in first ch-3 sp of pineapple, (ch 3, sc in next ch-3 sp of pineapple) 5 times; ch 1, work a shell in sp of next shell, ch 2, work a shell in sp of next shell; rep from * around, *ending last rep without working shell*; join.

Rnd 17: Sl st into sp of beg shell, work beg shell in same sp; * ch 2, sk next ch-1 sp, sc in first ch-3 sp of pineapple, (ch 3, sc in next ch-3 sp of pineapple) 4 times; ch 2, work a shell in sp of next shell; ch 2, work (trc, ch 3, trc) in ch-2 sp between shells; ch 2, work a shell in sp of next shell; rep from * around, *ending last rep without working shell*; join.

Rnd 18: Sl st into sp of beg shell, work beg shell in same sp; * ch 3, sk next ch-2 sp, sc in first ch-3 sp of pineapple, (ch 3, sc in next ch-3 sp of pineapple) 3 times; ch 3, work a shell in sp of next shell; ch 2, work (trc, ch 3, trc) in next ch-2 sp, ch 2, work (trc, ch 3, trc) in next ch-3 sp; ch 2, work (trc, ch 3, trc) in next ch-2 sp; ch 2, work a shell in sp of next shell; rep from * around, *ending last rep without working shell*; join.

Rnd 19: Sl st into sp of beg shell, work beg shell in same sp; * ch 3, sk next ch-3 sp, sc in first ch-3 sp of pineapple, (ch 3, sc in next ch-3 sp of pineapple) twice; ch 3, work a shell in sp of next shell; ch 2, † work (dc, ch 2, dc) in next ch-2 sp, work (dc, ch 2, dc) in next ch-3 sp †; rep from † to † twice; work (dc, ch 2, dc) in next ch-2 sp, ch 2, work a shell in sp of next shell; rep from * around, *ending last rep without working shell*; join.

Rnd 20: Sl st into sp of beg shell, work beg shell in same sp; * ch 3, sk next ch-3 sp, sc in first ch-3 sp of pineapple; ch 3, sc in next ch-3 sp of pineapple; ch 3, work a shell in sp of next shell, ch 3, sk next ch-2 sp, work a cluster in next ch-2 sp. [**To work cluster: Keeping last lp of each st on hook, work 3 dc in next ch-2 sp (4 lps now on hook—*Fig 1*), YO and draw through all 4 lps on hook = cluster made.**] † Ch 3, work a cluster in next ch-2 sp †; rep from † to † 5 times; ch 3, sk next ch-2 sp, work a shell in sp of next shell; rep from * around, *ending last rep without working shell*; join.

Rnd 21: Sl st into sp of beg shell, work beg shell in

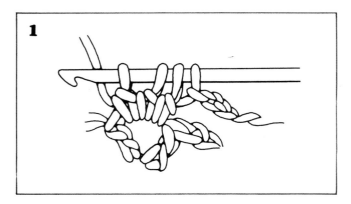

same sp; * ch 3, sk next ch-3 sp, sc in ch-3 sp at tip of pineapple; ch 3, work a shell in sp of next shell; † ch 2, work (trc, ch 2, trc) in next ch-3 sp †; rep from † to † 7 times; ch 2, work a shell in sp of next shell; rep from * around, *ending last rep without working shell*; join.

Rnd 22: Sl st into sp of beg shell, work beg shell in same sp; * sk next two ch-3 sps, work a shell in sp of next shell, ch 2, sk next ch-2 sp; † work (dc, ch 2, dc) in next ch-2 sp †; rep from † to † 14 times; ch 2, sk next ch-2 sp, work a shell in sp of next shell; rep from * around, *ending last rep without working shell*; join.

Rnd 23: Sl st into sp of beg shell, work beg cluster in same sp. **[To work beg cluster: Ch 3; keeping last lp of each st on hook, work 2 dc in same sp, YO and draw through all 3 lps on hook = beg cluster made.]** * Work a cluster (*see* Rnd 20) in sp of next shell, ch 3, sk next ch-2 sp, work a cluster in next ch-2 sp; † ch 3, work a cluster in next ch-2 sp †; rep from † to † 13 times; ch 3, sk next ch-2 sp, work a cluster in sp of next shell; rep from * around, *ending last rep without working cluster*; join with a sl st in top of beg cluster.

Rnd 24: Sl st across top of next (cluster, 3 chs and next cluster), then sl st into next ch-3 sp; ch 4, trc in same sp; * † ch 2, 2 trc in next ch-3 sp †; rep from † to † 12 times; sk next two ch-3 sps, 2 trc in next ch-3 sp; rep from * around, *ending last rep without working last 2 trcs*; join with a sl st in top of beg ch-4.

Rnd 25: * Ch 4, sk next trc, † dc in first trc of next 2-trc group; ch 4, sl st in 3rd ch from hook (for picot); ch 1, dc in next trc of same 2-trc group †; rep from † to † 11 times; ch 4, sk first trc of next 2-trc group, sl st in next trc of same 2-trc group; sl st in first trc of next 2-trc group; rep from * around, *ending last rep without working last sl st*.

Finish off; weave in all ends.

Edging No. 1 (light)   Edging No. 2 (dark)

ELEGANT EDGINGS

What a quick and easy way to add a touch of class to a simple pillow case, sheet, towel—or even the hem of a ready-made skirt. Just crochet an elegant edging. Here are two different edgings, both based upon the ever-popular pineapple motif. You'll want to make yards of these edgings to trim your household linen as well as your gift items.

EDGING NO. 1

Size

Approx 4¼" deep × desired length

Materials

American Thread Puritan Crochet Thread in ecru
Size 7 steel crochet hook (or size required for gauge)

(*MATERIALS NOTE: Approx 30 yds of thread are required to complete one repeat of the pattern.*)

Gauge

One pattern repeat = 4¼" deep × 4¼" wide

Instructions

Ch 32.

Row 1: Work 2 dc in 4th ch from hook, ch 2, 3 dc in next ch (**foundation shell made**); * ch 3, sk next 7 chs; 3 dc in next ch, ch 2, 3 dc in next ch (**foundation shell made**); rep from * once more; ch 1, sk next ch, dc in next ch; ch 3, sk next ch, sc in next ch; ch 3, sk next ch, dc in next ch; ch 2, sk next 2 chs, dc in last ch.

Row 2: Ch 5, turn; dc in next dc, ch 3, sk sc, work (dc, ch 1, dc) in next dc; ch 1, work (3 dc, ch 2, 3 dc) in sp of next shell (**shell made**); ch 3, work 11 trc in sp of next shell (for base of pineapple); ch 3, work a shell in sp of next shell.

Row 3: Ch 4, turn; work a shell in sp of first shell, ch 3, sc in sp between first 2 trcs of pineapple, (ch 3, sc in sp between next 2 trcs of pineapple) 9 times; ch 1, work a shell in sp of next shell; sk next 3 dc of shell (*now and throughout patt*), work (ch 1, dc in next dc) twice; ch 3, sc in next ch-3 sp, ch 3, dc in next dc; ch 2, dc in 3rd ch of Tch.

55

Row 4: Ch 5, turn; dc in next dc, ch 3, sk sc, dc in next dc; ch 3, dc in next dc, work a shell in sp of next shell; ch 1, sc in first ch-3 sp of pineapple, (ch 3, sc in next ch-3 sp of pineapple) 8 times; ch 3, work a shell in sp of next shell.

Row 5: Ch 4, turn; work a shell in sp of first shell, ch 3, sk next ch-3 sp, sc in first ch-3 sp of pineapple; (ch 3, sc in next ch-3 sp of pineapple) 7 times, ch 1, work a shell in sp of next shell; ch 1, dc in next dc *(remember to sk next 3 dc of shell)*; * ch 3, sc in next ch-3 sp, ch 3, dc in next dc; rep from * once more; ch 2, dc in 3rd ch of Tch.

Row 6: Ch 5, turn; * dc in next dc, ch 3, sk next sc; rep from * once more; work (dc, ch 1, dc) in next dc, ch 1, work a shell in sp of next shell; ch 2, sc in first ch-3 sp of pineapple, (ch 3, sc in next ch-3 sp of pineapple) 6 times; ch 3, work a shell in sp of next shell.

Row 7: Ch 4, turn; work a shell in sp of first shell, ch 3, sk next ch-3 sp, sc in first ch-3 sp of pineapple; (ch 3, sc in next ch-3 sp of pineapple) 5 times, ch 2, work a shell in sp of next shell; (ch 1, dc in next dc) twice; * ch 3, sc in next ch-3 sp, ch 3, dc in next dc; rep from * once more; ch 2, dc in 3rd ch of Tch.

Row 8: Ch 5, turn; dc in next dc, * ch 3, sk next sc, dc in next dc; rep from * once more; ch 3, dc in next dc, work a shell in sp of next shell; ch 2, sc in first ch-3 sp of pineapple, (ch 3, sc in next ch-3 sp of pineapple) 4 times; ch 3, work a shell in sp of next shell.

Row 9: Ch 4, turn; work a shell in sp of first shell, ch 3, sk next ch-3 sp, sc in first ch-3 sp of pineapple; (ch 3, sc in next ch-3 sp of pineapple) 3 times, ch 2, work a shell in sp of next shell; ch 1, dc in next dc; * ch 3, sc in next ch-3 sp, ch 3, dc in next dc; rep from * twice more; ch 2, dc in 3rd ch of Tch.

Row 10: Ch 5, turn; * dc in next dc, ch 3, sk next sc; rep from * twice more; work (dc, ch 1, dc) in next dc, ch 1, work a shell in sp of next shell; ch 3, sc in first ch-3 sp of pineapple, (ch 3, sc in next ch-3 sp of pineapple) twice; ch 3, work a shell in sp of next shell.

Row 11: Ch 4, turn; work a shell in sp of first shell, ch 3, sk next ch-3 sp, sc in first ch-3 sp of pineapple; ch 3, sc in next ch-3 sp of pineapple; ch 3, work a shell in sp of next shell, (ch 1, dc in next dc) twice; * ch 3, sc in next ch-3 sp, ch 3, dc in next dc; rep from * twice more; ch 2, dc in 3rd ch of Tch.

Row 12: Ch 5, turn; dc in next dc, * ch 3, sk next sc, dc in next dc; rep from * twice more; ch 3, dc in next dc, work a shell in sp of next shell; ch 3, sk next ch-3 sp, sc in ch-3 sp at tip of pineapple; ch 3, work a shell in sp of next shell.

Row 13: Ch 4, turn; work a shell in sp of first shell, ch 1, work a shell in sp of next shell; ch 1, dc in next dc, * ch 3, sc in next ch-3 sp, ch 3, dc in next dc; rep from * 3 times more; ch 2, dc in 3rd ch of Tch.

Row 14: Ch 5, turn; * dc in next dc, ch 3, sk next sc; rep from * 3 times more, work (dc, ch 1, dc) in next dc; ch 1, work a shell in sp of next shell; ch 2, sc in sp of next shell.

Row 15: Ch 2, turn; work a shell in sp of next shell, ch 3, sk next ch-1 sp, work a shell in next ch-1 sp (between dcs); ch 3, sk next two ch-3 sps, work a shell in next dc; ch 1, sk next ch-3 sp, dc in next dc; ch 3, sc in next ch-3 sp, ch 3, dc in next dc; ch 2, dc in 3rd ch of Tch.

Rep Rows 2 through 15 to desired length, ending by working Row 14.

Finish off; weave in ends.

Then work one row of edging across top edge (long edge without shells) as follows: Make a slip knot on hook, join with a sc in first sp, work 2 sc in same sp as joining; work 3 sc in each rem sp across. Finish off; weave in ends.

EDGING NO. 2

Size

Approx 5¼" deep × desired length

Materials

American Thread Puritan or Giant Crochet Thread in brown
Size 7 steel crochet hook (or size required for gauge)

(MATERIALS NOTE: Approx 30 yds of thread are required to complete one repeat of the pattern.)

Gauge

One pattern repeat = 5¼" deep × 3" wide

Instructions

Edging is first worked in a strip of shells along top edge to the total desired length; then pineapple design is worked along one edge of the shell strip.

SHELL STRIP: Ch 15.

Row 1: Work 2 dc in 7th ch from hook, ch 2, 2 dc in next ch (**first foundation shell made**); ch 5, next 5 chs, 2 dc in next ch, ch 2, 2 dc in last ch (**2nd foundation shell made**).

Row 2: Ch 5, turn; work (2 dc, ch 2, 2 dc) in sp of first shell (**for shell**); ch 3, sc in ch-5 sp (between shells); ch 3, work a shell in sp of last shell.

Row 3: Ch 5, turn; work a shell in sp of first shell, ch 5, work a shell in sp of last shell.

Rep Rows 2 and 3 to desired total length (ending by working Row 3), having a total number of lps in a multiple of 4 + 1 across long edge next to last shell worked. [NOTE: To determine a multiple, multiply 4 (one pattern repeat) by the number of repeats needed for length (one repeat measures 3″ long). Then add 1 to this total for the total number of lps needed to complete edging in pineapple design. For example, if a 15″ length of lace is desired: 4 lps (one pattern repeat) × 5 repeats (each repeat measures 3″ long) = 20 lps + 1 = 21 total lps needed to complete a 15″ length of lace.]

Do not finish off; continue with pineapple design across long edge (along end of rows) of shell strip as follows.

PINEAPPLE DESIGN: Row 1: Ch 3, work a shell in first lp (turning ch-5 sp), * ch 3, sc in next lp, ch 3, work 10 trc in next lp (for base of pineapple); ch 3, sc in next lp, ch 3, work a shell in next lp; rep from * across.

Row 2: Ch 5, turn; work a shell in sp of first shell, * ch 5, dc in first trc of pineapple, (ch 1, dc in next trc of pineapple) 9 times; ch 5, work a shell in sp of next shell; rep from * across.

Row 3: Ch 5, turn; work a shell in sp of first shell, * ch 5, sc in first ch-1 sp of pineapple, (ch 3, sc in next ch-1 sp of pineapple) 8 times; ch 5, work a shell in sp of next shell; rep from * across.

Row 4: Ch 5, turn; work a shell in sp of first shell, * ch 5, sc in first ch-3 sp of pineapple, (ch 3, sc in next ch-3 sp of pineapple) 7 times; ch 5, work a shell in sp of next shell; rep from * across.

Row 5: Ch 5, turn; work a shell in sp of first shell, * ch 5, sc in first ch-3 sp of pineapple, (ch 3, sc in next ch-3 sp of pineapple) 6 times; ch 5, work a shell in sp of next shell; rep from * across.

Row 6: Ch 5, turn; work a shell in sp of first shell, * ch 5, sc in first ch-3 sp of pineapple, (ch 3, sc in next ch-3 sp of pineapple) 5 times; ch 5, work (2 dc, ch 2, 2 dc, ch 2, 2 dc) in sp of next shell (**for double shell**); rep from * across, *ending last rep by working a shell (instead of a double shell) in sp of last shell.*

Row 7: Ch 5, turn; work a shell in sp of first shell, ch 5, sc in first ch-3 sp of pineapple, (ch 3, sc in next ch-3 sp of pineapple) 4 times; ch 5, work a shell in first sp of next double shell.

Leave rem sts unworked; continue by working point of first pineapple as follows.

FIRST PINEAPPLE POINT: Row 1: Ch 5, turn; work a shell in sp of first shell, ch 5, sc in first ch-3 sp of pineapple, (ch 3, sc in next ch-3 sp of pineapple) 3 times; ch 5, work a shell in sp of next shell.

Row 2: Ch 5, turn; work a shell in sp of first shell, ch 5, sc in first ch-3 sp of pineapple, (ch 3, sc in next ch-3 sp of pineapple) twice; ch 5, work a shell in sp of next shell.

Row 3: Ch 5, turn; work a shell in sp of first shell, ch 5, sc in first ch-3 sp of pineapple; ch 3, sc in next sp of pineapple, ch 5, work a shell in sp of next shell.

Row 4: Ch 5, turn; work a shell in sp of first shell, ch 5, sc in sp of pineapple; ch 5, work a shell in sp of next shell.

Row 5: Ch 5, turn; work a shell in sp of first shell, work a shell in sp of next shell.

Row 6: Turn; sl st in next dc and then into sp of first shell, ch 3, dc in same sp; 2 dc in sp of next shell.

Row 7: Ch 5, turn; sk next 2 dc, sc in top of ch-3. Finish off; weave in ends.

Work point of each rem pineapple as follows.

NEXT PINEAPPLE POINT: Hold edging with pineapple point just made at top and to your right. Join with a sl st in next sp of double shell (next to pineapple just completed).

Row 1: Ch 3, work (dc, ch 2, 2 dc) in same sp as joining; ch 5, sc in first ch-3 sp of pineapple, (ch 3, sc in next ch-3 sp of pineapple) 4 times; ch 5, work a shell in first sp of next double shell.

Rows 2 through 8: Rep Rows 1 through 7 of first pineapple point. Finish off; weave in ends.

When all pineapple points have been completed, work one row of edging across top edge (along un-worked long edge of Shell Strip) as follows: Make a slip knot on hook, join with a sc in first lp; * ch 5, sc in next lp; rep from * across. Finish off; weave in all ends.

OVAL PINEAPPLE PLACEMAT

For over 100 years, the pineapple has been the symbol of hospitality. What better way to welcome your guests than to serve them dinner on a pineapple placemat!

Size
Approx 15″ × 19″

Materials
American Thread Puritan Crochet Thread:
    550 yds kelly green
Size 0 steel crochet hook (or size required for gauge)

(*MATERIALS NOTE: Thread is used doubled throughout patt.*)

Gauge
With 2 strands of thread in dc, 17 sts = 3″

Instructions
With 2 strands of thread, ch 32. (*Note: All rnds are worked on right side.*)

Rnd 1: Work 2 dc in 4th ch from hook (3 unused chs count as first dc), dc in each of the next 27 chs, work 5 dc in last ch. **Continuing on opposite side of starting chain**, work dc in each of the next 27 sts, 2 dc in last st; join with a sl st in top of ch-3.

Rnd 2: Ch 3, (2 dc in next dc, dc in next dc) twice, dc in each of next 24 dc; (2 dc in next dc, dc in next dc) 4 times, dc in each of next 24 dc; 2 dc in next dc, dc in next dc, 2 dc in next dc; join with a sl st in top of beg ch-3.

Rnd 3: Ch 3, (2 dc in next dc, dc in next dc) 3 times, dc in each of next 24 dc; (2 dc in next dc, dc in next dc) 6 times, dc in each of next 24 dc; (2 dc in next dc, dc in next dc) twice, 2 dc in last dc; join with a sl st in top of beg ch-3.

Rnd 4: Ch 1, work (sc, ch 3, sc) in same st as joining; * ch 3, sk one dc, sc in next dc; ch 3, sc in next dc; (ch 3, sk one dc, sc in next dc) 4 times; (ch 3, sk 2 dc, sc in next dc) 3 times; ch 3, sk one dc, sc in next dc; (ch 3, sk 2 dc, sc in next dc) 3 times; (ch 3, sk one dc, sc in next dc) 4 times; ch 3, sc in next dc, ch 3, sk one dc, work (sc, ch 3, sc) in next dc; rep from * once more, *ending last rep without working (sc, ch 3, sc) in next dc*; join with a sl st in beg sc.

Rnd 5: Sl st into first ch-3 sp; ch 4, work (trc, ch 2, 2 trc) in same sp; ch 2, sk next ch-3 sp, work (dc, ch 1, dc) in next ch-3 sp **(for single shell)**; * ch 2, sk next ch-3 sp, work (2 trc, ch 2, 2 trc) in next ch-3 sp; ch 2, sk next ch-3 sp, work a single shell in next ch-3 sp; rep from * around, ch 2, sk last ch-3 sp; join with a sl st in top of beg ch-4.

Rnd 6: Sl st in next trc and then into ch-2 sp (between trcs); ch 4 (counts as first trc of pineapple), work 7 trc in same sp (for base of large pineapple); ch 1, sk next ch-2 sp, work (2 dc, ch 2, 2 dc) in sp of next single shell **(for shell)**; * ch 1, sk next ch-2 sp, work 8 trc in next ch-2 sp (between trcs) for base of large pineapple; ch 1, sk next ch-2 sp, work a shell in sp of next single shell; rep from * around, ch 1, join with a sl st in top of beg ch-4.

Rnd 7: Ch 4, dc in next trc of pineapple, (ch 1, dc in next trc of pineapple) 6 times; ch 1, work a shell in sp of next shell: * ch 1, dc in first trc of next pineapple, (ch 1, dc in next trc of pineapple) 7 times; ch 1, work a shell in sp of next shell; rep from * around, ch 1, join with a sl st in 3rd ch of beg ch-4.

Rnd 8: Ch 1, * sc in first ch-1 sp of pineapple, (ch 2, sc in next ch-1 sp of pineapple) 6 times; ch 2, work a shell in sp of next shell, ch 2; rep from * around, join with a sl st in beg sc.

Rnd 9: Ch 1, * sc in first ch-2 sp of pineapple, (ch 2, sc in next ch-2 of pineapple) 5 times; ch 2, work (2 dc, ch 2, 2 dc, ch 2, 2 dc) in sp of next shell, ch 2; rep from * around, join with a sl st in beg sc.

Rnd 10: Ch 1, * sc in first ch-2 sp of pineapple, (ch 2, sc in next ch-2 sp of pineapple) 4 times; ch 2, sk next ch-2 sp, work (dc, ch 1, dc) in next ch-2 sp **(for single shell)**; ch 2, work a single shell in next ch-2 sp; ch 2, sk next ch-2 sp; rep from * around, join with a sl st in beg sc.

Rnd 11: Ch 1, * sc in first ch-2 sp of pineapple, (ch 2, sc in next ch-2 sp of pineapple) 3 times; (ch 3, work single shell in sp of next single shell) twice, ch 3; rep from * around, join with a sl st in beg sc.

Rnd 12: Ch 1, * sc in first ch-2 of pineapple, (ch 2, sc in next ch-2 sp of pineapple) twice; ch 3, work a single shell in sp of next single shell; ch 5, work a single shell in sp of next single shell, ch 3; rep from * around, join with a sl st in beg sc.

Rnd 13: Ch 1, * sc in first ch-2 sp of pineapple, ch 2, sc in next ch-2 sp of pineapple; ch 3, work a single shell in sp of next single shell; ch 3, work a single shell in 3rd (center) ch of ch-5 (between single shells); ch 3, work a single shell in sp of next single shell, ch 3; rep from * around, join with a sl st in beg sc.

Rnd 14: Ch 1, * sc in ch-2 sp at tip of large pineapple, ch 3, work (dc, ch 2, dc, ch 2, dc) in sp of next single shell; ch 3, work 6 trc in sp of next single shell; (for base of small pineapple); ch 3, work (dc, ch 2, dc, ch 2, dc) in sp of next single shell, ch 3; rep from * around, join with a sl st in beg sc.

Rnd 15: Sl st in each of next 3 chs, sl st in next dc and then into ch-2 sp; ch 6, * work single shell in next ch-2 sp; ch 3, sk next ch-3 sp, dc in first trc of next pineapple, (ch 1, dc in next trc of pineapple) 5 times; ch 3, sk next ch-3 sp, work single shell in next ch-2 sp; ch 3, dc in next ch-2 sp; sk next two ch-3 sps (on each side of large pineapple), dc in next ch-2 sp, ch 3; rep from * around, *ending last rep without working last dc and ch 3*; join with a sl st in 3rd ch of beg ch-6.

Rnd 16: Ch 1, * sc in next ch-3 sp, ch 3, work a single shell in sp of next single shell; ch 4, sk next ch-3 sp, sc in first ch-1 sp of pineapple, (ch 2, sc in next ch-1 sp of pineapple) 4 times; ch 4, sk next ch-3 sp, work a single shell in sp of next single shell; ch 3, sc in next ch-3 sp, ch 5, sk sp between dcs; rep from * around, *ending last rep by working ch 1 (instead of ch 5); then join with a trc in beg sc (this brings thread into position to beg next rnd).*

Rnd 17: Work (ch 3, dc, ch 2, 2 dc) in sp under joining trc **(for beg shell)**; * ch 3, sk next ch-3 sp, work a single shell in sp of next single shell; ch 3, sk next ch-4 sp, sc in first ch-2 sp of pineapple, (ch 2, sc in next ch-2 sp of pineapple) 3 times; ch 3, sk next ch-4 sp, work a single shell in sp of next single shell; ch 3, sk next ch-3 sp, work (2 dc, ch 2, 2 dc) in next ch-5 sp **(for shell)**; rep from * around, *ending last rep without working last shell*; join with a sl st in top of ch-3 of beg shell.

Rnd 18: Sl st in next dc and then into sp of beg shell; ch 3, work (dc, ch 2, 2 dc, ch 2, 2 dc) in same sp; ch 4, work a single shell in sp of next single shell;

ch 3, sc in first ch-2 sp of pineapple, (ch 2, sc in next ch-2 sp of pineapple) twice; ch 3, work a single shell in sp of next single shell; ch 4, work (2 dc, ch 2, 2 dc, ch 2, 2 dc) in sp of next shell; rep from * around, *ending last rep without working (2 dc, ch 2, 2 dc, ch 2, 2 dc) in sp of next shell*; join with a sl st in top of beg ch-3.

Rnd 19: Sl st in next dc and then into next ch-2 sp, work beg shell in same sp; * ch 2, work a shell in next ch-2 sp, ch 5, work a single shell in sp of next single shell; ch 3, sc in first ch-2 sp of pineapple, ch 2, sc in next ch-2 sp of pineapple; ch 3, work a single shell in sp of next single shell; ch 5, sk next ch-4 sp, work a shell in next ch-2 sp; rep from * around, *ending last rep without working last shell*; join with a sl st in top of ch-3 of beg shell.

Rnd 20: Sl st in next dc and then into sp of beg shell, work beg shell in same sp; * ch 3, sc in next ch-2 sp (between shells); ch 3, work a shell in sp of next shell; ch 5, work a single shell in sp of next single shell; ch 3, sc in ch-2 sp at tip of pineapple, ch 3, work a single shell in sp of next single shell; ch 5, work a shell in sp of next shell; rep from * around, *ending last rep without working last shell*; join with a sl st in top of ch-3 of beg shell.

Rnd 21: Sl st in next dc and then into sp of beg shell, work beg shell in same sp; * ch 2, work a shell in sc (between shells); ch 2, work a shell in sp of next shell; ch 4, work a shell (instead of a single shell) in sp of next single shell; sk next two ch-3 sps (on each side of pineapple), work a shell in sp of next single shell; ch 4, work a shell in sp of next shell; rep from * around, *ending last rep without working last shell*; join with a sl st in top of ch-3 of beg shell.

Finish off; weave in all ends.

KITCHEN KUTIES

designed by Kathie Schroeder

Brighten up your kitchen with this cheery set! Decorate a pair of terry cloth towels, and then make two hot plate mats to match. A quick and easy gift to delight everyone on your list!

KITCHEN TOWEL SET

Materials
Aunt Lydia's Heavy Rug Yarn in 70-yd skeins:
    1 skein each of tangerine and sunset
Size G aluminum crochet hook
Kitchen terry cloth towel (approx 16" × 24") in
    color and print of your choice
2 Buttons (⅞" diameter) in color(s) of your choice

Gauge
None specified

Instructions
Cut towel in half widthwise, with each piece measuring approx 16" wide × 12" long.

FIRST TOWEL: Work across cut end of one piece as follows: With sharp point of a scissors, make 41 holes evenly spaced across cut edge, approx ⅜" from edge. With right side facing, join tangerine with a sl st in first hole to your right.

Row 1: Ch 1, sc in same hole as joining and in each rem hole across = 41 sc.

Row 2: Ch 1, turn; sc in each sc across.

Row 3: Rep Row 2.

Row 4: Ch 2, turn; dc in first sc and in each rem sc across = 41 dc. (*NOTE: Do not count ch-2 as one dc*).

Row 5: Ch 2, turn; dc in first dc, * sk next dc, dc in next dc; rep from * across = 21 dc.

Row 6: Rep Row 5 = 11 dc.

Row 7: Rep Row 5 = 6 dc.

Row 8: Ch 2, turn; dc in first dc and in each rem dc across = 6 dc. Continue by working tab as follows.

Rows 9 through 15: Rep Row 8, 7 times.

Row 16: Ch 2, turn; sk first dc, dc in each of next 3 dc, sk next dc, dc in last dc = 4 dc. Finish off; then continue with edging as follows.

Edging: With right side facing, use sunset and work one row in sc evenly spaced around edge of crocheted top. Finish off; weave in all ends. Sew button to center front, approx 1¼" up from towel edge. Fold over tab and button through sp between sts at end of tab.

SECOND TOWEL: Work same as other towel, reversing colors (sunset for main color, instead of tangerine, and edged with tangerine, instead of sunset).

HOT PLATE MATS

Sizes

Smaller mat measures approx 8¼" diameter; larger mat measures approx 10" diameter (measured from point to point)

Materials

Aunt Lydia's Heavy Rug Yarn in 70-yd skeins:
    2 skeins each of tangerine and sunset
Size J aluminum crochet hook (or size required for gauge)

(MATERIALS NOTE: Yarn is used doubled throughout patt.)

Gauge

With 2 strands, in sc, 5 sts = 2"

Instructions

SMALLER MAT: With 2 strands of tangerine, ch 4, join with a sl st to form a ring. (NOTE: All rnds are worked on right side.)

Rnd 1: Ch 3 (counts as first dc), work 11 dc in ring; join with a sl st in top of beg ch-3 = 12 dc.

Rnd 2: Ch 1, work (sc, ch 2, sc) in same st as joining; work (sc, ch 2, sc) **in back lp** (lp away from you) in each rem dc around. (NOTE: Do not join; work continuous rnds, unless otherwise specified. Use a small safety pin or piece of yarn in contrasting color and mark first st of rnd; move marker at beg of each rnd.)

Rnd 3: Work (sc, ch 2, sc) in each ch-2 sp around.

Rnd 4: Work (2 sc, ch 2, 2 sc) in each ch-2 sp around.

Rnd 5: * Sk next sc, sc **in back lp** of next sc, work (sc, ch 2, sc) in ch-2 sp; sc **in back lp** of next sc, sk next sc; rep from * around, join with a sl st **in back lp** of beg sc. Finish off tangerine.

Rnd 6: With right side facing, join 2 strands of sunset with a sl st **in back lp** of 2nd sc (st to the right of first ch-2 sp). Working **in back lp** of sts, ch 1, 2 sc in same st as joining; * work (sc, ch 2, sc) in ch-2 sp, 2 sc in next sc; sk 2 sc, 2 sc in next sc; rep from * to last ch-2 sp, work (sc, ch 2, sc) in last ch-2 sp, 2 sc in next sc; sk last sc, join with a sl st **in back lp** of beg sc. Finish off and weave in ends.

LARGER MAT: With 2 strands of sunset, ch 4, join with a sl st to form a ring. (NOTE: All rnds are worked on right side.)

Rnd 1: Ch 3 (counts as first dc), work 11 dc in ring; join with a sl st in top of beg ch-3 = 12 dc.

Rnd 2: Ch 1, work (sc, ch 2, sc) in same st as joining; work (sc, ch 2, sc) **in back lp** (lp away from you) in each rem dc around, join with a sl st in beg sc. Finish off sunset.

Rnd 3: With right side facing, join 2 strands of tangerine with a sl st in any ch-2 sp around. Ch 1, work (sc, ch 2, sc) in same sp as joining and in each rem ch-2 sp around. (NOTE: Do not join; work continuous rnds, unless otherwise specified. Use a small safety pin or piece of yarn in contrasting color and mark first st of rnd; move marker at beg of each rnd.)

Rnds 4 through 6: Rep Rnds 4 through 6 of Smaller Mat, following same color changes. At end of Rnd 6, do not join; do not finish off—continue with sunset.

Rnd 7: * Sk next sc, sc **in back lp** in each of next 2 sc, work (sc, ch 2, sc) in ch-2 sp; sc **in back lp** in each of next 2 sc, sk next sc; rep from * around.

Rnd 8: Rep Rnd 7. At end of rnd, join with a sl st **in back lp** of beg sc. Finish off and weave in all ends.

FLORAL PILLOW

designed by Mary Thomas

Here's a new way to use the old-favorite granny square. Our floral pillow, which resembles a field of flowers, is easy to make, and you'll be delighted when you see how it brightens any room in your house.

Size

Approx 14″ square before edging

Materials

American Thread Dawn Sayelle Knitting Worsted Size Yarn:
    8 oz white
    2 oz each of golf green, watermelon, turquoise, lemon, lilac, scarlet, hot orange, true blue and pink

Size G aluminum crochet hook (or size required for gauge)
14″ square, knife-edge pillow form

Gauge

One floral motif = 3¼″ square

Instructions

FLORAL MOTIF: Make 4 in each of the following 2-rnd center colors: watermelon, turquoise, lemon, lilac, scarlet, hot orange, true blue and pink (32 motifs total). With center color, ch 3, join with a sl st to form a ring.

[NOTE: All motifs use the same color for Rnd 3 (golf green) and Rnd 4 (white).]

63

Rnd 1 (right side): Continuing with center color, ch 1, work 8 sc in ring; join with a sl st in beg sc. (*NOTE: All following rnds are worked on right side.*)

Rnd 2: Continuing with center color, ch 1, pull up lp on hook to measure approx ½″; work puff st in same st as joining [**To make puff st: Work (YO, insert hook in st and draw up ½″ lp) twice (5 lps now on hook—*Fig 1*); YO and draw through all 5 lps on hook, ch 1 = puff st made**]. Work another puff st in same st as joining; work 2 puff sts in each rem sc around; join with a sl st in top of beg puff st. Finish off center color.

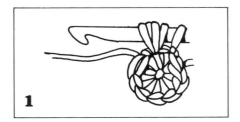

Rnd 3: With right side facing, join golf green with a sl st in sp between any 2 puff sts; ch 1, work (2 sc, ch 2, 2 sc) in same sp as joining for beg corner. * Sc in each of next 3 sps (between puff sts), work (2 sc, ch 2, 2 sc) in next sp for corner; rep from * 3 times more, ending last rep without working corner; join with a sl st in beg sc. Finish off golf green.

Rnd 4: With right side facing, join white with a sl st in any ch-2 corner sp; ch 2, work (hdc, ch 1, 2 hdc) in same sp as joining. * Hdc in each of next 7 sc along side, work (2 hdc, ch 1, 2 hdc) in next ch-2 corner sp; rep from * 3 times more, ending last rep without working corner; join with a sl st in top of beg ch-2. Finish off, leaving approx 12″ sewing length.

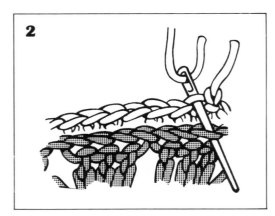

ASSEMBLING: To join, hold two motifs with right sides tog, positioned (when possible) with yarn end (left for sewing) in upper right hand corner. Thread

3				

1	2	3	4
5	6	7	8
4	3	2	1
8	7	6	5

1 = watermelon
2 = turquoise
3 = lemon
4 = lilac
5 = scarlet
6 = hot orange
7 = true blue
8 = pink

matching yarn in tapestry or yarn needle. Carefully matching sts on both motifs, sew with overcast st **in outer lps** only (*Fig 2*) across side, beg and end with corner st. Continuing to join in this manner, join motifs first into rows; then, sew rows tog, being sure that all four-corner junctions are firmly joined. Weave in all yarn ends. Join 16 motifs each for front and back sections of pillow as shown in *Fig 3*. (*NOTE: Sections are joined later after edging.*)

EDGING: (*NOTE: Edging is worked only around edges of one section.*) With right side facing, join white with a sl st **in back lp** (*lp away from you*) of center st at any outer corner.

Rnd 1: Working **in back lp** of each st, ch 1, sc in same st as joining; sc in each rem st and in each joining around edge, join with a sl st in beg sc. Now continue by working **in both lps** of sts.

Rnd 2: Ch 4, do not turn; work (dc, ch 1) in each sc around, join with a sl st in 3rd ch of beg ch-4.

Rnd 3: Ch 4, do not turn; dc in same st as joining (*beg shell made*); work (dc, ch 1, dc) in each rem dc around (*for shells*), join with a sl st in 3rd ch of beg ch-4.

Rnd 4: Do not turn, sl st in ch-1 sp of first shell; ch 4, sc in sp before next shell; * ch 1, dc in ch-1 sp of next shell; ch 1, sc in sp before next shell; rep from * around; ch 1, join with a sl st in 3rd ch of beg ch-4. Finish off; weave in ends.

Finishing

Join sections tog as follows. Hold sections with wrong sides tog and section without edging facing you. Thread white into tapestry or yarn needle. Carefully matching sts, sew with overcast st through scs in first rnd of edging on one section and back lp of sts on other section (*without edging*). Sew 3 sides closed; then insert pillow form and complete rem side. Finish off; weave in ends.

Above, left:
PINK PINEAPPLE DOILY
Above, right:
GRANNY SQUARE VEST
Left:
ELEGANT EDGINGS 1 & 2

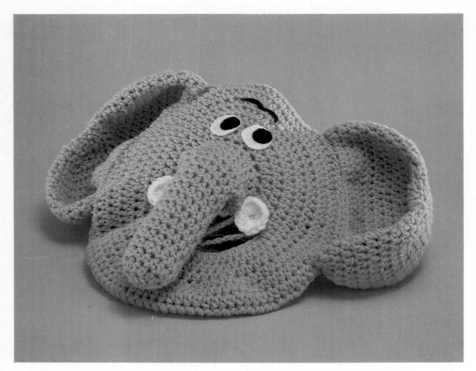

Left:
ELEPHANT PAJAMA BAG
Below:
CUDDLY CAT FAMILY
Opposite, top:
RATTLE TOYS
Opposite, bottom:
LION PAJAMA BAG *(left)*
SUNFLOWER HAND PUPPET *(right)*

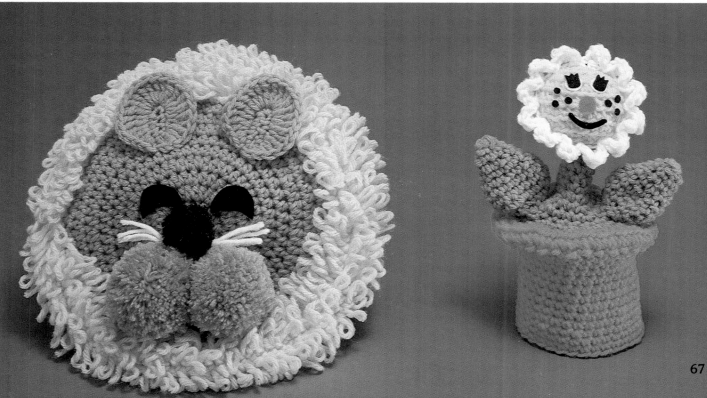

Left:
RIBBON BABY BONNET
Below, left:
GOLDFISH MOBILE
Below, right:
BABY'S BOTTLE HOLDER
Opposite:
TRADITIONAL BABY LAYETTE

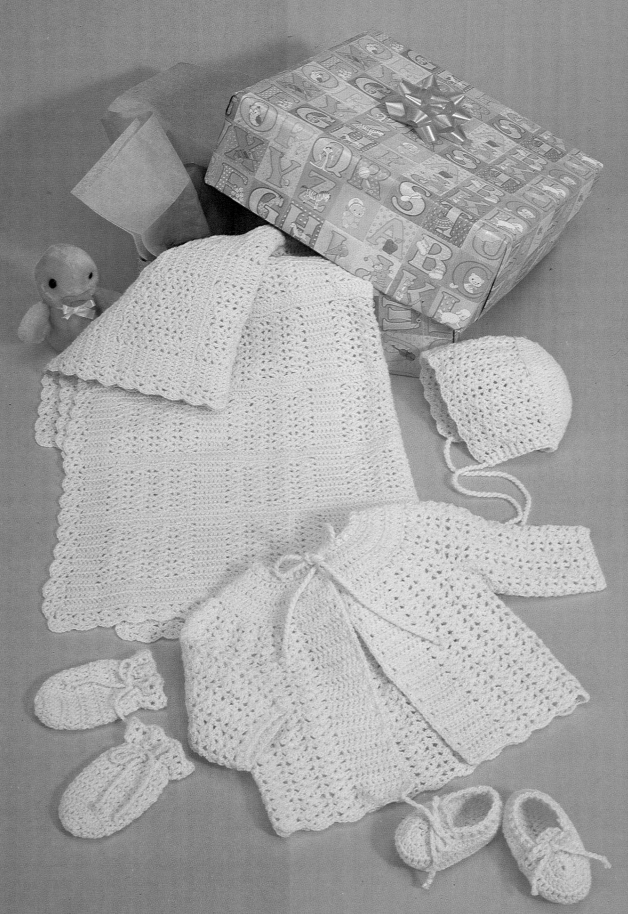

Above, left:
ROCKET WALL HANGING
Above, right:
LACE COLLAR
Left:
OVAL PINEAPPLE PLACEMAT
Opposite:
WINDOW VIEW WALL HANGING

Above, left:
FREDOM RIPPLE AFGHAN
Above, right:
KITCHEN KUTIES
Left:
EASY FILET CROCHET PLACEMAT
Opposite, top left:
PURSE
Opposite, top right:
SPIDER-WEB-LACE SHAWL
Opposite, bottom:
HEART SACHET & PINCUSHION *(left)*
GRANNY BOOKMARK *(right)*

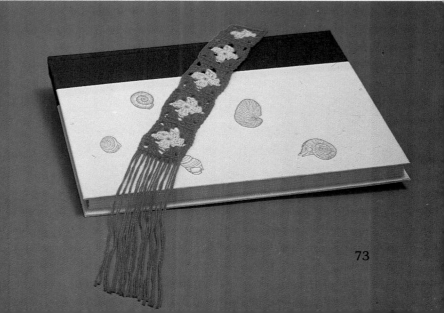

Above, left:
FLORAL PILLOW
Above, right:
DOILY PILLOWS
Left:
COZY SLIPPERS
Opposite:
GRANNY RAINBOW AFGHAN

74

Left:
FREDDIE FROG
Below:
BABY BARBARA JEAN
Opposite:
MOUSE WEDDING PARTY

Left:
CHERIE CHEERLEADER &
FOOTBALL FREDDIE
Below:
RAINBOW WINDOW HANGING
Opposite:
HIM & HER DOLLS

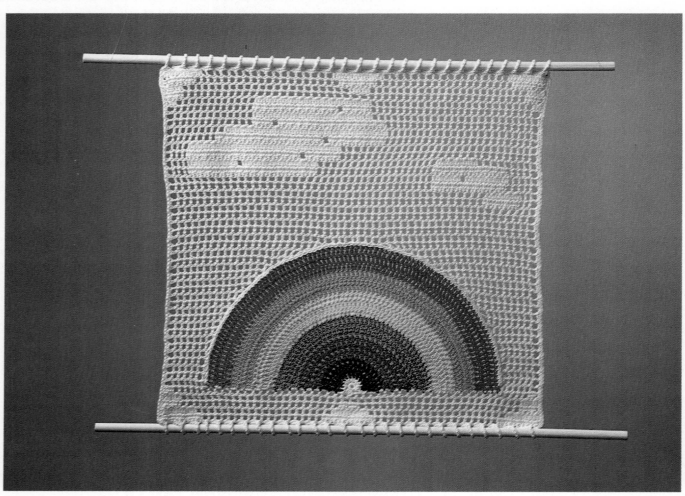

Left:
CACTUS GARDEN
Below, left:
BABY BLUE EYES
Below, middle:
TURTLE PINCUSHION
Below, right:
HAT & MITTENS LAPEL PIN

DOILY PILLOWS

Add a romantic touch to any room in your house with these two doily pillows in the pineapple design. One pillow is a square in a popcorn pineapple design, while the round pillow is created with the traditional pineapple motif. If you prefer, either pillow design can be used simply as an elegant doily.

ROUND DOILY PILLOW

Size

Pillow measures approx 16″ diameter; doily measures approx 15″ diameter.

Materials

American Thread Puritan or Giant Crochet Thread:
    300 yds brown
Size 7 steel crochet hook (or size required for gauge)
16″ round, knife-edge pillow form (covered with
    blue fabric or in a color of your choice)

Gauge

First 9 rnds = 6¼″ diameter

Instructions

Ch 6, join with a sl st to form a ring. (*NOTE: All rnds are worked on right side.*)

Rnd 1: Work 8 sc in ring, join with a sl st in beg sc.

Rnd 2: Ch 1, sc in same st as joining; * ch 3, sc in next sc; rep from * around; ch 3, join with a sl st in beg sc = 8 ch-3 sps.

Rnd 3: Sl st into first ch-3 sp; ch 1, work (sc, 3 dc, sc) in same sp **(first petal made)**; * ch 3, work (sc, 3 dc, sc) in next ch-3 sp **(petal made)**; rep from * 6 times more, join with a dc in beg sc of first petal (*brings thread into position to beg next rnd*) = 8 petals.

Rnd 4: Ch 11, trc (triple crochet) in first sp (under joining dc just made); * ch 4, work (trc, ch 7, trc) in next ch-3 sp (between petals); rep from * around; ch 4, join with a sl st in 4th ch of beg ch-11 = 8 ch-7 sps.

Rnd 5: Sl st in each of next 3 chs, work (sl st, ch 3, 2 dc, ch 3, 3 dc) in next ch (center ch of beg ch-7); * ch 3, sk next ch-4 sp, work (3 dc, ch 3, 3 dc) in 4th (center) ch of next ch-7; rep from * around; ch 3, sk last ch-4 sp, join with a sl st in top of beg ch-3.

Rnd 6: Work a beg dc-cluster over same st as joining and next 2 dc. [**To work beg dc-cluster: Ch 3; keeping last lp of each st on hook, work dc in each of next 2 dc (3 lps now on hook— Fig 1); YO and draw through all 3 lps on hook = beg dc-cluster made.**] Ch 1, work (dc, ch 1) 4 times in next ch-3 sp (between 3-dc groups); work a dc-cluster over next 3 dc. [**To work dc-cluster: Keeping last lp of each st on hook, work dc in each of next 3 dc (4 lps now on hook); YO and draw through all 4 lps on hook = dc-cluster made.**] * Ch 3, sk next ch-3 sp, work a dc-cluster over next 3 dc; ch 1, work (dc, ch 1) 4 times in next ch-3 sp (between 3-dc groups); work a dc-cluster over next 3 dc; rep from * around; ch 1, sk last ch-3 sp, join with a dc in top of beg dc-cluster (*brings thread into position to beg next rnd*).

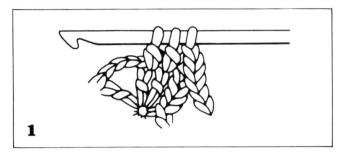

1

Rnd 7: Ch 4, 2 trc in first sp (under joining dc just made); * ch 7, sk next cluster and next 2 dc, sc in next ch-1 sp; ch 7, sk next 2 dc and next cluster, 3 trc in next ch-3 sp; rep from * around, *ending last rep without working 3 trc in next ch-3 sp*; join with a sl st in top of beg ch-4.

Rnd 8: Ch 4, 2 trc in same st as joining; * ch 3, sk next trc, 3 trc in next trc; ch 3, sc in next ch-7 sp; ch 9, sc in next ch-7 sp; ch 3, 3 trc in next trc; rep from * around, *ending last rep without working 3 trc in next trc*; join with a sl st in top of beg ch-4.

Rnd 9: Work a beg trc-cluster in same st as joining. [**To work beg trc-cluster: Ch 4; keeping last lp of each st on hook, work 2 trc in same st as joining (3 lps now on hook); YO and draw through all 3 lps on hook = beg trc-cluster made.**] * Ch 7, sk next 2 trc, work a trc-cluster in next ch-3 sp (between 3-trc groups). [**To work trc-cluster: Keeping last lp of each st on hook, work 3 trc in ch-3 sp (4 lps now on hook); YO and draw through all 4 lps on hook = trc cluster made.**] Ch 7, work a trc-cluster in same sp (where prev cluster was worked); ch 7, sk next 2 trc, work a trc-cluster in next trc (3rd trc of 3-trc group); work a picot in top of cluster just made.

[**To work picot: Ch 3, sl st back into top of cluster just made = picot made.**] Sk next ch-3 sp, work (trc-cluster, ch 7, trc-cluster) in 5th (center) ch of next ch-9; work a picot in top of cluster just made; sk next ch-3 sp, work a trc-cluster in next trc (first trc of next 3-trc group); rep from * around, *ending last rep without working trc-cluster in next trc (first trc of next 3-trc group)*; join with a sl st in top of beg trc-cluster.

Rnd 10: Sl st in each of next 3 chs, work (sl st, ch 7, trc) in next ch (center ch of beg ch-7). * † ch 5, work (trc, ch 3, trc) in 4th (center) ch of next ch-7 †; rep from † to † once; ch 5, work a trc-cluster in 4th (center) ch of next ch-7; work a picot in top of cluster just made, rep from † to † once; now rep from * around, *ending last rep without repeating from † to † once*; ch 5, join with a sl st in 4th ch of beg ch-7.

Rnd 11: Sl st into next ch-3 sp, work (beg trc-cluster, ch 3, trc-cluster) in same sp (**beg cluster shell made**); * ch 3, sk next ch-5 sp, work 9 trc in next ch-3 sp (for base of pineapple); ch 3, sk next ch-5 sp, work (trc-cluster, ch 3, trc-cluster) in next ch-3 sp (**cluster shell made**); work (ch 3, sc in next ch-5 sp) twice; ch 3, work a cluster shell in next ch-3 sp; rep from * around, *ending last rep without working cluster shell*; join with a sl st in top of beg cluster. (*NOTE: Work end of each following rnd in this manner, without working cluster shell at end of last rep and joining rnd with a sl st in top of beg cluster.*)

Rnd 12: Sl st into sp of beg cluster shell, work a beg cluster shell in same sp; * ch 3, sk next ch-3 sp, sc in first trc of pineapple, (ch 3, sc in next trc of pineapple) 8 times; ch 3, sk next ch-3 sp, work a cluster shell in sp of next cluster shell; ch 5, sk next ch-3 sp, sc in next ch-3 sp; ch 5, sk next ch-3 sp, work a cluster shell in sp of next cluster shell; rep from * around (*remember to end and join rnd as before*).

Rnd 13: Sl st into sp of beg cluster shell, work a beg cluster shell in same sp; * ch 3, sk next ch-3 sp, sc in first ch-3 sp of pineapple, (ch 3, sc in next ch-3 sp of pineapple) 7 times; ch 3, sk next ch-3 sp, work a cluster shell in sp of next cluster shell; ch 3, sc in next ch-5 sp, ch 5, sc in next ch-5 sp; ch 3, work a cluster shell in sp of next cluster shell; rep from * around.

Rnd 14: Sl st into sp of beg cluster shell, work a beg cluster shell in same sp; * ch 3, sk next ch-3 sp, sc in first ch-3 sp of pineapple, (ch 3, sc in next ch-3 sp of pineapple) 6 times; ch 3, sk next ch-3 sp, work a cluster shell in sp of next cluster shell; ch 5, sk next ch-3 sp, sc in next ch-5 sp; ch 5, sk next ch-3 sp, work a cluster shell in sp of next cluster shell; rep from * around.

Rnd 15: Sl st into sp of beg cluster shell, work a beg

cluster shell in same sp; * ch 3, sk next ch-3 sp, sc in first ch-3 sp of pineapple, (ch 3, sc in next ch-3 sp of pineapple) 5 times; ch 3, sk next ch-3 sp, work a cluster shell in sp of next cluster shell; ch 3, sc in next ch-5 sp; ch 5, sc in next ch-5 sp; ch 3, work a cluster shell in sp of next cluster shell; rep from * around.

Rnd 16: Sl st into sp of beg cluster shell, work a beg cluster shell in same sp; * ch 3, sk next ch-3 sp, sc in first ch-3 sp of pineapple, (ch 3, sc in next ch-3 sp of pineapple) 4 times; ch 3, sk next ch-3 sp, work a cluster shell in sp of next cluster shell; ch 7, sk next ch-3 sp, sc in next ch-5 sp; ch 7, sk next ch-3 sp, work a cluster shell in sp of next cluster shell; rep from * around.

Rnd 17: Sl st into sp of beg cluster shell, work a beg cluster shell in same sp; * ch 3, sk next ch-3 sp, sc in first ch-3 sp of pineapple, (ch 3, sc in next ch-3 sp of pineapple) 3 times; ch 3, sk next ch-3 sp, work a cluster shell in sp of next cluster shell; ch 3, sc in next ch-7 sp; ch 11, sc in next ch-7 sp; ch 3, work a cluster shell in sp of next cluster shell; rep from * around.

Rnd 18: Sl st into sp of beg cluster shell, work a beg cluster shell in same sp; * ch 3, sk next ch-3 sp, sc in first ch-3 sp of pineapple, (ch 3, sc in next ch-3 sp of pineapple) twice; ch 3, sk next ch-3 sp, work a cluster shell in sp of next cluster shell; ch 9, sk next ch-3 sp, work (3 trc, ch 3, 3 trc) in 6th (center) ch of next ch-11, ch 9, sk next ch-3 sp, work a cluster shell in sp of next cluster shell; rep from * around.

Rnd 19: Sl st into sp of beg cluster shell, work a beg cluster shell in same sp; * ch 3, sk next ch-3 sp, sc in first ch-3 sp of pineapple, ch 3, sc in next ch-3 sp of pineapple; ch 3, sk next ch-3 sp, work a cluster shell in sp of next cluster shell; ch 5, sc in next ch-9 sp; ch 5, work a dc-cluster (see instructions in Rnd 6) over next 3 trc; ch 3, work (dc, ch 3) 4 times in next ch-3 sp (between 3-trc groups); work a dc-cluster over next 3 trc; ch 5, sc in next ch-9 sp; ch 5, work a cluster shell in sp of next cluster shell; rep from * around.

Rnd 20: Sl st into sp of beg cluster shell, work a beg cluster shell in same sp; * ch 3, sk next ch-3 sp, sc in ch-3 sp at tip of pineapple; ch 3, sk next ch-3 sp, work a cluster shell in sp of next cluster shell; work (ch 7, sc in next ch-5 sp) twice; work (ch 7, sk next ch-3 sp, sc in next ch-3 sp) twice; ch 7, sk next ch-3 sp, work (sc in next ch-5 sp, ch 7) twice; work a cluster shell in sp of next cluster shell; rep from * around.

Rnd 21: Sl st into sp of beg cluster shell; work a beg cluster shell in same sp; * sk next two ch-3 sps (on each side of pineapple), work a cluster shell in sp of next cluster shell; ch 7, † sc in next ch-7 sp; ch 3, work (3 dc, ch 3, 3 dc) in 4th (center) ch of next ch-7; ch 3, sc in next ch-7 sp †; ch 5, work (3 dc, ch 3, 3 dc) in 4th (center) ch of next ch-7; ch 5, rep from † to † once; ch 7, work a cluster shell in sp of next cluster shell; rep from * around.

Finish off; weave in all ends.

Finishing

Block doily out to size (see *Finishing Techniques* on page 12). Then position doily on top of covered pillow form, having right side facing up. With matching sewing thread, tack in place.

SQUARE DOILY PILLOW

Size

Pillow measures approx 14" square; doily measures approx 13" across (from side to side)

Materials

American Thread Giant Crochet Thread:
    250 yds blue
Size 7 steel crochet hook (or size required for gauge)
14" square, knife-edge pillow form (covered with brown fabric or in a color of your choice)

Gauge

First 4 rnds = 3¾" across (from side to side)

Instructions

Ch 10, join with a sl st to form a ring. (*NOTE: All rnds are worked on right side.*)

Rnd 1: Ch 4 (counts as first trc—triple crochet), work 4 trc in ring; * ch 5, work 5 trc in ring; rep from * twice more; ch 5, join with a sl st in top of beg ch-4 = 4 5-trc groups.

Rnd 2: Ch 4, sk next 3 trc, trc in next trc; ch 4, work a 2-trc cluster over same st (where last trc was just worked) and 3rd (center) ch of next ch-5. [**To work 2-trc cluster: Keeping last lp of each st on hook, work trc in same st and 3rd ch of next ch-5 (3 lps now on hook—*Fig 2*); YO and draw**

through all 3 lps on hook = 2-trc cluster made.] * Ch 7, work a 2-trc cluster over same ch (3rd ch of ch-5) and first trc of next 5-trc group; ch 4, work a 2-trc cluster over same st (first trc of 5-trc group) and last trc of same 5-trc group; ch 4, work a 2-trc cluster over same st and 3rd ch of next ch-5; rep from * twice more. Ch 7, work a 2-trc cluster over same ch and joining sl st (at end of prev rnd); ch 4, join with a sl st in top of beg ch-4.

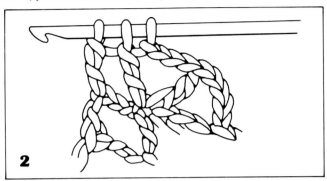

Rnd 3: Ch 4, sk next trc, work (trc, ch 4, trc) in top of next cluster; work 7 trc in next ch-7 sp (for base of pineapple), trc in top of next cluster. * Work (ch 4, 2-trc cluster over same cluster and top of next cluster) twice; ch 4, trc in top of same cluster; work 7 trc in next ch-7 sp (for base of pineapple), trc in top of next cluster; rep from * twice more. Ch 4, work a 2-trc cluster over same cluster and joining sl st; ch 4, join with a sl st in top of beg ch-4.

Rnd 4: Ch 4, sk next trc, trc in next trc; ch 4, work 2 trc in each of next 7 trc of pineapple; ch 4, work a 2-trc cluster over next trc and top of next cluster. * Ch 4, work a 2-trc cluster over same cluster and top of next cluster; ch 4, work a 2-trc cluster over same cluster and next trc; ch 4, work 2 trc in each of next 7 trc of pineapple; ch 4, work a 2-trc cluster over next trc and top of next cluster; rep from * twice more. Ch 4, work a 2-trc cluster over same cluster and joining sl st; ch 4, join with a sl st in top of beg ch-4.

Rnd 5: Ch 1, sc in next trc. * Ch 4, trc in first trc of pineapple, (ch 1, trc in next trc of pineapple) 13 times; ch 4, sc in top of next cluster; ch 4, work 5 trc in top of next cluster; ch 4, sc in top of next cluster; rep from * around, *ending last rep without working sc in top of next cluster;* join with a sl st in beg sc.

Rnd 6: Sl st in each of next 4 chs, ch 1. * Sc in first ch-1 sp of pineapple (between first 2 trcs), work (ch 3, sc in next ch-1 sp of pineapple) 12 times; ch 8, sk next two ch-4 sps, work a 5-trc cluster over next 5 trc. [**To work 5-trc cluster: Keeping last lp of each st on hook, work trc in each of next 5 trc (6 lps now on hook); YO and draw through all 6 lps on hook = 5 trc cluster made.**] Ch 8, sk

next two ch-4 sps; rep from * around, join with a sl st in beg sc.

Rnd 7: Sl st into first ch-3 sp of pineapple, work beg PC (popcorn) in same sp. [**To work beg PC: Ch 4, work 4 trc in first ch-3 sp of pineapple; drop lp from hook, insert hook in top of ch-4; hook dropped lp (*Fig 3*) and pull through st on hook = beg PC made.**] * Ch 2, work PC in next ch-3 sp of pineapple. [**To work PC: Work 5 trc in next ch-3 sp of pineapple; drop lp from hook, insert hook in top of first trc of 5-trc group just made; hook dropped lp and pull through st on hook = PC made.**] Work (ch 2, PC in next ch-3 sp of pineapple) 10 times; ch 7, sk next ch-8 sp, work 5 trc with ch 2 between each trc in top of next 5-trc cluster; ch 7, sk next ch-8 sp, work PC in first ch-3 sp of next pineapple; rep from * around, *ending last rep without working PC in first sp of next pineapple;* join with a sl st in top of beg PC.

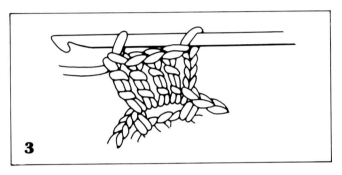

Rnd 8: Ch 1, * sc in first ch-2 sp (between PCs) of pineapple, (ch 3, sc in next ch-2 sp of pineapple) 10 times; ch 6, sk next ch-7 sp, (trc in next trc, ch 3) twice; 3 trc in next trc, (ch 3, trc in next trc) twice; ch 6, sk next ch-7 sp; rep from * around, join with a sl st in beg sc.

Rnd 9: Sl st into first ch-3 sp of pineapple, work beg PC in same sp. * Work (ch 2, PC in next ch-3 sp of pineapple) 9 times; ch 6, sk next ch-6 sp, † 2 trc in next trc; ch 3, sk next ch-3 sp, trc in next trc; ch 3, sk next ch-3 sp, 2 trc in next trc †; work 3 trc in next trc (center trc of 3-trc group), rep from † to † once; ch 6, sk next ch-6 sp, work PC in first ch-3 sp of next pineapple; rep from * around, *ending last rep without working PC in first ch-3 sp of next pineapple;* join with a sl st in top of beg PC.

Rnd 10: Ch 1, * sc in first ch-2 sp of pineapple, (ch 3, sc in next ch-2 sp of pineapple) 8 times; ch 6, sk next ch-6 sp, trc in next trc, 2 trc in next trc; † ch 3, sk next ch-3 sp, trc in next trc; ch 3, sk next ch-3 sp, 2 trc in next trc, trc in next trc †; ch 2, trc in next trc, 2 trc in next trc; trc in next trc, ch 2, trc in next trc, 2 trc in next trc; rep from † to † once; ch 6, sk next ch-6 sp; rep from * around, join with a sl st in beg sc.

Rnd 11: Sl st into first ch-3 sp of pineapple, work beg PC in same sp. * Work (ch 2, PC in next ch-3 sp of pineapple) 7 times; ch 7, sk next ch-6 sp, † trc in each of next 3 trc; ch 3, sk next ch-3 sp, trc in next trc; ch 3, sk next ch-3 sp, trc in each of next 3 trc †; ch 6, sk next ch-2 sp, work a 4-trc cluster over next 4 trc. [**To work 4-trc cluster: Keeping last lp of each st on hook, work trc in each of next 4 trc (5 lps now on hook); YO and draw through all 5 lps on hook = 4-trc cluster made.**] Ch 6, sk next ch-2 sp, rep from † to † once; ch 7, sk next ch-6 sp, work PC in first ch-3 sp of next pineapple; rep from * around, *ending last rep without working PC in first ch-3 sp of next pineapple*; join with a sl st in top of beg PC.

Rnd 12: Ch 1, * sc in first ch-2 sp of pineapple, (ch 3, sc in next ch-2 of pineapple) 6 times; ch 11, sk next ch-7 sp, † trc in each of next 2 trc; ch 3, sk next trc and next ch-3 sp, trc in next trc; ch 3, sk next ch-3 sp and next trc, trc in each of next 2 trc †; ch 9, sk next ch-6 sp, work (sc, ch 5, sc) in top of 4-trc cluster; ch 9, sk next ch-6 sp, rep from † to † once; ch 11, sk next ch-7 sp; rep from * around, join with a sl st in beg sc.

Rnd 13: Sl st into first ch-3 sp of pineapple, work beg PC in same sp. * Work (ch 2, PC in next ch-3 sp of pineapple) 5 times, ch 8, sc in next ch-11 sp; † ch 8, work a 2-trc cluster (*see instructions in Rnd 2*) over next 2 trc; ch 2, sk next ch-3 sp, trc in next trc; ch 2, sk next ch-3 sp, work a 2-trc cluster over next 2 trc †; ch 8, sc in next ch-9 sp; ch 4, work 7 trc in next ch-5 sp (at tip of 4-trc cluster); ch 4, sc in next ch-9 sp, rep from † to † once; ch 8, sc in next ch-11 sp; ch 8, work PC in first ch-3 sp of next pineapple; rep from * around, *ending last rep without working PC in first ch-3 sp of next pineapple*; join with a sl st in top of beg PC.

Rnd 14: Ch 1, * sc in first ch-2 sp of pineapple, (ch 3, sc in next ch-2 sp of pineapple) 4 times; work (ch 8, sc in next ch-8 sp) twice; † ch 8, work a 3-trc cluster over next 3 sts (sk ch-2 sps). [**To work 3-trc cluster: Keeping last lp of each st on hook, work trc in top of next cluster, next trc, and next cluster (4 lps now on hook); YO and draw through all 4 lps on hook = 3 trc cluster made.**] Ch 8, sc in next ch-8 sp, ch 8 †; sk next ch-4 sp, work 2 trc in each of next 7 trc; ch 8, sk next

ch-4 sp, sc in next ch-8 sp; rep from † to † once; sc in next ch-8 sp, ch 8; rep from * around, join with a sl st in beg sc.

Rnd 15: Sl st into first ch-3 sp of pineapple, work beg PC in same sp. * Work (ch 2, PC in next ch-3 sp of pineapple) 3 times; work (ch 8, sc in next ch-8 sp) 5 times; ch 5, 2 trc in next trc, trc in each of next 12 trc; 2 trc in next trc, ch 5, work (sc in next ch-8 sp, ch 8) 5 times, work PC in first ch-3 sp of next pineapple; rep from * around, *ending last rep without working PC in first ch-3 sp of next pineapple*; join with a sl st in top of beg PC.

Rnd 16: Ch 1, * sc in first ch-2 sp of pineapple, (ch 3, sc in next ch-2 sp of pineapple) twice; 3 sc in next ch-8 sp, work (ch 8, sc in next ch-8 sp) 4 times; ch 8, sk next ch-5 sp, work a 2-trc cluster over next 2 trc, (ch 2, work a 2-trc cluster over next 2 trc) 7 times, ch 8, sk next ch-5 sp, work (sc in next ch-8 sp, ch 8) 4 times, 3 sc in next ch-8 sp; rep from * around, join with a sl st in beg sc.

Rnd 17: Sl st into first ch-3 sp of pineapple, work beg PC in same sp. * Ch 2, work PC in next ch-3 sp of pineapple; work (ch 8, sc in next ch-8 sp) 5 times, ch 5, work (2-trc cluster, ch 3, 2-trc cluster) in top of next cluster; work (ch 3, 2-trc cluster in top of next cluster) 6 times; ch 3, work (2-trc cluster, ch 3, 2-trc cluster) in top of next cluster, ch 5, work (sc in next ch-8 sp, ch 8) 5 times; work PC in first ch-3 sp of next pineapple; rep from * around, *ending last rep without working PC in first ch-3 sp of next pineapple*; join with a sl st in top of beg PC.

Rnd 18: Ch 1, * work (sc, ch 3, sc) in ch-2 sp at tip of pineapple, 3 sc in next ch-8 sp; work (ch 8, sc in next ch-8 sp) 4 times; ch 8, sk next ch-5 sp, work (sc, ch 3, sc) in each of next 9 ch-3 sps (between clusters); ch 8, sk next ch-5 sp, work (sc in next ch-8 sp, ch 8) 4 times, 3 sc in next ch-8 sp; rep from * around, join with a sl st in beg sc.

Finish off; weave in all ends.

Finishing

Block doily out to size (see *Finishing Techniques* on page 12). Then position doily on top of covered pillow form, having right side facing up. With matching sewing thread, tack in place.

EASY FILET
CROCHET PLACEMAT

designed by Ernestine H. Giesecke

If you've never tried filet crochet before, here's a good beginning project. You'll find it easy and fun to do, and, in addition, you'll create a lovely placemat, which you'll be proud to use.

Size

Approx 18″ wide by 13″ high

Materials

American Thread Puritan crochet cotton:
    500 yds ecru *(for each placemat)*
Size 5 steel crochet hook (or size required for gauge)

Gauge

6 blocks (bls) or 6 spaces (sps) = 2″; 6 rows = 2″.

Filet Instructions

Filet designs are worked from charts of squares, some of which are filled in. The filled-in squares are **blocks** and the open squares are **spaces**. Blocks are filled in with dc, and spaces are left open, as mesh. As filet patterns are designed with squares, it is important that you work to a gauge in which each space (sp) and each block (bl) is exactly as wide as it is high. Look at the chart in *Fig 1*. You will work Row 1 and all odd-numbered rows reading the chart from right to left; and Row 2 and all even-numbered rows, reading from left to right.

Instructions

Loosely ch 176.

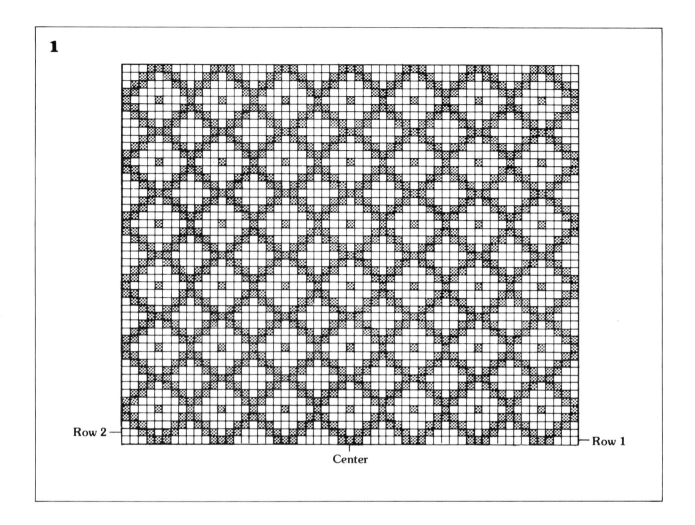

1

Row 2 ⎯ | ⎯ Row 1

Center

Row 1: Dc in 7th ch from hook (first sp made); (ch 2, sk 2 ch, dc in next ch) twice: 2 more sps made [Look at Row 1 of the chart: you will see these 3 sps are indicated by 3 open squares]; * dc in each of next 9 chs (3 bls made) [indicated by filled-in squares on chart]; (ch 2, sk 2 ch, dc in next ch) 5 times (5 sps made); rep from * 5 times; dc in each of next 9 chs; (ch 2, sk 2 ch, dc in next ch) 3 times; ch 5, turn. Now compare your first row to the chart.

From this point on, you will work only from the chart. It is important that when a row is to begin with

a sp, you end the preceding row with ch 5, turn; and that when a row is to begin with a bl, you end the preceding row with ch 3, turn. Now work through last row of chart; at end, do not ch or turn.

EDGING: Rnd 1: Work 2 hdc in each sp and bl and in each row around mat, working 5 hdc in each corner; at end, join with a sl st.

Rnd 2: Sl st in each hdc around, taking care to work loosely enough to keep work flat. Finish off, weave in thread ends. Place mat on a padded ironing board, lightly steam press.

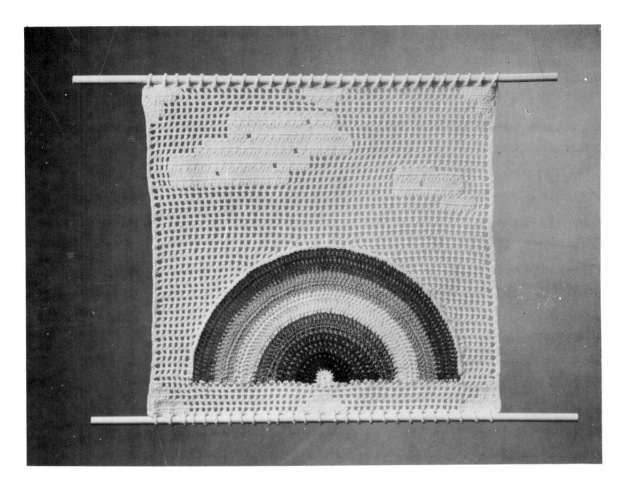

RAINBOW WINDOW HANGING

designed by Ernestine H. Giesecke

Everyone loves a rainbow, and here's a delightful rainbow to hang in your window. The white background, which is worked first, is made in filet crochet where joined double crochets are worked to form the blocks. After the white background has been completed, the colored rainbow is worked in. Follow the chart: each square is a space (sp) and each filled-in square is a block (bl).

Size

Approx 12" square

Materials

American Thread Puritan crochet thread
    500 yd white
       175 yds each: purple, national blue, kelly
         green, buttercup, orange and red
Size 1 steel crochet hook (or size required for gauge)
Size 16 tapestry needle
Two 18" wooden dowels (3/8" diameter)
   painted white

Gauge

4 sps (each sp is 1 dc + 1 ch) = 1"; 4 rows = 1".

Instructions

BACKGROUND: Note piece is worked upside down, that is, from top to bottom. Ch 106.

Row 1 (right side of work): Work jdc (joined double crochet). [**To work jdc: YO, insert hook into 3rd ch from hook and pull lp through; YO and pull through 2 lps, leaving 2 lps on hook; YO, insert hook into same ch, pull lp through, YO and pull through 2 lps on hook; YO and pull through rem 3 lps on hook = jdc made.**] Dc in next ch (one bl made). (Jdc in ch, dc in next ch) 4 times: five bls made; (ch 1, sk 1 ch, dc in next ch: sp made) 18 times; you should have 18 sps. Work (jdc in ch, dc in next ch) 6 times; (ch 1, sk 1 ch, dc in next ch) 18 times; and (jdc in ch, dc in next ch) 5 times; ch 2, turn.

Row 2: Jdc in jdc, dc in dc (first bl of row 2 made). Follow chart in *Fig 1* across.

Rows 3 through 5: Follow chart. After last bl of Row 5, ch 4, turn.

Row 6: Sk 1 ch, dc in dc (first sp of Row 6 made— ch 4 is counted as dc and ch 1; the dc in dc following completes your first sp.) Follow chart across row.

Rows 7 through 23: Follow chart, working bls and sps as shown. (NOTE: *At this point, you begin shaping for insertion of rainbow later.*)

Row 24: From side edge, work 21 sps, sk 1 ch, tr in dc, turn.

Row 25: Sk tr, sl st in dc, ch-1 sp, next dc and ch-1 sp (4 sl sts), ch 2; sk dc and ch-1 sp, dc in dc; work to end of row (18 sps); ch 4, turn.

Row 26: Work 16 sps, sk 1 ch, tr in dc, turn.

Row 27: Sk tr; sl st in dc and in ch-1 sp, ch 2. Sk first dc and ch-1 sp, dc in next dc, work to end of row (14 sps); ch 4, turn.

Row 28: Work 13 sps, sk 1 ch, tr in dc, ch 2, turn.

Row 29: Sk tr, dc and ch-1 sp; dc in next dc, work to end of row (12 sps); ch 4, turn.

Row 30: Work 11 sps, ending with dc, tr in last dc, ch 2, turn.

Row 31: Sk tr, dc and ch-1 sp; dc in next dc, work to end of row (10 sps); ch 4, turn.

Row 32: Work 9 sps, ending with dc, tr in last dc; ch 4, turn.

Row 33: Sk tr, dc and ch-1 sp; dc in next dc, work to end (8 sps); ch 4, turn.

Row 34: Work 8 sps, sk 2 ch, on the ch-4, tr in next ch; ch 4, turn.

Row 35: Sk tr, dc, and ch-1 sp, dc in next dc; work 7 sps; ch 4, turn.

Row 36: Work 7 sps, ch 4, turn.

Row 37: Work 7 sps; ch 4, turn.

Row 38: Work 7 sps; ch 2, turn.

Row 39: Sk first dc, sk 1 ch, dc in next dc; work 6 sps; ch 4, turn.

Rows 40 through 42: Work even on 6 sps. Finish off thread.

OPPOSITE SIDE: With wrong side of Row 23 facing you, having left the center 8 sps unworked, join thread with a sl st in 8th dc from last worked dc. Work as follows (Rows are numbered to correspond with opposite side):

Row 24: Ch 2, sk dc where you joined and ch-1 sp; dc in next dc, work in patt to end of row (21 sps); ch 4, turn.

Row 25: Work 18 sps, sk next ch-1 sp, tr in next dc, turn.

Row 26: Sk tr, sl st in dc and ch-1 sp, ch 2, sk next dc; ch 1 and dc in next dc, work to end (16 sps); ch 4, turn.

Row 27: Work 14 sps, ending with dc, sk ch-1 sp, tr in next dc, ch 2, turn.

Row 28: Sk tr; sk dc and ch, dc in next dc; work for 13 sps, ch 4, turn.

Row 29: Work 12 sps, ending with a dc, sk ch-1 sp, tr in next dc, ch 2, turn.

Row 30: Sk tr; sk dc and ch, dc in next dc; work 11 sps, ch 4, turn.

Row 31: Work 10 sps, finishing as Row 29, ch 2, turn.

Row 32: Begin as Row 30, work 9 sps, ch 4, turn.

Row 33: Work 9 sps, ch 2, turn.

Row 34: Sk first dc and ch-1 sp, dc in next dc, work 8 sps, ch 4, turn.

Row 35: Work 8 sps, ch 2, turn.

Row 36: Sk first dc and ch-1 sp, dc in next dc, work 7 sps, ch 4, turn.

Row 37: Work 7 sps, ch 4, turn.

Row 38: Work 7 sps, ch 4, turn.

Row 39: Work 6 sps, ch 4, turn.

Rows 40 through 42: Work 6 sps even, ch 4, turn.

Row 43: This row forms base of Rainbow. Work 6 sps, ch 79; work dc in first dc on opposite side of panel, work 6 sps, ch 2, turn.

Row 44: Work 1 bl, 5 sps; (ch 1, sk 1 ch, dc in next ch) 40 times.(NOTE: *The 40th dc is in the first dc of the 6 sps on the other side of the rainbow.*) Work 4 sps, 1 bl; ch 2, turn.

Rows 45 through 48: Follow chart. Finish off thread.

RAINBOW INSERT: With white, ch 3, join with a sl st to make a lp and attach with sl st to dc between sps 26 and 27 on Row 43. Be sure the right side of the work is facing you.

Row 1: Ch 1, sl st to next dc to right of joined lp (the right side of the work is still facing you), work 6 sc in ch-3 lp, sl st to next dc to left of joined lp, ch 1, sl st to next dc on the left side, turn.

Row 2: (NOTE: *Wrong side of work is now facing you: all odd-numbered rows will be worked with the right side facing you, all even-numbered rows will be worked with the wrong side facing you.*) Work 2 sc in each sc of Row 2 (12 sc), join with sl st in next dc row on base, finish off white.

Row 3: With purple, join with a sl st to last sc of Row 2, ch 2, sl st to the next dc of the base row, now turn your work. (*NOTE: This method of joining will be used each time you change colors, except you will be joining in a dc instead of a sc.*) Work 1 dc in each sc, sl st to next dc in base, ch 2, sl st in next base row, turn (you will have worked 12 dc in Row 3). (*NOTE: From this point on count ch-2 of each row as a dc; at end of every row and after ch-2 at beg of every row, join insert to base with a sl st.*)

Row 4: 2 dc in next st; (1 dc in next st, 2 dc in next st) 5 times, sl st, ch 2, sl st, **turn**; (18 dc).

Row 5: Dc in each st, sl st, break off purple (18 dc).

Row 6: Join blue as in Row 3, counting ch-2 as first dc; dc in next dc, 2 dc in next dc, 2 dc in next dc, (1 dc in next 2 dc, 2 dc in next dc) 5 times, sl st, ch 2, sl st, **turn**; (24 dc).

Row 7: Rep Row 3, having instead 24 dc.

Row 8: Rep Row 4, working instruction in parentheses 7 times (32 sts); finish off blue.

Row 9: Join green as in Row 3; Rep Row 3, having 32 sts.

Row 10: Rep Row 4, working instruction in parentheses 11 times (48 sts).

Row 11: Rep Row 3, finish off green (48 sts).

Row 12: Joining yellow as in Row 3, Rep Row 4, working instruction in parentheses 15 times (64 sts).

Rows 13 and 14: Rep Row 3 (64 sts); at end, finish off yellow.

Row 15: Joining orange as in Row 3, counting ch-2 as first dc, work 1 dc in next 2 sts, 2 dc in next dc, (1

dc in next 3 dc, 2 dc in next dc) 15 times. Sl st, ch 2, sl st, **turn**; (80 dc).

Rows 16 and 17: Rep Row 3 (80 sts). At end, finish off orange.

Row 18: Joining red as in Row 3, counting ch-2 as first dc, work 1 dc in next 3 sts, 2 dc in next dc; (1 dc in next 4 dc, 2 dc in next dc) 15 times, sl st, ch 2, sl st, **turn**; (96 sts).

Rows 19 and 20: Rep Row 3 (96 sts). Finish off red.

ASSEMBLING: Join white and work 1 sc loosely in each st around insert, finish off white. Weave all ends in with tapestry needle. Using needle threaded with white, loosely stitch rounded insert to background. Match st 46 with center of Row 23, sts 23 and 69 with Row 29.

EDGING: Hold Rainbow with right side facing and top at top; join white with an sc in upper right-hand corner sp. Along top edge, you are going to work ch-lps for insertion of dowels, as follows: * ch 9 (lp made), work 4 sc (2 sc in each sp and in each bl) along edge; rep from * across, adjusting spacing of sc as needed to end with a ch-9 lp in left-hand corner; sc along side of work, placing 2 sc in each row, adjusting to keep work flat; work bottom as for top edge, with ch-9 lps; work final side in sc, join with a sl st to first sc, finish off.

Lightly spray finished piece with starch, press on padded ironing board, using press cloth. Insert dowels in ch-9 lps at top and bottom.

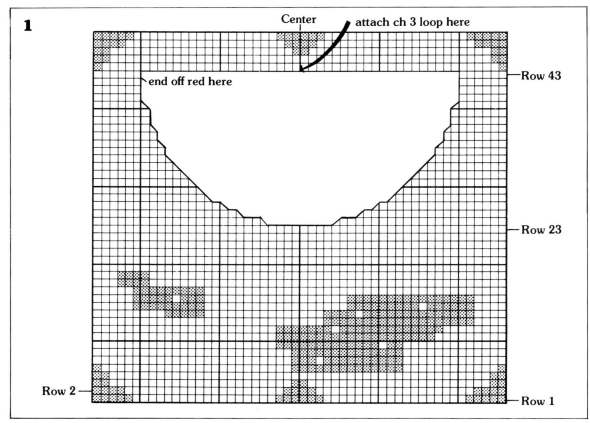

Kid's Bazaar

BABY BLUE EYES

designed by Sue Penrod

Baby Blue Eyes is designed as the perfect little first doll for a baby. Small enough for tiny fingers to clasp with love, she'll be a beloved object for baby girls and boys alike.

Size

Approx 7″ tall

Materials

American Thread Dawn Wintuk Sport Yarn:
    2 oz white
    1 oz pink
    3 yds true blue
    1½ yds lemon
Size F aluminum crochet hook (or size required for gauge)
Polyester fiber *(for stuffing)*

Gauge

In sc, 5 sts = 1″

Instructions

HEAD: With pink, ch 4, join with a sl st to form a ring.

Rnd 1: Work 2 sc in each ch around = 8 sc. [*NOTE: Do not join rnds (unless otherwise* specified); work continuous rnds. Use a small safety pin or piece of yarn in contrasting color and mark first st of rnd; move marker at beg of each rnd.]

Rnd 2: Work 2 sc in each sc around = 16 sc.

Rnd 3: Rep Rnd 2 = 32 sc.

Rnds 4 through 8: Work 5 rnds even. (NOTE: To "work even", work one sc in each st around for specified number of rnds, without increasing or decreasing.)

Rnd 9: Sc in each of next 15 sc, work puff st in next sc for nose. [**To work puff st: Keeping last lp of each st on hook, work 3 dc in next sc (4 lps now on hook—**Fig 1**); Yo and draw through all 4 lps on hook = puff st made.**] Sc in each of rem 16 sc.

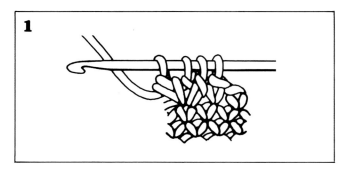

Rnd 10: Sc in each of next 15 sc, sc in top of puff st, sc in each of rem 16 sc = 32 sc.

Rnd 11: Work even.

Rnd 12: * Sc in each of next 2 sc, sk one sc, sc in next sc; rep from * around = 24 sc.

Rnd 13: * Sc in next sc, sk one sc, sc in next sc; rep from * around = 16 sc.

Rnd 14: * Sk next sc, sc in next sc; rep from * to last 2 sc, sk next sc; sc in last sc, changing to white (for collar). [**To change color: Work last sc until 2 lps rem on hook; finish off pink, tie in white (leave ends on inside of doll) and complete st (YO and draw through both lps on hook) = color changed.**] You should now have 8 sc; continue with white and work collar as follows.

COLLAR: Rnd 1: Mark back lp (lp away from you) of first sc (use marker different from beg of rnd) for working dress later. **Working in front lp of each st around**, work (sl st, ch 2, 2 dc) in first sc (where back lp was marked), 3 dc in each rem sc around; join with a sl st in top of beg ch-2 = 23 dc.

Rnd 2: Ch 3, do not turn; * sc **in both lps** of next dc, ch 2; rep from * around, join with a sl st in first ch of beg ch-3. Finish off; weave in end. Now work dress as follows.

DRESS: Hold head with collar just worked at top.

Rnd 1: Hold collar back toward you and work **in unused lp** of each st around (lps left unworked in Rnd 1 of Collar) as follows: Join white with a sl st in marked lp, ch 2, dc in same lp as joining; 2 dc in each rem lp around, join with a sl st in top of beg ch-2 = 15 dc. **Continue by working in both lps of sts**.

Rnd 2: Ch 2, do not turn; 2 dc in next dc, * dc in next dc, 2 dc in next dc; rep from * around, join with a sl st in top of beg ch-2 = 23 dc.

Rnd 3: Ch 2, do not turn; dc in next dc, 2 dc in next dc; * dc in each of next 2 dc, 2 dc in next dc; rep from * around, join with a sl st in top of beg ch-2 = 31 dc.

Rnd 4: Ch 2, do not turn; dc in next dc and in each rem dc around, join with a sl st in top of beg ch-2.

Rnds 5 through 12: Rep Rnd 4, 8 times.

Rnd 13 (bottom edging): Ch 3, do not turn; * sc **in front lp** of next dc, ch 2; rep from * around, join with a sl st in first ch of beg ch-3.

Finish off; weave in end. Lightly stuff doll (do not overstuff; doll should be very cuddly). Continue by working bottom of dress as follows.

BOTTOM: Hold doll with bottom edging just worked at top.

Rnd 1: Hold bottom edging back toward you and work **in unused lp** of each st around (left unworked in prev rnd) as follows: Join white with a sl st in any st around, ch 3, dc in each rem st around; join with a sl st in top of beg ch-3 = 31 dc (counting beg ch-3).

Rnd 2: Ch 1, sc in same st as joining; * sk next dc, sc in next dc; rep from * around = 16 sc. (NOTE: Do not join; work continuous rnds. Mark first st of rnd as before.)

Rnd 3: * Sk next sc, sc in next sc; rep from * around = 8 sc.

Rnd 4: Rep Rnd 3 = 4 sc.

Finish off, leaving approx 8" sewing length. Thread into tapestry or yarn needle; weave through sts of last rnd. Draw up tightly and fasten securely.

SLEEVES AND HANDS (make 2): With white, leave approx 8" end for sewing sleeve to dress later, ch 2.

Rnd 1: Work 12 dc in 2nd ch from hook. [NOTE: Do not join (work continuous rnds), unless otherwise specified. Mark first st of rnd as before.]

Rnd 2: Dc in each dc around = 12 dc.

Rnd 3: Rep Rnd 2.

Rnd 4: Dc in each of first 10 dc, hdc in next dc, sc in last dc; join with a sl st **in front lp** of beg dc.

Rnd 5 (sleeve edging): Working **in front lp** of each st around (back lps will be used later for working hand), ch 3, * sc in next st, ch 2; rep from * around, join with a sl st in first ch of beg ch-3. Finish off; weave in end. Continue by working hand as follows.

Rnd 6: Hold sleeve edging back toward you and work **in back (unused) lp** of sts as follows: Join pink with a sl st in any st around, ch 2, hdc in each rem st around; join with a sl st in top of beg ch-2 = 12 hdc (counting beg ch-2).

Rnd 7: Ch 1, **turn**; sc **in both lps** in each hdc around, ending by working last sc in top of ch-2; join with a sl st in beg sc = 12 sc.

Finish off, leaving approx 8″ sewing length. Thread into tapestry or yarn needle; weave through sts of last rnd. Draw up tightly and fasten securely. Thread beg sewing length (at top of sleeve) into tapestry or yarn needle. Sew sleeve to side of dress, approx 2 rnds down from collar.

BONNET: Beg at center back, with white, ch 4, join with a sl st to form a ring.

Rnd 1 (right side): Ch 3, work 21 dc in ring; join with a sl st in top of beg ch-3 = 22 dc (counting beg ch-3)

Rnd 2: Ch 3, do not turn; dc in next dc and in each rem dc around, join with a sl st in top of beg ch-3.

Rnd 3: Ch 3, do not turn; dc in each of next 2 dc, 2 dc in next dc; * dc in each of next 6 dc, 2 dc in next dc; rep from * once more, dc in each of rem 4 dc; join with a sl st in top of beg ch-3 = 25 dc.

Rnds 4 and 5: Rep Rnd 2, twice. Finish off.

Rnd 6 (brim): **Turn**; with wrong side of bonnet now facing you, join white with a sl st in 3rd dc to the left of joining; ch 1, sc in same dc as joining, 2 dc in each of next 7 dc; 2 dc **in back lp** in each of next 4 dc (front lps will be used to work hair later), 2 dc **in both lps** in each of next 7 dc, sc **in both lps** of next dc.

Finish off (rem sts are left unworked for back of neck), leaving approx 14″ sewing length (for sewing bonnet to head later).

HAIR: Hold bonnet with brim edge facing you. Working under brim in 4 unused lps at center top, join lemon with a sl st in first st to your right; (ch 6, sc in next st) twice, ch 6, sl st in last st.

Finish off; weave in ends. Place bonnet on head; sew in place.

EYES: With single strand of true blue, embroider 2 eyes in satin st (**Fig 2**) as shown in photo.

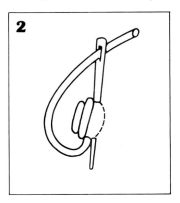

TIE: With true blue, make a chain to measure approx 18″ long.

Finish off, knot and trim each end of tie. Place tie around neck of doll (under collar) and tie into a bow.

FREDDIE FROG

designed by Eleanor Denner

Freddie Frog is so realistic that you'd better not let him catch grandma unaware! From his curling red tongue to his bumpy back, Freddy looks as though he just hopped out of the pond to pay a visit.

Size
Approx 6½″ body length

Materials
American Thread Dawn Sayelle Knitting Worsted Size Yarn:
   3 oz grass green
   1 oz nile green
   ½ oz white
   3 yds each of black and flame
Size G aluminum crochet hook (or size required for gauge)
Polyester fiber (*for stuffing*)

Gauge
In sc, 4 sts = 1″

Instructions
BACK: Beg at mouth edge, with grass green, ch 9.

Row 1 (wrong side): Sc in 2nd ch from hook and in each rem ch across = 8 sc.

Row 2: Ch 1, turn; 2 sc in first sc, sc in each sc across to last sc, 2 sc in last sc = 10 sc.

Row 3: Ch 1, turn; sc in each sc across.

Row 4: Rep Row 2 = 12 sc.

Rows 5 through 9: Rep Row 3, 5 times.

Row 10 (right side): Ch 1, turn; sc in each of first 3 sc, * work a bump. [**To work a bump: Ch 3, sl st in 3rd ch from hook = bump made**], sc in each of next 3 sc; rep from * twice more = 12 sc + 3 bumps.

Row 11: Ch 1, turn; *keeping bumps to right side of work*, sc in each sc across = 12 sc.

Row 12: Ch 1, turn; 2 sc in first sc, * work a bump (as before), sc in each of next 2 sc; rep from * to last sc, work a bump, 2 sc in last sc = 14 sc + 6 bumps.

Row 13: Rep Row 11 = 14 sc.

Row 14: Rep Row 12 = 16 sc + 7 bumps.

Row 15: Rep Row 11 = 16 sc.

Row 16: Ch 5, turn; sc in 2nd ch from hook and in each of next 3 chs, sc in each of next 2 sc; * work a bump, sc in each of next 2 sc; rep from * across = 20 sc + 7 bumps.

Row 17: Ch 5, turn; sc in 2nd ch from hook and in each of next 3 chs, sc in each sc across (*keeping bumps to right side of work*) = 24 sc.

Row 18: Ch 1, turn; sc in each of first 2 sc, * work a bump, sc in each of next 2 sc; rep from * across = 24 sc + 11 bumps.

Row 19: Rep Row 11 = 24 sc.

Row 20: Rep Row 18.

Row 21: Ch 1, turn; sk first sc, sc in each sc across to last 2 sc (*keep bumps to right side of work*); sk next sc, sc in last sc = 22 sc.

Row 22: Ch 1, turn; sk first sc, * sc in each of next 2 sc, work a bump; rep from * to last 3 sc; sc in next sc, sk next sc, sc in last sc = 20 sc + 9 bumps.

Row 23: Rep Row 21 = 18 sc.

Row 24: Rep Row 22 = 16 sc + 7 bumps.

Row 25: Rep Row 21 = 14 sc.

Finish off; weave in ends.

FRONT: Beg at mouth edge, with nile green, ch 9.

Rows 1 through 9: Reps Rows 1 through 9 of Back. At end of Row 9, you should have 12 sc.

Row 10: Ch 1, turn; sc in each sc across.

Row 11: Rep Row 10.

Row 12: Ch 1, turn; 2 sc in first sc, sc in each sc across to last sc, 2 sc in last sc = 14 sc.

Row 13: Rep Row 10.

Row 14: Rep Row 12 = 16 sc.

Row 15: Rep Row 10.

Row 16: Ch 5, turn; sc in 2nd ch from hook and in each of next 3 chs, sc in each sc across = 20 sc.

Row 17: Rep Row 16 = 24 sc.

Rows 18 through 20: Rep Row 10, 3 times.

Row 21: Ch 1, turn; sk first sc, sc in each sc across to last 2 sc; sk next sc, sc in last sc = 22 sc.

Rows 22 through 25: Rep Row 21, 4 times. At end of Row 25, you should have 14 sc. Finish off; weave in ends.

MOUTH INSET: With white, ch 9.

Rows 1 through 4: Rep Rows 1 through 4 of Back. At end of Row 4, you should have 12 sc.

Row 5: Ch 1, turn; sc in each sc across.

Row 6: Rep Row 5.

Row 7: Ch 1, turn; sk first sc, sc in each sc across to last 2 sc; sk next sc, sc in last sc = 10 sc.

Row 8: Rep Row 5.

Row 9: Rep Row 7 = 8 sc.

Row 10: Rep Row 5. Finish off; weave in ends.

ASSEMBLING: First, join half of Mouth Inset (5 rows) to Front (*other half of Mouth Inset will be joined to Back later*). Hold Front and Mouth Inset tog, having Front facing you and straight mouth edge across top. Carefully match 8 sts across top and 5 rows on each side. With nile green, beg at right corner of mouth and crochet edges tog in sc.

Then join Front and Back, attaching rem half of Mouth Inset. Hold Front and Back tog, having Back with bumpy side facing you and straight mouth edge across top. Carefully match sts and rows around, having rem half of Mouth Inset aligned with Mouth end of Back in same manner as before. With grass green, beg at right corner of Mouth and crochet edges tog in sc, leaving approx 2″ opening for stuffing. Stuff upper and lower sections of Mouth lightly and stuff body firmly; then close opening.

HIND LEGS (*make 2*): With grass green, leave approx 12″ end for sewing leg to body later, ch 10, join with a sl st to form a ring.

Rnd 1: Sc in each ch around = 10 sc. [*NOTE: Do not join; work continuous rnds. Mark first st of rnd (use small safety pin or piece of yarn in contrasting color); move marker at beg of each rnd.*]

Rnd 2: Sc in each sc around.

Rnds 3 through 11: Rep Rnd 2, 9 times.

Rnd 12: * Sc in next sc, sk next sc; rep from * around = 5 sc.

Rnd 13: Work 2 sc in each sc around = 10 sc.

Rnds 14 through 16: Rep Rnd 2, 3 times. At end of Rnd 16, do not finish off; continue with toes (closing end of leg) as follows: Hold opening closed, carefully matching 5 corresponding sts across; work (sc, ch 3) in each st across to last st, sl st in last st. Finish off; weave in end. Stuff leg and sew to back edge of body as shown in *Fig 1*.

FRONT LEGS (*make 2*): With grass green, leave approx 12″ end for sewing to body later, ch 12, join with a sl st to form a ring.

Rnd 1: Sc in each ch around = 12 sc. *Do not join; mark first st of rnd (as before).*

Rnd 2: Sc in each sc around.

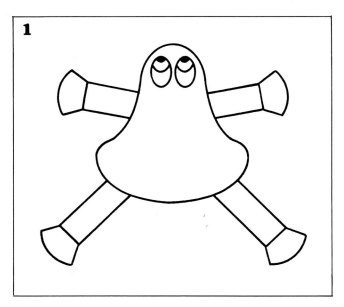

1

Rnds 3 through 6: Rep Rnd 2, 4 times.

Rnd 7: * Sc in next sc, sk next sc; rep from * around = 6 sc.

Rnd 8: Work 2 sc in each sc around = 12 sc.

Rnds 9 through 11: Rep Rnd 2, 3 times. At end of Rnd 11, do not finish off; work toes in same manner as Hind Legs, having 6 corresponding sts across (instead of 5 corresponding sts). Stuff leg and sew to side edge of body as shown in **Fig 1**.

EYES (make 2): With black, ch 3, join with a sl st to form a ring.

Rnd 1 (right side): Work 6 sc in ring, join with a sl st in beg sc. Finish off black.

Rnd 2: With right side facing, join white with a sl st in any sc around; ch 1, 2 sc in same st as joining and in each rem sc around; join with a sl st in beg sc = 12 sc. Finish off white.

Rnd 3: With right side facing, join grass green with a sl st in any sc around; ch 1, sc in same st as joining and in each rem sc around; **Do not join** = 12 sc. Continue by working back and forth in rows as follows:

  Row 1: Ch 1, turn; sk first sc, sc in each sc across to last 2 sc; sk next sc, sc in last sc = 10 sc.

  Rows 2 through 5: Rep Row 1 (prev row), 4 times. At end of Row 5, you should have 2 sc.

Finish off, leaving approx 8" sewing length. Stuff eye; then sew to top of head as shown in photo.

TONGUE: With flame, ch 10. Sc in 2nd ch from hook and in each rem ch across = 9 sc.

Finish off, leaving approx 6" sewing length. Thread into tapestry or yarn needle; sew this end of tongue to center back of mouth. Weave in all ends.

KIDS' PAJAMA BAGS

designed by Sue Penrod

Children will be delighted by these crocheted pajama bags, and they may be just the thing to encourage your youngsters to put their pajamas away neatly. The elephant can be "fed" through his smiling mouth, and the lion can be "plumped up" through an opening in the back. Just watch the smiles when children first lay eyes on these "practical" toys.

ELEPHANT PAJAMA BAG

Size

Approx 10½" diameter

Materials

American Thread Dawn Sayelle Knitting Worsted
    Size Yarn:
        7 oz steel gray
        6 yds white
Size I aluminum crochet hook (or size required for
    gauge)
Polyester fiber (*for stuffing trunk*)
Small pieces of felt in white and black
Tracing paper and pencil
White craft glue

Gauge

In hdc, 3 sts = 1"; 3 rnds = 1¼"

Instructions

TRUNK: Beg at tip, with steel gray, ch 4, join with a sl st to form a ring.

Rnd 1: Work 2 hdc in each ch around = 8 hdc. (*NOTE: Do not join; work continuous rnds, unless otherwise specified. Use a small safety pin or piece of yarn in contrasting color and mark first st of rnd; move marker at beg of each rnd.*)

Rnd 2: Work 2 hdc in each st around = 16 hdc.

Rnds 3 through 14: Work 12 rnds even. (*NOTE: To "work even", work one hdc in each st around for specified number of rnds, without increasing or decreasing.*)

Rnd 15: * Hdc in next st, 2 hdc in next st; rep from * around = 24 hdc.

Rnds 16 through 18: Work 3 rnds even. At end of Rnd 18, join with a sl st in beg hdc. Lightly stuff *trunk* (**do not overstuff**), to within 2 rnds from top (this will enable trunk to bend). Now work closure at top of trunk as follows.

Rnd 19: Mark front lp (*lp toward you*) of same st as joining (use marker different from beg of rnd) for beginning head later. Working **in back lp** (*lp away from you*) of each st around (front lps will be used to work head later), ch 1, hdc in same st as joining (where front lp was just marked) and in each rem st around; **Do not join** = 24 hdc. Continue by working continuous rnds **in both lps** of sts.

Rnd 20: * Sc in next st, sk next st; rep from * around = 12 sc.

Rnd 21: Rep Rnd 20 = 6 sc.

Rnd 22: * Sl st in next st, sk next st; rep from * around = 3 sl sts. Finish off; weave in end.

HEAD: Hold trunk with tip facing you and closure just worked at top.

Rnd 1: Working **in unused lps** (*left unworked in Rnd 19 of trunk*) around top edge, join steel gray with a sl st in marked lp; ch 1, work 2 hdc in same lp as joining and in each rem lp around; join with a sl st in beg hdc = 48 hdc. Continue by working **in both lps** of sts.

Rnd 2: Ch 20, sk same st as joining and next 19 sts (*for mouth opening*), hdc in each of next 28 sts. (*NOTE: Do not join. Continue by working continuous rnds.*)

Rnd 3: * Hdc in next ch, 2 hdc in next ch; rep from * 9 times more; ** hdc in next hdc, 2 hdc in next hdc; rep from ** 13 times more = 72 hdc.

Rnds 4 and 5: Work 2 rnds even.

Rnd 6: * Hdc in next st, 2 hdc in next st; rep from * around = 108 hdc.

Rnds 7 through 10: Work 4 rnds even. At end of Rnd 10, front of head is completed; continue with back as follows.

Rnd 11: * Hdc in each of next 3 sts, sk next st; rep from * around = 81 hdc.

Rnds 12 and 13: Work 2 rnds even.

Rnd 14: * Hdc in each of next 3 sts, sk next st; rep from * to last st, hdc in last st = 61 hdc.

Rnd 15: Work even.

Rnd 16: Rep Rnd 14 = 46 hdc.

Rnd 17: * Hdc in each of next 3 sts, sk next st; rep from * around to last 2 sts, hdc in each of last 2 sts = 35 hdc.

Rnd 18: Work even.

Rnd 19: * Dec (decrease) over next 2 sts. [**To make dec: YO, insert hook in next st and draw up a lp (3 lps now on hook), YO and draw through 2 lps on hook (2 lps now on hook); insert hook in next st and draw up a lp (3 lps now on hook), YO and draw through all 3 lps on hook = dec made.**] Rep from * to last st, hdc in last st = 18 hdc.

Rnd 20: * Dec over next 2 sts; rep from * 8 times = 9 hdc.

Rnd 21: Rep Rnd 19 = 5 hdc.

Finish off, leaving approx 6″ end; thread into tapestry or yarn needle. Weave through sts of last rnd; draw up tightly and fasten securely. Weave in ends.

EARS (make 2): With steel gray, leave approx 36″ end for sewing ear to head later, ch 50; join with a sl st in beg ch to form a ring, being careful not to twist chain.

Rnd 1: Hdc in same ch as joining, 2 hdc in next ch; * hdc in next ch, 2 hdc in next ch; rep from * around = 75 hdc. [*NOTE: Do not join; work continuous rnds (mark first st of rnd as before).*]

Rnds 2 through 5: Work 4 rnds even.

Rnd 6: * Hdc in each of next 14 sts, sk next st; rep from * around = 70 hdc.

Rnd 7: Work even.

Rnd 8: * Hdc in each of next 6 sts, sk next st; rep from * around = 60 hdc.

Rnd 9: Work even.

Rnd 10: * Hdc in each of next 4 sts, sk next st; rep from * around = 48 hdc.

Rnd 11: * Hdc in each of next 3 sts, sk next st; rep from * around = 36 hdc.

Rnd 12: Rep Rnd 11 = 27 hdc.

Rnd 13: * Hdc in each of next 2 sts, sk next st; rep from * around = 18 hdc.

Rnd 14: * Sl st in next st, sk next st; rep from * around = 9 sl sts.

Rnd 15: * Sl st in next st, sk next st; rep from * to last st, sl st in last st = 5 sl sts.

Finish off, leaving approx 6″ end; thread into tapestry or yarn needle. Weave through sts of last rnd; draw up tightly and fasten securely.

Thread beg sewing length into tapestry or yarn needle and sew beg edge of ear closed, having wrong sides of ear tog. Continuing with same sewing length, sew this edge of ear to side of head, approx 8 rnds from trunk and having approx 16 sts between ears at top of head. Cup ear forward.

BUTTONS (make 2): With white, ch 3, join with a sl st to form a ring.

Rnd 1: Ch 2, work 14 hdc in ring, join with a sl st in top of beg ch-2. Finish off, leaving approx 10″ sewing length. Thread into tapestry or yarn needle and sew one button to each corner of mouth.

LOOP FASTENERS: Join steel gray with a sl st in center st at lower edge of mouth; ch 1, sc in same st as joining; * ch 23, sl st back into sc just made; rep from * once more (2 lps made). Finish off and fasten ends securely.

EYES AND EYEBROWS: Trace outlines in *Fig 1*

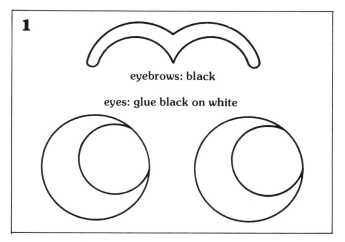

eyebrows: black

eyes: glue black on white

on paper. Cut outlines and use as patterns on felt as indicated. (NOTE: To prevent pattern pieces from slipping on felt, tape pieces in place with cellophane tape. Cut out felt pieces, then discard tape.) With glue, attach felt pieces as shown in photo.

LION PAJAMA BAG

Size

Approx 10½" diameter

Materials

American Thread Dawn Sayelle Knitting Worsted
  Size Yarn:
    6 oz lemon
    3 oz gold
    6 yds black
    1 yd white
Size I aluminum crochet hook (or size required for
  gauge)
Small piece of black felt
Tracing paper and pencil
White craft glue

Gauge

In hdc, 3 sts = 1"; 3 rnds = 1¼"

Pattern Stitch

(NOTE: Before beginning your project, we suggest working a sample swatch. Although the loop stitch is not difficult to do, it does require practice to become familiar with the technique and to be able to work with ease. To practice, ch 11, sc in 2nd ch from hook and in each rem ch across; ch 1, turn; then follow instructions below.)

LOOP STITCH (abbreviated LS): Insert hook in st and draw up a lp (2 lps now on hook). Wrap yarn twice around tip of left index finger; insert hook in front of yarn and through first lp on finger (*Fig 2*), draw lp through one lp on hook. Now bring left index finger down in front of work; sk first lp on finger and insert hook through 2nd lp on finger (*Fig 3*), draw lp through both rem lps on hook. Drop long lp off finger = LS made.

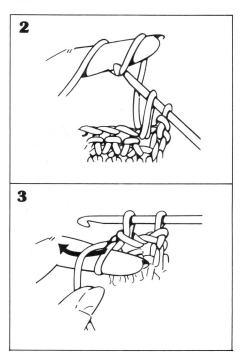

Instructions

Beg at center front, with gold, ch 4, join with a sl st to form a ring.

Rnd 1: Work 2 sc in each ch around = 8 sc. (NOTE: Do not join; work continuous rnds, unless otherwise specified. Use small safety pin or piece of yarn in contrasting color and mark first st of rnd; move marker at beg of each rnd.)

Rnd 2: Work 2 hdc in each st around = 16 hdc.

Rnd 3: Rep Rnd 2 = 32 hdc.

Rnd 4: Work even in hdc. (NOTE: To "work even", work one st in each st around, without increasing or decreasing.)

Rnd 5: * Hdc in next st, 2 hdc in next st; rep from * around = 48 hdc.

Rnds 6 and 7: Work 2 rnds even in hdc.

Rnd 8: Rep Rnd 5 = 72 hdc.

Rnd 9: Work even in hdc.

Rnd 10: Hdc in each st to last st; sc in last st, changing to lemon. (**To change colors: Insert hook in last st and draw up a lp; finish off gold. With lemon, YO and draw through both lps on hook = color changed.**) Continuing with lemon, work loop sts as follows.

Rnd 11: * LS in each of next 2 sts, 2 LS in next st; rep from * around = 96 LS.

Rnds 12 through 15: Work 4 rnds even in LS.

Rnd 16: * Sc in each of next 2 sts, dec; (**To make dec: Draw up a lp in each of next 2 sts, YO and draw through all 3 lps on hook = dec made.**) Rep from * 9 times more; LS in each rem st around = 86 sts.

Rnd 17 (lower back opening): Sc in first st, ch 38, sk next 28 sts (for opening); sc in next st (be careful not to twist chain), LS in each rem st around.

Rnd 18: LS in first sc, hdc in each of first 6 chs; * sk one ch, hdc in each of next 2 chs; rep from * 9 times more, hdc in each of last 2 chs; LS in next sc and in each rem LS around = 86 sts.

Rnd 19: LS in each st around = 86 LS.

Rnd 20: LS in each of first 30 sts; * sk one st, LS in each of next 3 sts; rep from * around = 72 LS.

Rnd 21: Work even in LS.

Rnd 22: * LS in each of next 3 sts, sk one st; rep from * around = 54 LS.

Rnd 23: Work even in LS.

Rnd 24: * LS in each of next 2 sts, sk one st; rep from * around = 36 sts.

Rnd 25: Work even in LS.

Rnd 26: Rep Rnd 24 = 24 LS.

Rnd 27: Work even in LS.

Rnd 28: * LS in next st, sk one st; rep from * around = 12 LS.

Rnd 29: Rep Rnd 28 = 6 LS.

Finish off, leaving approx 8″ end. Thread into tapestry or yarn needle; weave through sts of last rnd. Draw up tightly and fasten securely on inside. Weave in ends.

MUZZLE: With black, make 1″ diameter pompon (see instructions on page 11). Attach pompon securely to center front for nose. With gold, make two 2½″ diameter pompons and attach side by side, directly below nose (toward edge near back opening).

WHISKERS: Cut 6 strands of white, having each strand 5″ long. Knot 3 strands around st on each side of nose, just above gold pompons as follows: Fold 3 strands in half; insert hook under st (from outside edge toward nose), hook folded end of strands and pull through. Pull loose ends through folded section (**Fig 4**) and draw knot up firmly. Trim ends evenly.

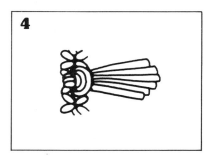

EYES: Trace outlines in **Fig 5** on paper. Cut outlines and use as patterns on black felt. (*NOTE: To prevent pattern pieces from slipping on felt, tape pieces in place with cellophane tape. Cut out felt pieces, then discard tape.*) With glue, attach felt pieces above nose as shown in photo.

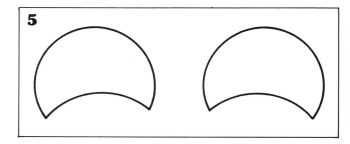

EARS (make 2): With gold, ch 5.

Rnd 1 (right side): Working in top lp only of each ch, sc in 2nd ch from hook and in each of next 2 chs, 3 sc in last ch. **Working on opposite side of starting chain in top lp only of each st,** sc in each of next 2 sts, 2 sc in last st; do not join. Continue by working **in both lps** of sts.

Rnd 2: Do not turn; work (sc, hdc) in first sc, work (dc, trc—triple crochet) in next sc [**To work TRC: (YO hook) twice; insert hook in st and draw up a lp (4 lps now on hook): work (YO and draw through 2 lps on hook) 3 times = trc made**]. Work 2 trc in next sc, 3 trc in next sc, 5 trc in next sc (*top of ear*); 3 trc in next sc, 2 trc in next sc, work (trc, dc) in next sc; work (hdc, sc) in next sc, sl st in last sc. Finish off, leaving approx 12″ sewing length. Position ear above eye as shown in photo, having top sts overlapping loop sts; sew ear in place along bottom edge and up center along foundation chain.

CUDDLY CAT FAMILY

designed by Sue Penrod

Our tiger-striped mother cat keeps a wary eye on her lively offspring. This charming set comes complete with its own basket.

Size

Mother cat measures approx 7½" long (without tail). Each kitten measures approx 4" long (without tail). Oval basket measures approx 8" × 12".

Materials

American Thread Dawn Sayelle Knitting Worsted
Size Yarn:
    6 oz chocolate brown
    3½ oz shaded oranges
    1½ oz each of orange and lemon
    1 yd white
Sizes F and I aluminum crochet hooks (or sizes
    required for gauge)
Polyester fiber (*for stuffing*)
Small piece of black felt
Tracing paper and pencil
White craft glue

Gauge

For kittens, with smaller size hook and single strand of yarn, in sc, 9 sts = 2"; 5 rnds = 1"

For mother cat, with larger size hook and single strand of yarn, in sc, 4 sts = 1"; 4 rnds = 1"

For basket, with larger size hook and 2 strands of yarn, in sc, 13 sts = 4"; 10 rnds = 3"

MOTHER CAT

Instructions

(*NOTE: All rnds are worked on right side.*)

BODY: Beg at center front of head, with larger size hook and single strand of shaded oranges, ch 4, join with a sl st to form a ring.

Rnd 1: Work 2 sc in each ch around = 8 sc. [*NOTE: Do not join; work continuous rnds (without joining), unless otherwise specified. Use a small safety pin or piece of yarn in contrasting color and mark first st of rnd; move marker at beg of each rnd.*]

Rnd 2: Work 2 sc in each sc around = 16 sc.

Rnd 3: Rep Rnd 2 = 32 sc.

Rnds 4 through 6: Work 3 rnds even. (*NOTE: To "work even", work one sc in each st around for specified number of rnds, without increasing or decreasing.*)

Rnd 7 (ears): Work ear **in front lp** (*lp toward you*) of first 3 sts as follows: Work (sc, hdc) in first sc (remember to work in front lp only), 2 dc in next sc, work (2 trc, ch 4, sc) in next sc [**To work trc (triple crochet): (YO hook) twice, insert hook in st and draw up a lp (4 lps now on hook); work (YO and draw through 2 lps on hook) 3 times = trc made].** One ear is now completed. Sc **in both lps** in each of next 3 sc; work other ear **in front lp** of next 3 sts as follows: Work (sc, ch 4, 2 trc) in next sc, 2 dc in next sc, work (hdc, sc) in next sc. Second ear is now completed. Sc **in both lps** in each rem sc around.

Rnd 8: Working behind first ear, sc in unused (back) lp in each of first 3 sts; sk all sts of first ear, sc **in both lps** in each of next 3 sc (between ears). Working behind other ear, sc in unused lp in each of next 3 sts; sk all sts of second ear, sc **in both lps** in each of rem 23 sc = 32 sc. **Continue by working in both lps of sts.**

Rnds 9 through 11: Work 3 rnds even.

Rnd 12: * Sc in each of next 2 sc, sk one sc, sc in next sc; rep from * around = 24 sc.

Rnd 13: * Sc in next sc, sk one sc, sc in next sc; rep from * around = 16 sc.

Rnd 14: Work even. Stuff and shape head; then continue with body as follows.

Rnd 15: * Sc in next sc, 2 sc in next sc; rep from * around = 24 sc.

Rnd 16: * Sc in each of next 2 sc, 2 sc in next sc; rep from * around = 32 sc.

Rnds 17 and 18: Work 2 rnds even.

Rnd 19 (marking rnd): (*NOTE: In this rnd, 2 sts are marked for sewing front legs to body later.*) Sc in each of first 20 sc; sc in next sc and mark st just made (*use marker different from beg of rnd*), sc in each of next 8 sc; sc in next sc and mark st just made, sc in each of rem 2 sc.

Rnds 20 and 21: Work 2 rnds even.

Rnd 22: * Sc in each of next 7 sc, 2 sc in next sc; rep from * around = 36 sc.

Rnds 23 through 30: Work 8 rnds even.

Rnd 31 (marking rnd): (*NOTE: In this rnd, 2 sts are marked for sewing hind legs to body later.*) Sc in each of first 23 sc; sc in next sc and mark st just made, sc in each of next 8 sc; sc in next sc and mark st just made, sc in each of rem 3 sc.

Rnd 32: * Sc in each of next 2 sc, sk one sc, sc in next sc; rep from * around = 27 sc.

Rnd 33: * Sc in next sc, sk one sc, sc in next sc; rep from * around = 18 sc. Stuff and shape body; then continue with tail as follows.

Rnd 34: Rep Rnd 33 = 12 sc.

Rnds 35 through 45: Work 11 rnds even.

Rnd 46: * Sc in next sc, sk one sc, sc in next sc; rep from * around = 8 sc.

Rnds 47 through 51: Work 5 rnds even. At end of Rnd 51, stuff tail lightly.

Rnd 52: * Sk one sc, sc in next sc; rep from * around = 4 sc.

Finish off, leaving approx 6" end. Thread into tapestry or yarn needle; weave through sts of last rnd. Draw up tightly and fasten securely.

FRONT LEGS (make 2): Beg at paw, with larger size hook and single strand of shaded oranges, ch 4, join with a sl st to form a ring.

Rnd 1: Work 2 sc in each ch around = 8 sc. [*NOTE: Do not join; work continuous rnds (mark first st of rnd as before.)*]

Rnd 2: Work 2 sc in each sc around = 16 sc.

Rnds 3 and 4: Work 2 rnds even.

Rnd 5: * Sc in each of next 2 sc, sk one sc, sc in next sc; rep from * around = 12 sc.

Rnds 6 through 17: Work 12 rnds even. At end of Rnd 17, finish off; weave in ends. Stuff leg lightly to within 2 rnds from top, pushing stuffing down into bottom of leg to shape paw.

At end of 2nd leg, leave approx 20" sewing length. Stuff leg as before; then thread sewing length into tapestry or yarn needle and sew opening closed, carefully matching 6 corresponding sc across. Continuing with same sewing length, sew top of other leg closed in same manner, having front of each paw facing same direction. Then sew this top edge of legs to body between first (*front*) set of markers, having front of paws facing forward.

HIND LEGS: Work same as front legs and sew to body between other set of markers, having front of paws facing forward.

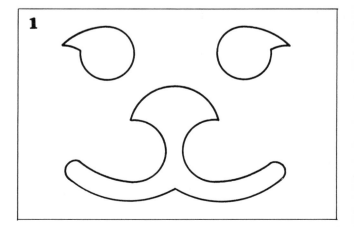

EYES, NOSE AND MOUTH: Trace outlines in *Fig 1* on paper. Cut outlines and use as patterns on black felt. (*NOTE: To prevent pattern pieces from slipping on felt, tape pieces in place with cellophane tape. Cut out felt pieces through tape, then discard tape.*) With glue, attach felt pieces as shown in photo.

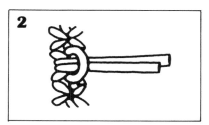

WHISKERS: Cut 4 strands of white, having each strand 4″ long. Knot 2 strands around st on each side of nose as follows: Fold 2 strands in half; insert hook under st toward nose, hook folded end of strands and pull through. Pull loose ends through folded section (*Fig 2*) and draw knot up firmly. Trim ends evenly.

KITTENS

Instructions

[*NOTE: Make one kitten in each of the following colors: shaded oranges, orange and lemon (3 total).*]

BODY: Beg at center front of head, with smaller size hook and single strand of yarn, ch 4, join with a sl st to form a ring. (*NOTE: All following rnds are worked on right side.*)

Rnd 1: Work 2 sc in each ch around = 8 sc. [*NOTE: Do not join; work continuous rnds (without joining). Mark first st of rnd; move marker at beg of each rnd.*]

Rnd 2: Work 2 sc in each sc around = 16 sc.

Rnds 3 and 4: Work 2 rnds even. (*NOTE: To "work even", work sc in each st around for specified number of rnds, without increasing or decreasing.*)

Rnd 5 (ears): Work ear **in front lp** (*lp toward you*) of first 2 sts as follows: Work (sc, hdc) in first sc (*remember to work in front lp only*), work (hdc, ch 3, sc) in next sc. One ear is now completed. Sc **in both lps** in each of next 2 sc, work other ear **in front lp** of next 2 sts as follows: Work (sc, ch 3, hdc) in next sc, work (hdc, sc) in next sc. Second ear is now completed. Sc **in both lps** in each rem sc around.

Rnd 6: Working behind first ear, sc in unused (back) lp in each of first 2 sts; sk all sts of first ear, sc **in both lps** in each of next 2 sc (between ears). Working behind second ear, sc in unused lp in each

of next 2 sts; sk all sts of second ear, sc **in both lps** in each of rem 10 sc = 16 sc. **Continue by working in both lps of sts**.

Rnd 7: * Sc in each of next 2 sc, sk one sc, sc in next sc; rep from * around = 12 sc. Stuff and shape head; then continue with neck shaping and body as follows.

Rnd 8: * Sc in next sc, sk one sc, sc in next sc; rep from * around = 8 sc.

Rnd 9: * Sc in next sc, 2 sc in next sc; rep from * around = 12 sc.

Rnd 10: Rep Rnd 9 = 18 sc.

Rnd 11 (marking rnd): (*NOTE: In this rnd, 2 sts are marked for sewing front legs to body later.*) Sc in each of first 11 sc, sc in next sc and mark st just made (*use marker different from beg of rnd*); sc in each of next 4 sc, sc in next sc and mark st just made, sc in rem sc.

Rnds 12 through 17: Work 6 rnds even.

Rnd 18 (marking rnd): (*NOTE: In this rnd, 2 sts are marked for sewing hind legs to body later.*) Sc in each of first 13 sc, sc in next sc and mark st just made; sc in each of next 3 sc, sc in last sc and mark st just made.

Rnd 19: Work even.

Rnd 20: * Sc in next sc, sk one sc, sc in next sc; rep from * around = 12 sc. Stuff body.

Rnd 21: Rep Rnd 20 = 8 sc.

Rnd 22: * Sk one sc, sc in next sc; rep from * around = 4 sc. Do not finish off; continue with tail as follows: Ch 7, sc in 2nd ch from hook and in each of next 5 chs.

Finish off, leaving approx 8″ sewing length; thread into tapestry or yarn needle. Fold tail in half lengthwise, having wrong side of sts facing outside of tail. First, secure tail to end of kitten; then sew edges tog.

FRONT LEGS (make 2): Beg at paw, with smaller size hook and single strand of yarn, ch 4, join with a sl to to form a ring.

Rnd 1: Work 2 sc in each ch around = 8 sc. [*NOTE: Do not join; work continuous rnds, (mark first st of rnd as before.)*]

Rnd 2: Work even.

Rnd 3: * Sc in each of next 2 sc, sk one sc, sc in next sc; rep from * once more = 6 sc.

Rnds 4 through 10: Work 7 rnds even. At end of Rnd 10, finish off; weave in ends. Do not stuff.

At end of 2nd leg, leave approx 16″ sewing length. Thread into tapestry or yarn needle; sew opening closed, carefully matching 3 corresponding sc across. Continuing with same sewing length, sew top of other leg closed in same manner, having front of each paw facing same direction. Then sew this top edge of legs to body between first (front) set of markers, having front of paws facing forward.

HIND LEGS: Work same as front legs and sew to body between other set of markers, having front of paws facing forward.

EYES, NOSE AND MOUTH: Using outlines in *Fig 3*, work in same manner as Mother Cat.

WHISKERS: Cut 2 strands of white, having each strand 2″ long. Knot one strand around st on each side of nose in same manner as Mother Cat. Fray end of strands and trim evenly.

BASKET

Instructions

Beg at center bottom, with larger size hook and 2 strands of chocolate brown, ch 17.

Rnd 1: Sc in 2nd ch from hook and in each of next 14 chs, work 4 sc in last ch. **Continuing on opposite side of starting chain**, sc in each of next 14 sts, 3 sc in last st; join with a sl st in beg sc = 36 sc.

Rnd 2: Ch 1, do not turn; 2 sc in same st as joining, sc in each of next 14 sc; 2 sc in each of next 4 sc, sc in each of next 14 sc; 2 sc in each of last 3 sc, join with a sl st in beg sc = 44 sc.

Rnd 3: Ch 1, do not turn; sc in same st as joining and in each rem sc around, join with a sl st in beg sc.

Rnd 4: Ch 1, do not turn; 2 sc in same st as joining, 2 sc in next sc, sc in each of next 14 sc; 2 sc in each of next 2 sc, (sc in next sc, 2 sc in each of next 2 sc) twice, sc in each of next 14 sc; (2 sc in each of next 2 sc, sc in next sc) twice, join with a sl st in beg sc = 56 sc.

Rnd 5: Rep Rnd 3.

Rnd 6: Ch 1, do not turn; sc in same st as joining, 2 sc in next sc; sc in next sc, 2 sc in next sc, sc in each of next 14 sc; (2 sc in next sc, sc in next sc) 3 times, 2 sc in each of next 2 sc, (sc in next sc, 2 sc in next sc) 3 times, sc in each of next 14 sc; (2 sc in next sc, sc in next sc) 3 times, 2 sc in each of next 2 sc, sc in next sc; 2 sc in last sc, join with a sl st in beg sc = 72 sc.

Rnds 7 and 8: Rep Rnd 3 twice.

Rnd 9: Ch 1, do not turn; sc in same st as joining, sc in next sc; 2 sc in next sc, sc in each of next 2 sc; 2 sc in next sc, sc in each of next 14 sc; 2 sc in next sc, sc in each of next 14 sc; 2 sc in next sc, (sc in each of next 2 sc, 2 sc in next sc) 7 times, sc in each of next 14 sc; 2 sc in next sc, (sc in each of next 2 sc, 2 sc in next sc) 5 times; join with a sl st in beg sc = 88 sc.

Rnds 10 and 11: Rep Rnd 3, twice.

Rnd 12: Ch 1, do not turn; sc in same st as joining, 2 sc in next sc; (sc in each of next 2 sc, 2 sc in next sc) twice, sc in each of next 14 sc; (2 sc in next sc, sc in each of next 2 sc) 4 times, 2 sc in next sc, sc in next sc, 2 sc in each of next 2 sc; sc in next sc, 2 sc in next sc; (sc in each of next 2 sc, 2 sc in next sc) 4 times, sc in each of next 14 sc; (2 sc in next sc, sc in each of next 2 sc) 4 times, 2 sc in next sc, sc in next sc; 2 sc in each of next 2 sc, sc in next sc; 2 sc in next sc, sc in each of next 2 sc; 2 sc in next sc, sc in last sc, join with a sl st in beg sc = 112 sc.

Rnds 13 and 14: Rep Rnd 3, twice. Bottom of basket is now completed; continue with side shaping as follows.

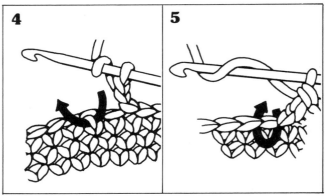

Rnd 15: Ch 2, do not turn; work FPdc (front post dc) around post of next sc. [**To work FPdc: YO, insert hook around post of next sc from front to back to front (*Fig 4*), hook yarn and draw lp back around st (3 lps now on hook); (YO and draw through 2 lps on hook) twice = FPdc made.**] Work BPdc (back post dc) around post of next sc. [**To work BPdc: YO, insert hook around post of next sc from back to front to back (*Fig 5*), hook yarn and draw lp back around st; (YO and draw through 2 lps on hook) twice = BPdc made.**] * Work FPdc around post of next sc, work BPdc around post of next sc; rep from * to last sc, work FPdc around post of last sc; join with a sl st in sp under beg ch-2.

Rnd 16: Ch 2, turn; work FPdc around post of next dc, * work BPdc around post of next dc, work FPdc around post of next dc; rep from * around, join with a sl st in sp under beg ch-2.

Rnd 17: Rep Rnd 16.

Finish off; weave in ends.

BABY BARBARA JEAN

designed by Sue Penrod

What little girl wouldn't love this adorable baby doll? Crochet her cuddly body, stuff, attach a sweet plastic doll head, and then just listen to the new "mommy" squeal with delight.

Size

Approx 17″ tall

Materials

Worsted weight yarn:
    4 oz turquoise
    ½ oz white
    ½ oz light pink

Size I aluminum crochet hook (or size required for gauge)
Plastic doll head with braids (5″ high, including neck)
Polyester fiber (*for stuffing*)
3 white heart-shaped buttons (½″ *length*)
1 yd, ¼″ wide white satin ribbon (optional—for replacing hair bows on doll head)

Gauge

In sc, worked in back lp of each st,
3 sts = 1″; 3 rnds = 1″

Instructions

COLLAR: Beg at neck edge, with turquoise, ch 14.

Row 1: Sc in 2nd ch from hook and in each rem ch across = 13 sc.

Row 2: Ch 1, turn. Working **in back lp** (*lp away from you*) of each sc across, work (sc, hdc) in first sc, work (dc, trc—triple crochet) in next sc, 2 trc in each of next 9 sc; work (trc, dc) in next sc, work (hdc, sc) in last sc = 26 sts. Finish off turquoise. Turn and work next row as follows.

Row 3 (trim): With white, first make a chain to measure approx 4″ long (for one tie). Then **with wrong side** of sts of last row facing you, continue with same white yarn and work sc in each sc of prev row across. **Do not finish off;** continue with same yarn and make a chain to measure approx 4″ long (for other tie). Finish off; knot and trim ends of ties.

BODY: Hold collar with neck edge (foundation chain edge) at top and wrong side of sts of first row facing you.

Rnd 1: Working **in unused lp** of each st of foundation chain (*between ties*), make a slip knot on hook with turquoise (leave approx 12″ sewing length for securing head to body later), then join with a sc in st at center back neck edge; sc in each of next 6 sts across neck edge to end of collar. Continuing at opposite end of collar, sc in each of next 6 sts across rem half of neck edge = 13 sc. [*NOTE: Do not join; work continuous rnds (without joining), unless otherwise specified. Use a small safety pin or piece of yarn in contrasting color and mark first st of rnd; move marker at beg of each rnd.*]

Rnd 2: Work 2 sc **in back lp** of each sc around = 26 sc. Continue by working **in back lp** of each st, unless otherwise specified.

Rnd 3: * Sc in next sc, 2 sc in next sc; rep from * around = 39 sc.

Rnd 4: Sc in each sc around.

Rnds 5 through 11: Rep Rnd 4, 7 times.

Rnd 12: * Sc in each of next 2 sc, 2 sc in next sc; rep from * around = 52 sc.

Rnd 13: Rep Rnd 4. At end of rnd, join with a sl st **in front lp** (*lp toward you*) of beg sc. **Do not finish off;** continue with waist edging as follows (body will be completed later):

WAIST EDGING: Rnd 1: (*NOTE: Place and leave marker for beg of rnd **in back lp** of first sc for continuing body later.*) Working **in front lp** of each st around, ch 3 (counts as first dc), dc in each of next 2 sc; * 2 dc in next sc, dc in each of next 3 sc; rep from * to last sc, 2 dc in last sc, join with a sl st in top of beg ch-3 = 65

dc. (*Back lps will be used later for completing body.*) Finish off turquoise; join white (for trim).

Rnd 2: Continuing with white, ch 1, sc in same st as joining; sc **in both lps** of each rem dc around, join with a sl st **in both lps** of beg sc. Finish off; weave in ends. Now complete body as follows.

BODY CONTINUED: Rnd 14: Hold body with edging just worked at top. Working **in unused lp** of each st behind edging (*hold edging down toward collar*), make a slip knot on hook with turquoise, then join with a sc in marked lp (*first st of rnd*), sc in each rem lp around = 52 sc. [*NOTE: Do not join; work continuous rnds (mark first st of rnd as before).*] Continue by working **in back lp** of each st.

Rnd 15: Sc in each sc around.

Rnds 16 through 19: Rep Rnd 15, 4 times. At end of Rnd 19, **do not finish off**.

Before working next rnd, insert head into neck opening, having face toward front of collar. Thread beg 12″ sewing length of body into tapestry or yarn needle and weave through sts around neck (under collar) twice. Draw up tightly to secure head; fasten end securely. Fold down collar; tie white chain ends into a bow. Stuff and shape body. Do not overstuff. Excess stuffing can change the shape of the entire doll. Continue with bottom closure as follows.

Rnd 20: * Sc in each of next 2 sc, sk next sc, sc in next sc; rep from * around = 39 sc.

Rnd 21: * Sc in next sc, sk next sc, sc in next sc; rep from * around = 26 sc.

Rnd 22: * Sk next sc, sc in next sc; rep from * around = 13 sc. **Before working next rnd, finish stuffing body.**

Rnd 23: * Sc in next sc, sk next sc; rep from * to last sc, sc in last sc = 7 sc.

Finish off, leaving approx 6″ sewing length. Thread into tapestry or yarn needle and weave through sts of last rnd. Draw up tightly and fasten securely. Fold waist edging down over body.

LEGS (make 2): Beg at top, with turquoise (leave approx 12″ sewing length for attaching leg later), ch 14, join with a sl st to form a ring.

Rnd 1: Sc in each ch around = 14 sc. [*NOTE: Do not join; work continuous rnds (mark first st of rnd as before).*] Continue by working **in back lp** of each st, unless otherwise specified.

Rnd 2: Sc in each sc around.

Rnds 3 through 13: Rep Rnd 2, 11 times. At end of Rnd 13, join with a sl st **in front lp** of beg sc. **Do**

not finish off; continue with bootie edging as follows (leg will be completed later).

BOOTIE EDGING: Rnd 1: (*NOTE: Place and leave marker for beg of rnd **in back lp** of first sc for continuing leg later.*) Ch 3, **Turn**. Working **in back lp** of each st around, * 2 dc in next sc; dc in next sc; rep from * to last sc, dc in last sc, join with a sl st in top of beg ch-3 = 21 dc (counting beg ch-3). (*Front lps will be used later to complete leg.*) Finish off turquoise; join white (for trim).

Rnd 2: Continuing with white, ch 1; **do not turn**; sc in same st as joining; sc **in both lps** of each rem dc around, join with a sl st **in both lps** of beg sc. Finish off; weave in ends. Now complete leg as follows.

LEGS CONTINUED: Rnd 14: Hold leg with edging just worked at top. Working **in unused lp** of each st behind edging (*hold edging down over leg*), make a slip knot on hook with turquoise, then join with a sc in marked lp (*first st of rnd*), sc in each of next 6 lps, 2 sc in each of rem 7 lps (for front of bootie) = 21 sc. (*NOTE: Do not join; work continuous rnds as before.*) Continue by working **in back lp** of each st.

Rnd 15: Sc in each of next 12 sc, 2 sc in each of next 4 sc, sc in each of rem 5 sc = 25 sc.

Rnd 16: Sc in each sc around.

Rnds 17 through 19: Rep Rnd 16, 3 times.

Rnd 20: * Sc in next sc, sk next sc; rep from * to last sc, sc in last sc = 13 sc. **Before working next rnd, lightly stuff and shape lower part of leg.**

Rnd 21: * Sl st in next sc, sk next sc; rep from * to last sc, sl st in last sc = 7 sl sts. *Finish off and close opening in same manner as bottom closure of body.*

Lightly stuff upper part of leg to within one rnd from top. Thread beg sewing length into tapestry or yarn needle; pinch opening closed and sew across. Then sew this edge **to front** (*unused*) **lps** of sts at front bottom outer edge of body, having front of bootie facing forward and 3 sts free between legs.

ARMS (*make 2*)**:** Beg at top, with turquoise (leave approx 12″ sewing length for attaching arm later), ch 14, join with a sl st to form a ring.

Rnd 1: Sc in each ch around = 14 sc. [*NOTE: Do not join; work continuous rnds (mark first st of rnd*

as before).] Continue by working **in back lp** of each st, unless otherwise specified.

Rnd 2: Sc in each sc around.

Rnds 3 through 11: Rep Rnd 2, 9 times. At end of Rnd 11, join with a sl st **in front lp** of beg sc. **Do not finish off**; continue with sleeve edging as follows (arm will be completed later.)

SLEEVE EDGING: Rnd 1: (*NOTE: Place and leave marker for beg of rnd **in back lp** of first sc for continuing arm later.*) Working **in front lp** of each st around, ch 3 (counts as first dc), 2 dc in next sc, * dc in next sc, 2 dc in next sc; rep from * around, join with a sl st in top of beg ch-3 = 21 dc. (*Back lps will be used later to complete arm.*) Finish off turquoise; join white (for trim).

Rnd 2: Continuing with white, ch 1, sc in same st as joining, sc **in both lps** of each rem dc around, join with a sl st **in both lps** of beg sc. Finish off; weave in ends. Now complete arm as follows.

ARMS CONTINUED: Rnd 12: Hold arm with edging just worked at top. Working **in unused lp** of each st behind edging (*hold edging down over arm*), make a slip knot on hook with pink, then join with a sc in marked lp, sc in each rem lp around = 14 sc. (*NOTE: Do not join; work continuous rnds as before.*) Continue by working **in both lps** of sts.

Rnd 13: Sc in each sc around.

Rnds 14 through 16: Rep Rnd 13, 3 times.

Rnd 17: * Sk next sc, sl st in next sc; rep from * around = 7 sl sts.

Rnd 18: * Sl st in next st, sk next st; rep from * to last st, sl st in last st = 4 sl sts. *Finish off and close opening in same manner as bottom closure of body. Fold edging down over hand.*

Lightly stuff and shape arm to within one rnd from top. Sew opening closed in same manner as top of leg and then sew arm to side of body, approx 1 rnd down from neck.

BUTTONS: With white sewing thread, sew 3 buttons evenly spaced halfway down center front of body, just below collar.

HAIR BOWS (optional): Cut ribbon into 4 equal lengths (9″ each). Tie one bow at top and bottom of each braid, replacing bows on doll head.

HIGH SCHOOL SWEETHEARTS

designed by Sue Penrod

It's the day of the big game, and Football Freddie is ready to go out onto the field and make a touch-down! Can he do any less when Cherie Cheerleader is there to cheer him on. Crochet this pair in your favorite school colors!

FOOTBALL FREDDIE

Size

Approx 12″ tall (without helmet)

Materials

Worsted weight yarn:
 1½ oz dark red
 1½ oz white
 12 yds light pink

Size H aluminum crochet hook (or size required for gauge)
Plastic boy doll head with freckles (3″ high, including neck)
Plastic doll hands (1½″ long, including wrist)
Polyester fiber (*for stuffing*)

Gauge

In sc, 4 sts = 1″; 4 rnds = 1″

Instructions

(*NOTE: Throughout patt, all rnds are worked on right side, unless otherwise specified.*)

BODY: Beg at neck edge, with red (leave approx 12″ sewing length for attaching head later), ch 12 loosely, join with a sl st in beg ch to form a ring. (NOTE: *Before proceeding, check size of ring by slipping up over neck of doll head. If sts are too tight, start again and work chains looser. Remove head before continuing.*)

Rnd 1: Ch 1, sc in same ch as joining and in each rem ch around to last ch; sc in last ch, changing to white. [**To change color: Continuing with red, work last sc until 2 lps rem on hook; drop red (do not cut—will be used again), join white (leave end on inside of doll); with white, YO and draw through both lps on hook = color changed.**] Continuing with white, join with a sl st in beg sc = 12 sc.

Rnd 2: With white, ch 1, sc in same st as joining and in each rem sc around to last sc; sc in last sc, changing to red (finish off white). Continuing with red only, join with a sl st in beg sc.

Rnd 3: Ch 1, work 2 sc in same st as joining and in each rem sc around = 24 sc. [NOTE: *Do not join; work continuous rnds (without joining), unless otherwise specified. Use a small safety pin or piece of yarn in contrasting color and mark first st of rnd; move marker at beg of each rnd.*]

Rnd 4: * Sc in each of next 2 sc, 2 sc in next sc; rep from * around = 32 sc.

Rnd 5: Sc in each of next 5 sc, sc **in back lp** (*lp away from you*) in each of next 5 sc (*front lps will be used later for attaching arm*); sc **in both lps** in each of next 11 sc, sc **in back lp** in each of next 5 sc (*front lps will be used later for attaching other arm*); sc **in both lps** in each of rem 6 sc. Continue by working **in both lps** of sts.

Rnd 6: Sc in each sc around = 32 sc.

Rnds 7 through 12: Rep Rnd 6, 6 times. At end of Rnd 12, join with a sl st in beg sc.

Rnd 13: Ch 1, sc in same st as joining and in each rem sc around; join with a sl st in beg sc. Finish off red; join white (*for pants*). Continuing with white only, work as follows.

Rnd 14: Ch 1, sc **in back lp** (*lp away from you*) in same st as joining and in each rem sc around, join with a sl st **in both lps** of beg sc = 32 sc. (*Front lps are left unworked—this forms a ridge around waistline.*) Continue by working **in both lps** of sts.

Rnd 15: Ch 1, sc in same st as joining and in each rem sc around, join with a sl st in beg sc.

Rnds 16 through 19: Rep Rnd 15, 4 times. [NOTE: *At end of Rnd 19, do not join rnd. Continue by working continuous rnds (without joining); mark first st of rnd as before.*]

Rnd 20: Sc **in both lps** in each of next 12 sc, sc **in back lp** in each of next 12 sc (front lps will be used later for attaching legs); sc **in both lps** in each of rem 8 sc. Continue by working **in both lps** of sts.

Rnd 21: * Sk next sc, sc in each of next 3 sc; rep from * around = 24 sc. **Do not finish off**.

Before working next rnd, insert head into neck opening, having back of head at side of body where rnds begin. Thread beg end into tapestry or yarn needle and weave through sts around neck edge twice. Draw up tightly to secure head; fasten end securely. Stuff and shape body; do not overstuff. Excess stuffing can change the shape of the entire doll. Continue as follows.

Rnd 22: * Sk next sc, sc in next sc; rep from * around = 12 sc. Before working next rnd, finish stuffing body.

Rnd 23: Rep Rnd 22 = 6 sc.

Finish off, leaving approx 6″ end. Thread into tapestry or yarn needle; weave through sts of last rnd. Draw up tightly and fasten securely.

LEGS (*make 2*) Beg at top, with white (leave approx 12″ sewing length for attaching leg later), ch 12, join with a sl st in beg ch to form a ring.

Rnd 1: Ch 1, sc in same ch as joining and in each rem ch around, join with a sl st in beg sc = 12 sc.

Rnd 2: Ch 1, sc in same st as joining and in each rem sc around, join with a sl st in beg sc.

Rnds 3 through 8: Rep Rnd 2, 6 times.

Rnd 9: Ch 1, sc in same st as joining and in each rem sc around, join with a sl st in beg sc.

Rnd 10: Rep Rnd 9.

Rnd 11: Ch 1, sc in same st as joining; * sk next sc, sc in each of next 2 sc; rep from * to last 2 sc, sk next sc, sc in last sc; join with a sl st in beg sc = 8 sc. Finish off white; join red (for stocking). Continue with red only and work as follows.

Rnd 12: Ch 1, sc **in back lp** in same st as joining and in each rem sc around, join with a sl st **in both lps** of beg sc = 8 sc. (*Front lps are left unworked— this forms a ridge at bottom edge of pants.*) Continue by working **in both lps** of sts.

Rnds 13 through 17: Rep Rnd 9, 5 times. At end of Rnd 17, finish off red; join white (for shoe). Continue as follows.

Rnd 18: Ch 1, sc in same st as joining, sc in next sc, 2 sc in each of next 4 sc (for front of shoe); sc in each of rem 2 sc, join with a sl st in beg sc = 12 sc.

Rnd 19: Ch 1, sc in same st as joining; sc in each of next 3 sc, 2 sc in each of next 4 sc, sc in each of rem 4 sc; join with a sl st in beg sc = 16 sc.

Rnd 20: Ch 1, sc in same st as joining and in each rem sc around, join with a sl st in beg sc.

Rnd 21: Ch 1, sc in same st as joining and in each rem sc around to last sc; sc in last sc, changing to blue (finish off white). Continuing with blue only (for sole of shoe), join with a sl st in beg sc.

Rnd 22: With blue, rep Rnd 23. Before working next rnd, lightly stuff lower part of leg.

Rnd 23: Ch 1, sc in same st as joining; * sk next sc, sc in next sc; rep from * to last sc, sk last sc, join with a sl st in beg sc = 8 sc.

Rnd 24: Rep Rnd 26 = 4 sc. Finish off and close opening in same manner as bottom of body.

Lightly stuff upper part of leg to within one rnd from top. Thread beg sewing length into tapestry or yarn needle. Pinch opening closed and sew across. Then sew this edge to 6 lps (*half of 12 unworked lps*) at front bottom outer edge of body, having front of shoe facing forward.

ARMS (*make 2*): Beg at top, with red (leave approx 12" sewing length for attaching arm later), ch 10, join with a sl st in beg ch to form a ring.

Rnd 1: Ch 1, sc in same ch as joining and in each rem ch around, join with a sl st in beg sc = 10 sc.

Rnd 2: Ch 1, sc in same st as joining and in each rem sc around to last sc; sc in last sc, changing to white (*for stripe—do not finish off red*). Continuing with white, join with a sl st in beg sc.

Rnd 3: With white, ch 1, sc in same st as joining and in each rem sc around to last sc; sc in last sc, changing to red (*finish off white*). Continuing with red only, join with a sl st in beg sc.

Rnd 4: Ch 1, sc in same st as joining and in each rem sc around, join with a sl st in beg sc. Finish off red; join pink. Continuing with pink only, work as follows.

Rnd 5: Ch 1, sc **in back lp** in same st as joining and in each rem sc around, join with a sl st **in both lps** of beg sc. (*Front lps are left unworked—this forms a ridge at bottom edge of sleeve.*) Continue by working **in both lps** of sts.

Rnd 6: Ch 1, sc in same st as joining and in each rem sc around, join with a sl st in beg sc.

Rnds 7 through 14: Rep Rnd 6, 8 times. At end of Rnd 14, finish off, leaving approx 10" sewing length. Lightly stuff lower part of arm. Insert hand into opening and secure in place in same manner as head.

Lightly stuff upper part of arm to within one rnd from top. Sew opening closed in same manner as top of leg. Then sew arm to 5 unworked lps at side of doll.

HELMET: Beg at center top, with white, ch 4, join with a sl st to form a ring.

Rnd 1: Work 2 sc in each ch around = 8 sc. [*NOTE: Do not join; work continuous rnds (mark first st of rnd as before).*]

Rnd 2: Work 2 sc in each sc around = 16 sc.

Rnd 3: * Sc in next sc, 2 sc in next sc; rep from * around = 24 sc.

Rnd 4: Sc in each sc around.

Rnds 5 and 6: Rep Rnd 4, twice. At end of Rnd 6, do not finish off; continue by working back and forth in rows for back shaping of helmet as follows.

> **Row 1:** Ch 1, turn; sc in each of next 16 sc (leave rem sts unworked).
>
> **Row 2:** Ch 1, turn; sc in each sc across.
>
> **Rows 3 through 7:** Rep Row 2, 5 times. At end of Row 7, do not finish off. Continue with face guard as follows: Ch 8, join with a sl st in opposite corner of helmet (insert hook in st from right to wrong side). Then sl st in next row above sl st just made. Ch 8, join with a sl st in corresponding row at opposite edge of helmet. Finish off; weave in ends.

Finishing

NUMBER ON SHIRT: With white, make 2 chains as follows: Ch 6 (for number one); finish off, leaving approx 6" sewing length. Then ch 16 (for zero); finish off, leaving approx 8" sewing length. Having wrong side of chains facing up, sew "10" in place on front of shirt.

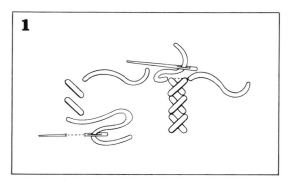

SHOELACES (*make 2*): Thread 14" strand of red into tapestry or yarn needle. Beg at center top of shoe and work 3 cross sts down center front of shoe (one st in each rnd), ending back at top of shoe (see *Fig 1*). Tie lace into a bow; knot and trim each end of lace.

CHERIE CHEERLEADER

Size

Approx 13″ tall

Materials

Worsted weight yarn:
  2 oz dark red
  2 oz white
  15 yds light pink
Size H aluminum crochet hook (or size required for gauge)
Plastic girl doll head with open-and-shut eyes (3½″ high, including neck)
Plastic ladies hands (2″ long, including wrist)
Polyester fiber *(for stuffing)*

Gauge

In sc, 4 sts = 1″; 4 rnds = 1″

Instructions

(NOTE: Throughout patt, all rnds are worked on right side, unless otherwise specified.)

BODY: Beg at neck edge, with white (leave approx 12″ end for securing head later), ch 8 loosely, join with a sl st in beg ch to form a ring. *(NOTE: Before proceeding, check size of ring by slipping up over neck of doll head. If too tight, start again and work chains looser. Remove head before continuing.)*

Rnd 1: Ch 1, sc in same ch as joining and in each rem ch around, join with a sl st in beg sc = 8 sc.

Rnd 2: Ch 1, sc in same st as joining and in each rem sc around, join with a sl st in beg sc.

Rnd 3: Ch 1, 2 sc in same st as joining and in each rem sc around, join with a sl st in beg sc = 16 sc.

Rnd 4: Ch 1, sc in same st as joining, 2 sc in next sc; * sc in next sc, 2 sc in next sc; rep from * around, join with a sl st in beg sc = 24 sc.

Rnds 5 through 14: Rep Rnd 2, 10 times. At end of Rnd 14, join with a sl st **in back lp** *(lp away from you)* of beg sc (instead of both lps). Finish off white; join red (for panties)—leave ends on inside of doll. With red only, continue as follows.

Rnd 15: Ch 1, sc in same lp as joining (**back lp** of beg sc); sc **in back lp** of each rem sc around, join

with a sl st **in both lps** of beg sc = 24 sc. *(Front lps will be used later to work skirt.)* Continue by working **in both lps** of sts.

Rnd 16: Ch 1, sc in same st as joining and in each rem sc around, join with a sl st in beg sc.

Rnds 17 through 19: Rep Rnd 16, 3 times. At end of Rnd 19, **do not finish off**.

Insert head into neck opening, having back of head at side of doll where rnds were joined. Thread beg end into tapestry or yarn needle and weave through sts around neck edge twice. Draw up tightly to secure head; fasten end securely. Stuff and shape body. Do not overstuff. Excess stuffing can change the shape of the entire doll. Continuing with same yarn, work bottom closure of body as follows.

Rnd 20: Ch 1, sc in same st as joining; sk next sc, sc in next sc; * sc in next sc, sk next sc, sc in next sc; rep from * around, join with a sl st in beg sc = 16 sc.

Rnd 21: Ch 1, sc in same st as joining, sk next sc, * sc in next sc, sk next sc, rep from * around, join with a sl st in beg sc = 8 sc. Before working next rnd, finish stuffing body.

Rnd 22: Rep Rnd 21 = 4 sc.

Finish off, leaving approx 6″ sewing length. Thread into tapestry or yarn needle and weave through sts of last rnd. Draw up tightly and fasten securely.

SKIRT: Hold doll with back facing you (side where rnds were joined) and bottom closure of body just worked at top.

Rnd 1: Working **in unused lp** of each st in first rnd of skirt at waist, make a slip knot on hook with red, then join with a sc in lp at center back, sc in each rem lp around; join with a sl st **in both lps** of beg sc. Finish off; weave in ends.

Rnd 2: Working **in back lp** of each st around, ch 3, dc in same st as joining, 2 dc in each rem sc around; join with a sl st in top of beg ch-3 = 48 dc (counting beg ch-3). *(Front lps will be used later for waist edging of skirt.)* Continue by working **in both lps** of sts.

Rnd 3: Ch 3, dc in next dc and in each rem dc around, join with a sl st in top of beg ch-3.

Rnd 4: Ch 1, sc in same st as joining; * ch 1, sc in next sc; rep from * around, ch 1, join with a sl st in beg sc.

Finish off; weave in ends. Then work edging around waist of skirt as follows.

WAIST EDGING: Hold doll with back facing you and head at top.

Rnd 1: Working **in unused lp** of each st in first rnd of skirt at waist, make a slip knot on hook with red, then join with a sc in lp at center back, sc in each rem lp around; join with a sl st **in both lps** of beg sc. Finish off; weave in ends.

LEGS *(make 2):* Beg at top, with red (leave approx 12″ end for attaching leg later), ch 12, join with a sl st in beg ch to form a ring.

Rnd 1: Ch 1, sc in same ch as joining and in each rem ch around, join with a sl st **in front lp** (*lp toward you*) of beg sc = 12 sc.

Rnd 2 (pantie ruffle): Ch 1, sc in same lp as joining (front lp of beg sc), * ch 2, sc **in front lp** of next sc; rep from * around, join with a sl st **in both lps** of beg sc. (*Back lps will be used to work next rnd.*) Finish off red; weave in end. Continue with leg as follows.

Rnd 3: Hold leg with ruffle (*last rnd*) just worked at top. Working **in unused (back) lp** of each st behind ruffle, make a slip knot on hook with pink, then join with a sc in any lp around; sc in each rem lp around, join with a sl st **in both lps** of beg sc = 12 sc. Continue by working **in both lps** of sts.

Rnd 4: Ch 1, sc in same st as joining and in each rem sc around, join with a sl st in beg sc.

Rnds 5 through 9: Rep Rnd 4, 5 times.

Rnd 10: Ch 1, sc in same st as joining; * sc in each of next 4 sc, sk one sc; rep from * once more; sc in last sc, changing to red (for striping). (**To change color: Continuing with pink, work last sc until 2 lps rem on hook; finish off pink, join red. With red, YO and draw through both lps on hook = color changed.**) Continuing with red, join with a sl st in beg sc = 10 sc.

Rnd 11: With red, ch 1, sc in same st as joining and in each rem sc around, changing to white in last sc (*do not finish off red—will be used again for striping*). Continuing with white, join with a sl st in beg sc.

Rnd 12: With white, ch 1, sc in same st as joining and in each rem sc around, changing to red in last sc (*do not finish off white*). Continuing with red, join with a sl st in beg sc.

Rnds 13 through 18: Rep Rnds 11 and 12, 3 times.

Rnd 19: With red, ch 1, sc in same st as joining; sc in each of next 2 sc, 2 sc in each of next 4 sc (for front of foot), sc in each of next 2 sc; sc in last sc, changing to white (for shoe). Continuing with white only (finish off red), join with a sl st in beg sc = 14 sc. Continue as follows.

Rnd 20: Ch 1, sc in same st as joining; sc in each of next 4 sc, 2 sc in each of next 4 sc (for front of shoe), sc in each of rem 5 sc; join with a sl st in beg sc = 18 sc.

Rnds 21 through 23: Rep Rnd 4, 3 times. At end of Rnd 23, lightly stuff lower part of leg. Then work as follows.

Rnd 24: Ch 1, sc in same st as joining; sk next sc, * sc in next sc, sk next sc; rep from * around, join with a sl st in beg sc = 9 sc.

Rnd 25: Ch 1, sc in same st as joining; * sk next sc, sc in next sc; rep from * around, join with a sl st in beg sc = 5 sc. Finish off and close opening in same manner as bottom of body.

Lightly stuff upper part of leg. Thread beg sewing length into tapestry or yarn needle and sew open beg round edge to bottom of doll, having front of shoe facing forward.

ARMS *(make 2):* Beg at top, with white (leave approx 12″ sewing length for attaching arm later), ch 8, join with a sl st to form a ring.

Rnd 1: Sc in each ch around = 8 sc. [*NOTE: Do not join; work continuous rnds, unless otherwise specified (mark first st of rnd as before).*]

Rnd 2: Sc in each sc around.

Rnds 3 through 13: Rep Rnd 2, 11 times. At end of Rnd 13, join with a sl st in beg sc. Finish off, leaving approx 10″ sewing length. Insert hand into opening and secure in place in same manner as head.

Lightly stuff and shape arm. Thread beg sewing length into tapestry or yarn needle and sew open round beg edge to side of doll, approx 3 rnds down from neck.

Finishing

POMPONS: With equal amounts of red and white, make two 2″ diameter pompons (*see instructions on page 11*). Tie one pompon to each hand.

SHOELACES *(make 2):* Thread 14″ strand of red into tapestry or yarn needle. Beg at center top of shoe and work 3 cross sts down center front of shoe (one st in each rnd), ending back at top of shoe (see **Fig 1**). Tie lace into a bow; knot and trim each end of lace.

LETTER ON SWEATER: With red, make a chain to measure approx 4″ long; finish off, leaving approx 10″ sewing length. Having wrong side of chain facing up, sew chain to front of sweater in the shape of a "P". Weave in ends.

HIM AND HER DOLLS

designed by Eleanor Denner

These appealing 37″ tall dolls seem to have personalities all their own, and can even share their owner's hand-me-downs, as most size Toddler 2 garments will fit them. The dolls, their shoes and hair are made in Aunt Lydia's Heavy Rug Yarn; their outfits are made in Worsted Size yarn. Features are cut from felt and attached with glue.

Materials

FOR GIRL DOLL:
Aunt Lydia's Heavy Rug Yarn in 70-yd skeins:
    15 pink (*for body*)
    4 brown (*for hair*)
    1 black (*for shoes*)

American Thread Dawn Sayelle Knitting Worsted Size Yarn:
    8 oz lemon (*For dress*)
    8 oz white (*for pinafore and panties*)
Two ⅜″-diameter round ball type black buttons (*for shoes*)
One ¾″-diameter white button (*for pinafore*)
Three ⅜″-diameter white or yellow buttons (*for dress*)
One pair lace trimmed real child's stretch socks in size 3½ to 6½
Small pieces light brown (*for eyes*) and pink felt (*for mouth*)
White craft glue

Six 1-lb bags polyester fiber (*for stuffing*)
Size G aluminum crochet hook (or size required for gauge) (*for body*)
Size H aluminum crochet hook (or size required for gauge) (*for clothes and hair*)
Size J aluminum crochet hook (or size required for gauge) (*for clothes and hair*)

FOR BOY DOLL:
Aunt Lydia's Heavy Rug Yarn in 70-yd skeins:
    15 pink (*for body*)
    3 antique gold (*for hair*)
    1 red (*for sneakers*)
    1 white (*for sneakers*)
American Thread Dawn Sayelle Knitting Worsted Size Yarn:
    4 oz white (*for shirt*)
    4 oz royal blue (*for shirt*)
    8 oz bluebell (*for overalls*)
Two ¾"-diameter white buttons (*for shirt*)
Two sets overall-style metal buckles (1¾" wide) and buttons (*for overalls*)
One pair real child's stretch socks in size 3½ to 6½
Small pieces of blue felt (*for eyes*), pink felt (*for mouth*)
White craft glue
Six 1-lb bags polyester fiber (*for stuffing*)
Size G aluminum crochet hook (or size required for gauge) (*for body*)
Size H aluminum crochet hook (or size required for gauge) (*for clothes and hair*)

Gauge
(for body) With Size G hook and Aunt Lydia's Heavy Rug Yarn in hdc, 4 sts = 1", in sc, 4 sts = 1"
(for girl's hair) With Size H hook and Aunt Lydia's Heavy Rug Yarn, 3 dc = 1"
(for girl's dress and panties) With Size H hook and Worsted Weight Yarn, 3 dc = 1", 2 rows dc = 1"
(for girl's pinafore) With Size J hook and Worsted Weight Yarn, 3 sps (each sp is 1 dc + 1 ch) = 2"
(for shoes) With Size H hook and Aunt Lydia's Heavy Rug Yarn in hdc, 4 sts = 1", in sc, 4 sts = 1"
(for boy's shirt and overalls) With Size H hook and Worsted Weight Size Yarn, 7 dc = 2"

GIRL DOLL

Doll Body
First you will make two separate legs; these are then joined and the body is worked in one piece with them to the neck; head and arms are worked separately, then sewn on.

Instructions
FOOT AND LEG: With pink Aunt Lydia's Heavy Rug Yarn and size G hook, starting at toe, ch 4.

Row 1: Sc in 2nd ch from hook and each ch across: you should have 3 sc; ch 1, turn.

Row 2: Sc in each sc, ch 1, turn.

Row 3: 2 sc in first sc; sc in next sc; 2 sc in last sc; you should have 5 sc; ch 1, turn.

Row 4: Rep Row 2.

Row 5: 2 sc in first sc; sc in each of next 3 sc; 2 sc in last sc = 7 sc; ch 1, turn.

Rows 6 through 21: Sc in each sc, ch 1, turn.

Row 22: Sk first sc; sc in each of next 4 sc; sk next sc; sc in last sc; you should have 5 sc; do not ch; turn. (*NOTE: This last row is heel end of sole.*)

Row 23: Sl st in first sc, ch 1; sc in each of next 4 sc; continue working in sc along side of sole, working one sc in each row (22 sc along side); sc in each of 3 sc across toe; sc in each of 22 rows along side: you should have 51 sc (see **Fig 1**). Join with a sl st to starting ch-1. Finish off yarn.

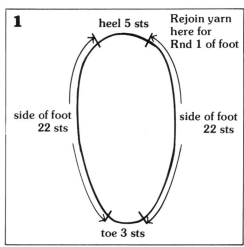

FOOT: (*NOTE: From now on, you will work in rnds, not rows, without joining. Mark beg of each rnd, and carry marker up entire foot and leg, moving it as you complete each rnd; a safety pin can be used for a marker.*)

Rnd 1: Rejoin yarn with a sl st at point indicated in **Fig 1**. Sc in each st.

Rnd 2 (mark for foot shaping): Sc across 14 sc (mark last st for end of side of foot); * dec. [**To make dec: (Pull up a lp in next sc) twice; YO and pull through all 3 lps on hook = dec made.**] Rep from * 13 times: mark last st for end of toe section; sc in each of next 9 sc: you should have 37 sc.

Rnd 3: Sc in each sc around.

Rnd 4: Sc across 14 sts; dec as before across toe sts up to marker for end of toe section; sc in each of next 9 sc = 30 sc.

Rnds 5 and 6: Rep Rnds 3 and 4 = 26 sc.

Rnds 7 and 8: Rep Rnds 3 and 4 = 24 sc.

BEGIN LEG: Continuing to mark beg of rnds, work in hdc for 2″. At this point, stop and stuff foot firmly. You will not stuff again until body is completed.

Increase Rnd: Hdc around, increasing 3 sts evenly spaced = 27 hdc.

Work even in hdc for 3″ more (5″ from start of leg). Rep Inc Rnd: 30 sts; work even in hdc for 4″ more (9″ from start of leg). Rep Inc Rnd: 33 sts. Work even in hdc on 33 sts until leg measures 14″ from floor when standing on foot. On last rnd, work to within 2 sts of end, sc in next st, sl st in last st. Finish off yarn.

Make another Foot and Leg exactly the same.

JOINING FOR BODY: Hold each leg with heel side facing you and fold in half to find center st at each inner side, and mark this st (see *Fig 2*).

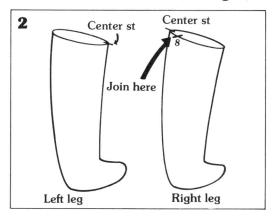

Rnd 1: On Right Leg, count back 8 sts from marked center st and join yarn with a sl st in this st; ch 2 (counts as first hdc of rnd; mark as first st), hdc in each of next 7 sts, ch 4 for crotch; pick up left leg, hdc in marked center st and in each st around left leg to ch-4; hdc in each ch; hdc around right leg to first st = 70 hdc (counting starting ch-2 as a st).

Rnd 2: Continue to work in rnds, not joining, but marking beg of each rnd; hdc to ch-4 of crotch, hdc in side of each ch not worked in before (*Fig 3*), hdc in each st around = 74 hdc. Work even in hdc until body measures 7″, then on next rnd, dec 3 sts evenly spaced.

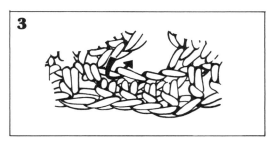

Work even on 71 hdc until body measures 13″ Finish off yarn.

At this point, stop and stuff each leg firmly; use a long stick, dowel, knitting needle or long wooden spoon to push stuffing well down in each leg. As you work, roll leg back and forth between hands to settle stuffing (otherwise, legs will be a bit knobbly). Stuff legs as full as you can, keeping nice shape. When legs are fully stuffed, stuff body, also firmly, up to about 2″ from where you are working.

SHOULDERS: Hold body with back toward you and mark center 15 sts for back, 20 sts for left shoulder, 16 sts for front, and 20 sts for right shoulder (see *Fig 4*). Join yarn with a sl st in first st of back, as indicated in *Fig 4*.

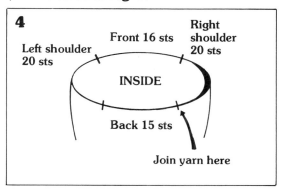

Rnd 1: Ch 2 (counts as first hdc of rnd), hdc in each of next 14 sts; * dec. **(To work dec: In next st, work an hdc until 3 lps are on hook; insert hook in next st and pull lp through: 4 lps on hook; hook yarn and draw through all 4 lps = dec made)** 10 times *; (left shoulder decs worked); hdc across next 16 sts for front; for right shoulder decs, rep from * to * once: you should have 51 sts.

Rnd 2: Work even in hdc.

Rnd 3: Hdc in first 15 sts for back; for left shoulder, dec as before 5 times; hdc in next 16 sts for front; for right shoulder, dec as before 5 times = 41 sts. At this point, stop and stuff body up to point where you are working. Stuff firmly.

Rnd 4: Hdc in first 15 sts for back; for left shoulder dec once; hdc in next st, dec once; hdc in next 16 sts for front, for right shoulder dec once; hdc in next st, dec once = 37 sts.

Rnd 5: Hdc in first 14 sts; dec 3 times; hdc in next 11 sts; dec 3 times = 31 sts. Stuff firmly.

Rnds 6 and 7: Work even in hdc; stuff firmly, finish off yarn.

HEAD: Entire head is worked in sc, in rnds. (*NOTE: Do not join rnds, but mark beg of each rnd and move marker up as you work.*) Work is begun at top of head.

Rnd 1: Ch 2, 6 sc in 2nd ch from hook.

Rnd 2: 2 sc in each sc: you should have 12 sc.

Rnd 3: * Sc in first sc, 2 sc in next sc; rep from * around = 18 sc.

Rnd 4: * Sc in each of next 2 sc, 2 sc in next sc; rep from * around = 24 sc.

Rnd 5: * Sc in each of next 3 sc, 2 sc in next sc; rep from * around = 30 sc.

Rnd 6: * Sc in each of next 4 sc, 2 sc in next sc; rep from * around = 36 sc.

Rnd 7: Sc in each sc around.

Rnd 8: * Sc in each of next 5 sc, 2 sc in next sc; rep from * around = 42 sc.

Rnd 9: Sc in each sc around.

Rnd 10: * Sc in each of next 6 sc, 2 sc in next sc; rep from * around = 48 sc.

Rnd 11: Sc in each sc around.

Rnd 12: * Sc in each of next 7 sc, 2 sc in next sc; rep from * around = 54 sc.

Rnd 13: Sc in each sc around.

Rnd 14: * Sc in each of next 8 sc, 2 sc in next sc; rep from * around = 60 sc. Work even on 60 sc until head measures 4″ from beg.

Shaping Rnds: Rnd 1: 2 sc in each of first 4 sc; sc in each of next 8 sc; 2 sc in each of next 4 sc (this forms cheeks and face front); sc in each sc around = 68 sc.

Rnds 2 through 7: Work even in sc.

Rnd 8: Work 3 sc, dec 4 times. **(To make dec: Draw up a lp in next sc, draw up a lp in next sc, YO and draw through all 3 lps = dec made)**; sc in each of next 6 sts; dec as before 4 times; sc in each sc around = 60 sc. Work even for 3 rnds.

Decrease Rnds: Rnd 1: * Sc in each of next 8 sc, dec as before, once; rep from * around = 54 sc.

Rnd 2: * Sc in each of next 7 sts, dec once; rep from * around = 48 sc.

Rnd 3: * Sc in each of next 6 sts, dec once; rep from * around = 42 sc.

Rnd 4: * Sc in each of next 5 sts, dec once; rep from * around = 36 sc.

At this point, begin stuffing head. Stuff firmly to about an inch from where you are working. Be sure to stuff cheeks to round them out.

Rnd 5: * Sc in each of next 4 sts, dec once; rep from * around = 30 sc.

Rnd 6: * Sc in each of next 3 sts, dec once; rep from * around = 24 sc.

Rnd 7: * Sc in each of next 2 sc, dec once; rep from * around = 18 sc. Continue stuffing as you work.

Rnd 8: * Sc in next sc, dec once; rep from * around = 12 sc

Rnd 9: Dec around = 6 sc. Stuff.

Rnd 10: Sc in each sc. Finish off, leaving an 18″ yarn end for sewing. Complete stuffing. Pull yarn end up tightly and tack to close head.

Place head on body, with cheek area facing front and thread 18″ yarn end into tapestry needle. Firmly sew head to body.

ARMS (make 2): Starting at base of hand, ch 4, join with a sl st to form a ring.

Rnd 1: Ch 1, 8 hdc in ring. (NOTE: Do not join, but mark beg of rnds as before.)

Rnd 2: Work 2 hdc in each st around = 16 hdc.

Rnd 3: Rep Rnd 2 = 32 hdc. Work even for 2½″ from Rnd 3. This completes hand.

Dec Rnd: Dec 3 sts evenly spaced around = 29 hdc. Mark this rnd for ease in measuring later. Work even in hdc for 9″ from marked rnd, ch 1, **turn.**

Shoulder Shaping: Row 1: (NOTE: From this point on, arm is worked in rows, not rnds.) Hdc in each of next 21 sts, turn.

Row 2: Sl st across 3 sts, ch 1; hdc in next 14 sts, turn.

Row 3: Sl st across 3 sts, ch 1, hdc in next 7 sts, sl st in next st; fasten off, leaving an 18″ yarn end for sewing.

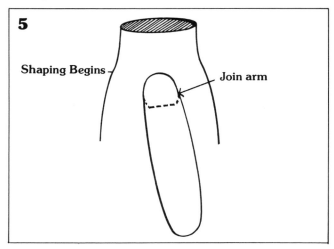

Stuff each arm firmly up to about 8″ from beg of hand; then stuff loosely for 2″ more, leave remainder unstuffed. Pin arm to shoulder (**Fig 5**) and adjust stuffing so arm lies fairly flat at joining point (otherwise, arm will stick straight out). Add more stuffing at top, if needed. Thread 18″ yarn end into tapestry needle and sew each arm in place.

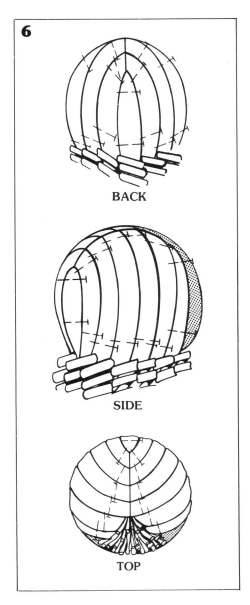

6

BACK

SIDE

TOP

HAIR: Hair is made with brown Aunt Lydia's Heavy Rug Yarn and size H hook.

Short Curls *(make 4):* Leaving a 2″ yarn end, make a sl knot on hook and ch 43; 2 dc in 4th ch from hook; 3 dc in each of next 25 chs; sc in next ch; dc in each of rem 14 chs; finish off yarn, leaving a 2″ yarn end.

Long Curls *(make 9):* Leaving a 2″ yarn end, make a sl knot on hook and ch 58; 2 dc in 4th ch from hook; 3 dc in each of next 25 chs; sc in next ch; dc in each of rem 29 chs; finish off yarn, leaving a 2″ yarn end.

Attaching Hair to Head: Following *Fig 6* use straight pins to pin curls to head, placing two Short Curls at each side at the front and Long Curls spaced around head. Readjust and pin until all curls are placed as you want them. Then thread brown yarn into tapestry needle and firmly stitch each curl strip in place, leaving the 2″ yarn ends on the Short Curls and on the first Long Curl strip on each side of face for bangs. On remaining curl strips, weave these yarn ends in and cut off. When all strips are secured, arrange bangs, "comb" down over forehead and trim to desired length.

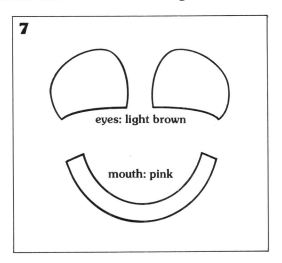

7

eyes: light brown

mouth: pink

EYES AND MOUTH: Trace outlines **in *Fig 7*** on paper. Cut outlines and use as pattern on felt. (*NOTE: To prevent pattern pieces from slipping on felt, tape pieces in place with cellophane tape. Cut out felt pieces through tape, then discard tape.*) With glue, attach felt pieces as shown in photo.

Dress

Instructions

SKIRT: Starting at bottom, with lemon in worsted-size yarn and size H hook, ch 159.

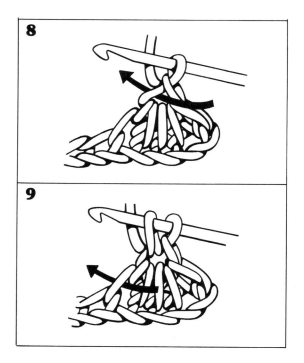

Rnd 1: Insert hook in 2nd ch from hook and draw up a lp; draw up a lp in each of next 3 chs; YO and draw through all 5 lps on hook; ch 1 for eye. (star st made) * insert hook in eye just made (**Fig 8**) and draw up a lp; insert hook into ch last worked (**Fig 9**) and draw up a lp; draw up a lp in each of next 2 chs, YO and draw through all 5 lps on hook; ch 1 for eye (another star st made); rep from * across = 78 star sts; join with a sl st to eye of first star st of row; ch 2, turn.

Rnd 2: Hdc in eye of each star st around = 78 hdc; join with a sl st to top of ch-2; ch 1, turn.

Rnd 3: Sc in first st (same place as joining), dc in next st; * sc in next st, dc in next st; rep from * around = 78 sts; join with a sl st to ch-1; ch 2, turn.

Rnd 4: * Sc in next dc, dc in next sc; rep from * around, join with a sl st to top of ch-2; ch 1, turn. Rep Rnds 3 and 4 until work measures 12″ from start, ending by working Row 3. At end of last row, ch 3, turn.

DRESS TOP BACK: From this point on, garment is worked in rows, not rnds.

Right Back: Row 1: Dc in each of next 13 sts (a total of 14 dc, counting turning ch-3 as a st); ch 3 turn.

Rows 2 through 9: Rep Row 1. At end of last row, do not ch. Finish off yarn.

Left Back: Hold garment with Right Back to your right. Join yarn with a sl st in first st to left of last st on first row of Right Back.

Row 1: Ch 3 (counts as first dc), dc in each of next 13 sts, ch 3, turn.

Rows 2 through 9: Rep Row 1. At end of last row, do not ch. Finish off yarn.

DRESS TOP FRONT: Hold work with Left Back to your right.

Row 1: Count in 10 sts from last st of Left Back (these are left unworked for underarm), join yarn with a sl st in 11th st, ch 3 (counts as first dc of row); dc in each of next 29 sts, ch 3, turn.

Rows 2 through 7: Dc in each st, ch 3, turn.

Row 8: Dc in 6 sts, ch 3, turn (this gives 7 sts for shoulder, counting turning ch as a st).

Row 9: Dc in each st across. Finish off yarn.

For other shoulder, hold work with first shoulder to your right, sk center 16 sts on Row 7 of front, join yarn with a sl st in 17th st, ch 3, dc in each st across (7 dc, counting ch-3 as a st); ch 3, turn. Dc in each st across. Finish off. Sew shoulder seams.

SLEEVES: Join yarn with a sl st at right-hand side of either underarm;

Rnd 1: Ch 3, dc in each of rem 9 sts left unworked for underarm, work 26 dc evenly spaced around armhole, working in sides of rows up back and down front; join with a sl st to top of starting ch, ch 3 (counts as first dc of next rnd), turn.

Rnds 2 through 6: Dc in each st around, join, ch 3, turn. At end of last rnd, do not ch. Finish off. Work second sleeve the same.

NECK EDGING: Hold garment with back facing you and join yarn with a sl st in base of first dc row at bottom of Left Back. Work (sc, ch 1) in each dc row up Left Back opening, in each st across neckline and in each row down Right Back opening; join with a sl st to first st. Finish off. Lightly steam dress. Sew a button in top dc row of Right Back, (sk a row, sew button in next row) twice. Use dc rows on opposite side as buttonholes.

Panties

Instructions

With white worsted-size yarn and size H hook, ch 76 and join with a sl st, being careful not to twist chain.

Rnd 1: Ch 4, sk joining st and next ch, * dc in next ch, ch 1, sk next ch; rep from * around, join with a sl st to 3rd ch of starting ch; ch 3, turn.

Rnd 2: Dc in each dc and each ch-1 sp around = 76 dc, counting turning ch-3 as a st; join with a sl st to top of ch-3; ch 3, turn.

Rnd 3: Dc in each dc around, join, ch 3, turn. Rep

Rnd 3 until piece measures 8″ from beg; ch 3, turn, as usual.

First Leg: Dc in each of next 37 dc, join with a sl st to top of ch-3.

Edging: Turn, (sc, ch 1) in each dc around. Finish off.

Second Leg: Hold garment with first leg to your right; join yarn with a sl st in first unworked dc to left of first leg, ch 3, dc in each dc around, join to top of ch-3.

Edging: Turn, (sc ch 1) in each dc around. Finish off yarn, leaving enough to sew any slight opening left at crotch. Weave in all yarn ends.

Pinafore

Intructions

Starting at neck of center back and working to hem of garment, with white worsted-size yarn and size J hook, ch 48.

Row 1: Dc in 6th ch from hook; ch 1, sk 1 ch; * dc in next ch, ch 1, sk next ch; rep from * across, ending dc in last ch: you should have 23 dc (counting starting ch as a st), and 22 sps. Ch 4, turn (ch-4 counts as first dc and ch-1 of next row).

Row 2: Dc in next dc; * ch 1, dc in next dc; rep from * across, working last dc in 3rd st of turning ch; ch 4, turn.

Rows 3 through 5: Rep Row 2.

Row 6: Dc in next dc; * ch 1, dc in next dc; rep from * 10 times = 12 sps; ch 4, turn.

Rows 7 through 10: Rep Row 2, working on the 12 sps only for underarm. At end of Row 10, ch 23, turn.

Row 11: Dc in 6th ch from hook, work as for Row 1 across ch, work as for Row 2 across remainder of row = 22 sps; ch 4, turn.

Rows 12 and 13: Rep Row 2, working on 22 sps.

Rows 14 through 20: Rep Row 2, working on 17 sps, end last row by working ch 13, turn.

Row 21: Rep Row 11.

Rows 22 and 23: Rep Row 2.

Rows 24 through 28: Rep Row 2 on 12 sps; at end of last row, ch 23, turn.

Row 29: Rep Row 11.

Rows 30 through 33: Rep Row 2. Finish off. Sew shoulder seams.

EDGING: Hold garment with upper corner of back neck edge at your right. Join yarn with a sc in corner, sc around neckline, placing sts to keep work flat, to opposite corner; work down back opening, working sc in first ch-sp; * sc in next dc, shell of 5 dc in next dc; rep from * down opening, working shell in corner; across bottom, * sc in base of dc row, shell of 5 dc in top of dc row; rep from * across bottom; work up opposite back opening as for previous side, join with a sl st to first sc. Finish off.

ARMHOLE TRIM: Join yarn with a sl st at right-hand corner of underarm; sc across underarm, work shell trim as for back opening around entire armhole; join with a sl st to first sc. Rep for opposite armhole. Finish off, weave in all loose yarn ends.

Mary Jane Shoes

Instructions

With black Aunt Lydia's Heavy Rug Yarn and size H hook, work exactly the same as for doll's foot through Rnd 5. Finish off yarn. Make second shoe exactly the same.

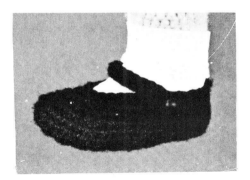

STRAPS: For Right Shoe, hold shoe with toe portion at your left; join yarn with a sl st in 11th st to left of center back of heel; ch 16, sc in 5th ch from hook and in each ch across, join with a sl st to 10th st to left of center heel back. Finish off. For Left Shoe, hold shoe with toe portion at your right; join yarn in 11th st from heel and work strap in same manner as before. Sew buttons opposite side where strap is joined.

BOY DOLL

Doll Body

Instructions

Follow directions under Girl Doll to hair.

HAIR: Hair is made with antique gold Aunt Lydia's Heavy Rug Yarn and size H hook.

Curls (make about 160): Make a sl knot on hook, leaving about a 2½″ yarn end, which is used later for attaching curl to head; ch 4, 3 sc in 2nd ch from hook; 3 sc in each of rem 2 chs. Finish off yarn, leaving a 2½″ yarn end.

Attaching Curls: With G crochet hook, or size used for doll body, hook one 2½″ yarn end of a curl and pull through a st on head; knot securely, with other 2½″ yarn end, leaving end untrimmed at this point; ends are used as filler with the curls and are trimmed later. Begin by attaching curls across front hairline, then around neckline; then fill in closely all around head; make more curls if needed. When finished, trim extra ends as desired.

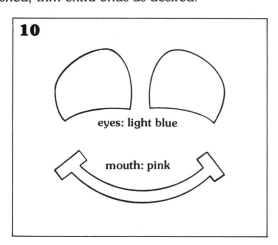

10

eyes: light blue

mouth: pink

EYES AND MOUTH: Using patterns in *Fig 10*, work in same manner as girl doll.

Shirt

Instructions

FRONT: With royal blue worsted-size yarn and size H hook, ch 40.

Row 1: Dc in 4th ch from hook and in each ch across = 38 dc (counting beg ch as a st); ch 3, turn (turning ch counts as first st of following row, throughout).

Row 2: Dc across to turning ch; in turning ch, work a dc, but work off last lp with white; drop royal, which will be picked up two rows later; with white, ch 3, turn.

Row 3: Dc in each dc across and in top of turning ch; ch 3, turn.

Row 4: Rep Row 2, substituting royal for white.

Continue in this manner, changing colors in same way, working 2 rows royal, 2 rows white, 2 rows royal, 2 rows white; you should have a total of 6 color stripes.

SLEEVES: At end of last row, change to royal, ch 15, remove hook from lp. Pulling yarn from outside of royal skein, join royal at opposite end of row, ch 13 and finish off. Insert hook in dropped lp at opposite end of row, turn.

SLEEVES AND FRONT: Row 1: Dc in 4th ch from hook and in each of rem 12 chs; dc across center 38 dc and in each of rem 13 chs: you should have 64 sts.

Continuing in patt, work one more row royal; then 2 rows white, 2 rows royal, 2 rows white; at end of last row, change to royal.

NECK AND SHOULDERS: Work 22 sts for shoulder (turning ch counts as a st). Finish off yarn. Sk center 20 sts for neck, rejoin yarn in next st, ch 3; dc in each st across. Finish off yarn.

BACK: Work same as front to Sleeves, where you will now divide work to provide back opening.

LEFT SLEEVE: With royal, at end of last row ch 15, turn; dc in 4th ch from hook and in each of rem 12 chs; dc across 19 dc on body of shirt = 32 sts; ch 3, turn.

Continue in color patt until you have 9 rows on sleeve portion (last row is royal). Finish off.

RIGHT SLEEVE: Attach royal at other underarm edge, ch 13. Finish off. Join royal at center back, ch 3, work in patt across body and 13 chs; complete to correspond to Left Sleeve. Finish off. Sew shoulder, side and underarm sleeve seams, matching sewing yarn to color of stripes.

EDGING: With royal, work one rnd of sc around each sleeve edge. Finish off.

NECKLINE: With royal, join yarn with a sl st in st at left top of back opening, 2 sc in same st; sc around neckline to opposite corner, 3 sc in corner; ch 3 (buttonhole lp), sc in base of next dc row; 2 sc in each of next 3 dc rows; ch 3 (buttonhole lp), sc in base of next dc row; continue to work 2 sc in each dc row down Right Back opening, then 2 sc in each dc row up Left Back opening. Join with a sl st to first sl st of rnd. Finish off. Weave in all yarn ends. Sew buttons opposite buttonhole lps. Lightly steam seams.

Overalls
Instructions

Sharting at waist, with bluebell in worsted-size yarn and size H hook, ch 80, join with a sl st, being careful not to twist.

Rnd 1: Ch 3 (counts as first dc of rnd here and throughout); dc in each ch around = 80 dc; join with a sl st to top of ch-3, **turn.** (*NOTE: Although you are working in rnds, each rnd is joined and turned. The ch-3 joining is used as center back.*)

Rnd 2: Dc in each dc around, join to top of ch-3; ch 3, turn. Rep Rnd 2 until piece measures 9″.

Divide for Legs: Dc in each of next 39 dc, join with a sl st to top of ch-3, turn; Rep Rnd 2 on 40 sts until leg measures 14″. Finish off. Join yarn with a sl st in first st unworked at point where first leg was ended; ch 3, dc in each st around, join with a sl st to top of ch-3, turn. Work as for first leg for 14″. Finish off. Sew any opening remaining between legs at crotch.

BIB: Hold garment with starting ch of waist at front and mark center front 20 sts for bib. Working on opposite side of ch from where first row of garment was worked, join yarn with a sl st in farthest right-hand bib st.

Row 1: Ch 3, dc in each of next 19 chs, ch 3, turn.

Rows 2 through 7: Dc in each st across, ch 3, turn. At end of last row, do not ch. Finish off.

STRAPS: Hold garment with back facing you. Leaving center 10 back sts unworked, join yarn in 6th st from center on either side.

Row 1: Ch 3, dc in each of next 4 sts, ch 3, turn.

Row 2: Dc across, ch 3, turn. Rep Row 2 until strap measures 14″. Finish off. Work second strap to correspond, joining yarn in 6th st from center on opposite side, as before.

Using overall buckle and button sets, sew a button

to each outer front corner of bib; attach buckle to each strap in front, adjust length to fit doll.

Sneakers
Instructions

With white Aunt Lydia's Heavy Rug Yarn and size H hook, work sole as for doll's foot patt through Row 23. On next row, work as for foot patt, but work **in back lp** (*lp away from you*) only on each st, thus forming a ridge. Finish off. Join red with a sl st in center st of toe.

Rnd 1: Dec 7 times. **(To make dec: Pull up a lp in next sc, pull up a lp in next sc, YO and pull through all 3 lps on hook = dec made.)** Sc in each of next 23 sts, dec as before 7 times, join with a sl st to center st of toe, ch 1, turn = 37 sc.

Rnd 2: Sc in each st, join, ch 1, turn.

Rnd 3: Dec as before 4 times; sc in each of next 20 sc, dec 4 times; join, ch 1, turn = 28 sc.

Rnd 4: Rep Rnd 2.

Rnd 5: Dec as before twice; sc in each of next 20 sts, dec twice, join, fasten off = 24 sc.

EDGING: Join white at center front toe with a sl st. (Sc, ch 1) in each row up front lacing edge of shoe; sc in each st around top edge of shoe, (ch 1, sc) in each row down other front lacing edge, fasten off. Ch-1 sps are used for eyelets for shoe laces.

TONGUE: With red, ch 6.

Row 1: Sc in 2nd ch from hook and in each ch across (5 sc), ch 1, turn.

Rows 2 through 10: Sc in each st across, ch 1, turn.

Row 11: Sk first st, sc in each of next 2 sts; sk next st, sc in last st. Finish off.

EDGING: Hold tongue with its first row to your right; join white with a sc in first row, sc in each row along side, 3 sc across last row of tongue, sc in each row along opposite side. Finish off. Sew tongue in shoe, with end without edging under toe portion. For lace, with white, ch 70. Fasten off. Weave in all yarn ends. Make second Sneaker exactly the same.

Just for Fun Bazaar

LITTLE STUFF

Here are some great quick and easy little projects you'll want to make for your next bazaar: a bookmark made of tiny granny squares; a lapel pin that looks like a hat and a pair of mittens; a pin cushion shaped like a turtle; a red heart that can be made into either a pin cushion or a sachet, and a hand puppet that's a flower growing out of a pot.

GRANNY BOOKMARK
designed by Judy Demain

Size
Approx 1¼" wide × 6¼" long before fringing

Materials
American Thread Puritan Crochet Bedspread and
    Tablecloth Cotton:
      18 yds red
      6 yds yellow
Size 3 steel crochet hook (or size required for gauge)

Gauge
One square = 1¼"

Instructions
SQUARE (make 5): With yellow, ch 4, join with a sl st to form a ring.
Rnd 1 (right side): Ch 3, 2 dc in ring; * ch 2, 3 dc

in ring; rep from * twice more, ch 2, join with a sl st in top of beg ch-3. Finish off yellow.

Rnd 2: With right side facing, join red with a sl st in any ch-2 sp; ch 3, work (2 dc, ch 3, 3 dc) in same sp as joining; * ch 1, work (3 dc, ch 3, 3 dc) in next ch-2 sp; rep from * twice more, ch 1, join with a sl st in top of beg ch-3. Finish off red, leaving approx 8" sewing length.

ASSEMBLING: Join 5 squares into one row. To join, hold two squares with right sides tog. Carefully matching sts of both squares across, beg in center corner st and sew with overcast st **in outer lps** only (**Fig 1**) across, ending in center st at next corner. When all squares have been joined, weave in all ends and lightly steam press joinings on wrong side.

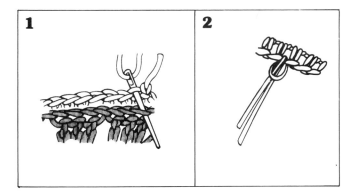

FRINGE: Fringe one short end of bookmark as follows: Cut 11 strands of red, having each strand 10″ long. Use one strand for each knot of fringe. Tie one knot (*Fig 2*) in each st across, beg and ending in center ch at each corner.

HAT AND MITTENS LAPEL PIN

designed by Joan Kokaska

Size

Hat measures approx 2¼″ long (with cuff and pompon); each mitten measures approx 1¾″ long.

Materials

American Thread Dawn Wintuk Sport Yarn:
    ½ oz tangerine
Size D aluminum crochet hook (or size required for gauge)
Small safety pin

Gauge

In sc, 11 sts = 2″

HAT
Instructions

Ch 15.

Row 1 (wrong side): Sc in 2nd ch from hook and in each rem ch across = 14 sc.

Row 2: Ch 1, turn; sc **in back lp** (*lp away from you*) in each sc across = 14 sc.

Rows 3 through 18: Rep Row 2, 16 times (9 ridges). At end of Row 18, do not finish off; join first and last rows tog as follows.

Finishing

Ch 1, turn; with wrong side now facing, hold first and last rows tog, carefully matching corresponding sts across. Sl st in each st across, working **in front lp** (*lp toward you*) in st of last row and in unused ch at base of first row.

Finish off, leaving approx 6″ end; thread into tapestry or yarn needle. Weave through rows around open end; draw up tightly and fasten securely for top of hat. Weave in ends. Turn hat right side out; fold up approx ½″ cuff.

Pompon

Make approx ½″ diameter pompon (see instructions on page 11) and attach securely to top of hat.

MITTENS (make 2)
Instructions

(*NOTE: Mitten is worked in one piece sideways.*)
Ch 23.

Row 1 (wrong side): Sl st in 2nd ch from hook and in each of next 3 chs (for cuff), sc in each of next 6 chs; sl st in each of next 2 chs, sc in each of next 6 chs; sl st in each of rem 4 chs (for cuff). [*NOTE: On each following row, work **in back lp** (lp away from you) of each st.*]

Row 2: Ch 1, turn; sl st in each of first 4 sl sts, sc in each of next 6 sc; sl st in each of next 2 sl sts, sc in each of next 6 sc; sl st in each of rem 4 sl sts.

Rows 3 and 4: Rep Row 2, twice. At end of Row 4, you should have 2 ridges. Continue with thumb shaping as follows.

Row 5: Ch 1, turn; sl st in each of first 4 sl sts, sc in each of next 3 sc; ch 2, sk 8 sts, sc in each of next 3 sc; sl st in each of rem 4 sl sts.

Row 6: Ch 1, turn; sl st in each of first 4 sl sts, sc in each of next 3 sc; sl st in each of next 2 chs, sc in each of next 3 sc; sl st in each of rem 4 sl sts.

Finish off, leaving approx 24″ end (for sewing length and for making chain to attach mitten to hat later).

Finishing

Fold mitten in half, having wrong sides tog and carefully matching corresponding side edges of mitten and thumb. Thread sewing length into tapestry or yarn needle; sew side edges tog (between seams, weave yarn across top of thumb and mitten).

Then continue with same yarn end and make a chain as follows: Insert hook in seam at cuff edge, hook yarn end and draw up a lp, ch 15.

Finish off and attach end of chain to inside of hat, having approx 1″ between edge of hat and mittens. Weave in all ends. Sew safety pin to side of hat at seam.

TURTLE PINCUSHION
designed by Eleanor Denner

Size
Approx 3″ tall × 4½″ long

Materials
American Thread Dawn Sayelle Knitting Worsted Size Yarn:
    1½ oz golf green
    10 yds white
    1 yd black
Size G aluminum crochet hook (or size required for gauge)
Polyester fiber (*for stuffing*)

Gauge
In sc, 4 sts = 1″

Instructions
SHELL: With golf green, ch 2.

Rnd 1: Work 6 sc in 2nd ch from hook. (*NOTE: Do not join; work continuous rnds. Use small safety pin or piece of yarn in contrasting color and mark first st of rnd; move marker at beg of each rnd.*)

Rnd 2: Work 2 sc in each sc around = 12 sc.

Rnd 3: * Sc in next sc, 2 sc in next sc; rep from * around = 18 sc.

Rnd 4: * Sc in each of next 2 sc, 2 sc in next sc; rep from * around = 24 sc.

Rnd 5: * Sc in each of next 3 sc, 2 sc in next sc; rep from * around = 30 sc.

Rnd 6: Sc in each sc around.

Rnds 7 through 11: Rep Rnd 6, 5 times. At end of Rnd 11, join with a sl st in beg sc. Finish off, leaving approx 18″ end for sewing bottom piece to shell later. Stuff inside of shell firmly; set aside. Now work bottom of shell as follows.

BOTTOM: With white, ch 2. Work Rnds 1 through 5 of Shell. At end of Rnd 5, join with a sl st in beg sc. Finish off; weave in ends. Thread sewing length (left at end of shell) into tapestry or yarn needle. Carefully matching sts of bottom piece and shell, sew with overcast st **in back lps only (*Fig 3*)** of corresponding sts around.

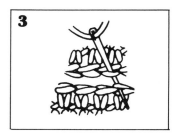

HEAD: With golf green, ch 2.

Rnds 1 through 3: Rep Rnds 1 through 3 of Shell.

Rnd 4: Sc in each sc around.

Rnd 5: Rep Rnd 4.

Rnd 6: * Dec (decrease) over next 2 sc. [**To make dec: Draw up a lp in each of next 2 sc (3 lps now on hook); YO and draw through all 3 lps on hook = dec made.**] Rep from * around = 9 sc.

Rnds 7 through 9: Rep Rnd 4, 3 times. At end of Rnd 9, finish off, leaving approx 12″ sewing length.

Stuff head, leaving last 3 rnds very lightly stuffed for neck. Thread sewing length into tapestry or yarn needle and sew neck edge closed. Continuing with same sewing length, sew neck edge to one end of shell, approx 2 rnds up from bottom edge. Tack each side of neck to shell (keeps head in upward position).

TAIL: With golf green, ch 5. Sc in 2nd ch from hook and in each of next 3 chs = 4 sc. Finish off, leaving approx 8″ sewing length. Thread into tapestry or yarn needle and sew this end of tail to bottom edge of shell at back.

FEET (*make 4*): With golf green, ch 2.

Rnd 1: Work 6 sc in 2nd ch from hook, join with a sl st in beg sc.

Rnd 2: Ch 1, do not turn; working **in back lp** (*lp away from you*) of each st, sc in same st as joining and in each rem sc around; join with a sl st in beg sc.

Finish off, leaving approx 8″ sewing length. Stuff foot. Thread end into tapestry or yarn needle and sew foot to bottom of turtle.

EYES: With single strand of black, embroider two French knots (**Fig 4**) to front of head as shown in photo.

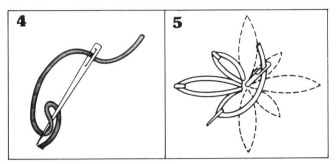

EMBROIDERED FLOWER: With single strand of white, work 8 lazy daisy sts on top of shell as shown in **Fig 5**.

HEART SACHET AND PINCUSHION
designed by Eleanor Denner

Sizes
Sachet: approx 4″ × 4″; pincushion: approx 6″ × 6″.

Materials for Sachet
American Thread Puritan Crochet Bedspread and Tablecloth Cotton:
    75 yds red
    125 yds white
Size 6 steel crochet hook (or size required for gauge)
Sachet powder (on cotton) or potpourri (encased in fine-mesh cloth) for filling

Materials for Pincushion
American Thread Dawn Wintuk Baby Yarn:
    ½ oz red
American Thread Dawn Wintuk Pompadour Baby Yarn:
    ½ oz white
Size D aluminum crochet hook (or size required for gauge)
Polyester fiber (*for stuffing*)

Gauge
In sc, for sachet, 9 sts = 1″; 9 rows = 1″;
In sc for pincushion, 5 sts = 1″; 6 rows = 1″

Instructions

[NOTE: *Instructions are the same for sachet and pincushion. Throughout patt, for sachet, use crochet cotton and size 6 steel hook (or size required for gauge); for pincushion, use baby yarn and size D aluminum hook (or size required for gauge).*]

HEART-SHAPED PIECES (*make 2*): Beg at bottom point, with red, ch 2.

Row 1: Sc in 2nd ch from hook.

Row 2: Ch 1, turn; 3 sc in sc.

Row 3: Ch 1, turn; 2 sc in first sc, sc in next sc, 2 sc in last sc = 5 sc.

Row 4: Ch 1, turn; 2 sc in first sc, sc in each sc to last sc, 2 sc in last sc = 7 sc.

Rows 5 through 12: Rep Row 4, 8 times. At end of Row 12, you should have 23 sc.

Row 13: Ch 1, turn; sc in each sc across.

Rows 14 through 18: Rep Row 13, 5 times. At end of Row 18, do not finish off; continue with top shaping as follows.

TOP SHAPING: First Half: Row 1: Ch 1, turn; sc in each of first 12 sc (leave rem sts unworked for 2nd Half).

Row 2: Ch 1, turn; sk first sc, sc in each rem sc across = 11 sc.

Rows 3 through 5: Rep Row 2, 3 times. At end of Row 5, you should have 8 sc.

Row 6: Ch 1, turn; sk first sc, sc in each of next 5 sc, dec over last 2 sc = 6 sc. **(To make dec: Draw up a lp in each of last 2 sc, YO and draw through all 3 lps on hook = dec made.)**

Row 7: Ch 1, turn; sk first st, dec over next 2 sc (as before), sc in next sc, dec over last 2 sc = 3 sc. Finish off; weave in ends.

TOP SHAPING: Second Half: Hold work with shaping just worked at top and to your right.

Row 1: With red, make a slip knot on hook; join with a sc in center st (where last sc of first row of other shaping was worked); sc in each of rem 11 sc across = 12 sc.

Rows 2 through 7: Rep Rows 2 through 7 of other shaping. At end of Row 7, finish off and weave in ends.

Assembling

Hold both heart-shaped pieces tog, carefully matching edges. With red, make a slip knot on hook; join with a sc in st at bottom point. Carefully matching corresponding rows and sts, work 2 sc in same st as joining, sc in each st and row around, leaving approx 2″ opening. Insert filling (polyester fiber, potpourri or sachet powder) and then sc opening closed; join with a sl st in beg sc. Finish off.

Ruffled Edging

Rnd 1: With last rnd just worked facing you, make a slip knot on hook with white and join with a sc in center sc of 3-sc group at bottom point. Ch 1, work (sc, ch 1) in each sc around to within one st at top center (between curved shapings); sk next 2 sc, then work (sc, ch 1) in each rem sc around; join with a sl st in beg sc.

Rnd 2: Do not turn; sl st into next ch-1 sp, ch 4, work (dc, ch 1) in same sp; work (dc, ch 1) twice in each ch-1 sp to within 4 ch-1 sps from top center (between curved shapings); work (dc, ch 1) in each of next 2 ch-1 sps, work hdc dec over 2 ch-1 sps. **[To make hdc dec: YO, insert hook in next ch-1 sp and draw up a lp; YO and draw through 2 lps on hook (2 lps now on hook), insert hook in next ch-1 sp and draw up a lp (3 lps now on hook); YO and draw through all 3 lps on hook = hdc dec made.]** Ch 1, work hdc dec over next 2 ch-1 sps; work (dc, ch 1) in each of next 2 ch-1 sps; work (dc, ch 1) twice in each rem ch-1 sp around; join with a sl st in 3rd ch of beg ch-4.

Rnd 3: Ch 1, do not turn; sc in same st as joining, ch 3, sc in 3rd ch from hook; * sk next ch-1 sp, sc in next st; ch 3, sc in 3rd ch from hook; rep from * around, join with a sl st in beg sc. Finish off; weave in ends.

SUNFLOWER HAND PUPPET

designed by Sue Penrod

Size

Approx 10″ long

Materials

American Thread Dawn Sayelle Knitting Worsted Size Yarn:
  ½ oz white
  1½ oz hot orange
  1½ oz nile green
  ¾ oz lemon
Size I aluminum crochet hook (or size required for gauge)
Polyester fiber (*for stuffing*)
Small felt pieces in white, black and orange
Tracing paper and pencil
White craft glue

Gauge

In sc, 3 sts = 1″

Instructions

BLOSSOM: With lemon, ch 4, join with a sl st to form a ring.

Rnd 1: Work 2 sc in each ch around = 8 sc. (*NOTE: Do not join; work continuous rnds, unless otherwise specified. Use a small safety pin or piece of yarn in contrasting color and mark first st of rnd; move marker at beg of each rnd.*)

Rnd 2: Work 2 sc **in back lp** (*lp away from you*) in each sc around = 16 sc.

Rnd 3: Rep Rnd 2 = 32 sc. Continue by working **in back lp** of sts, unless otherwise specified.

Rnd 4: Sc in each sc around.

Rnds 5 and 6: Rep Rnd 4, twice.

Rnd 7: * Sc in each of next 3 sc, sk next sc; rep from * around = 24 sc.

Rnd 8: * Sc in each of next 2 sc, sk next sc; rep from * around = 16 sc.

Rnd 9: * Sk next sc, sc **in both lps** of next sc; rep from * around to last 2 sc, sk next sc; sc **in both lps** of last sc, changing to nile green. [**To change color: Work last sc until 2 lps rem on hook, finish off lemon; with nile green, complete st (YO and draw through both lps on hook) = color changed.**] You should now have 8 sc. Stuff and shape head; then continue with nile green and work stem as follows.

STEM: (*NOTE: Work **in both lps** of sts, unless otherwise specified.*)

Rnd 1: Sc in each sc around = 8 sc.

Rnds 2 through 5: Rep Rnd 1, 4 times.

Rnd 6: * Sc in next sc, 2 sc in next sc; rep from * around = 12 sc.

Rnd 7: Rep Rnd 6 = 18 sc.

Rnd 8: * Sc in each of next 3 sc, 2 sc in next sc; rep from * around to last 2 sc, sc in each of last 2 sc = 22 sc.

Rnd 9: * Sc in each of next 5 sc; ch 5, sk next 5 sc (for opening to join base of leaf later), sc in each of next 6 sc; ch 5, sk next 5 sc (for opening to join base of other leaf later), sc in last sc.

Rnd 10: Working in each st and in each ch around, * sc in next st, 2 sc in next st; rep from * around, changing to hot orange in last sc = 33 sc. With hot orange, work flower pot as follows.

FLOWER POT: (*NOTE: Work **in both lps** of sts, unless otherwise specified.*)

Rnd 1: * Sc in next sc, 2 sc in next sc; rep from * to last sc, sc in last sc = 49 sc.

Rnd 2: * Work 2 sc in next sc, sc in each of next 2 sc; rep from * to last sc, 2 sc in last sc = 66 sc.

Rnd 3: Sc **in back lp** in each sc around. Continue by working **in both lps** of sts.

Rnd 4: * Sc in next sc, sk next sc; rep from * around = 33 sc.

Rnd 5: Sc in each sc around.

Rnds 6 through 16: Rep Rnd 5, 11 times. At end of Rnd 16, finish off and weave in ends.

LEAF (*make 2*)**:** With nile green, leave approx 8" end for sewing leaf to stem later, ch 12, join with a sl st to form a ring.

Rnd 1: Sc in each ch around = 12 sc. (*NOTE: Do not join; mark first st of rnd as before.*) Continue by working **in both lps** of sts.

Rnd 2: * Sc in next sc, 2 sc in next sc; rep from * around = 18 sc.

Rnd 3: Sc in each sc around.

Rnd 4: Rep Rnd 3.

Rnd 5: * Sc in each of next 2 sc, sk next sc; rep from * around = 12 sc.

Rnd 6: Rep Rnd 3.

Rnd 7: * Sc in each of next 3 sc, sk next sc; rep from * around = 9 sc.

Rnd 8: Rep Rnd 3.

Rnd 9: Rep Rnd 5 = 6 sc.

Rnd 10: * Sk next sc, sl st in next sc; rep from * around = 3 sl sts.

Finish off and weave in this end. Thread beg sewing length into tapestry or yarn needle and sew base edge of leaf to opening in stem, easing in leaf as necessary.

PETALS (*worked in one piece*)**:** With white, ch 24; join with a sl st in beg ch to form a ring, being careful not to twist ring.

Rnd 1: Ch 1, work (sc, hdc, dc, hdc, sc) in same ch as joining, sl st in next ch; * work (sc, hdc, dc, hdc, sc) in next ch, sl st in next ch; rep from * around. Finish off, leaving approx 12" sewing length. Thread into tapestry or yarn needle and sew ring of petals around head as shown in photo.

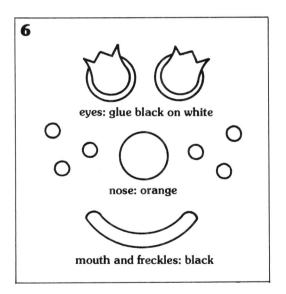

6

eyes: glue black on white

nose: orange

mouth and freckles: black

FACIAL FEATURES: Trace outlines in *Fig 6* on paper. Cut outlines and use as patterns on felt as indicated. (*NOTE: To prevent pattern pieces from slipping on felt, tape pieces in place with cellophane tape; cut out felt pieces through tape, then discard tape.*) With glue, attach felt pieces as shown in photo.

CACTUS GARDEN

designed by Kathie Schroeder

These cacti look so real that you'd expect to prick your fingers! Plant them in individual clay pots or group them for an unusual accent. Just be careful that no one waters them by mistake. All three of the cacti are easy to make with rug yarn and work up very quickly. They make perfect housewarming gifts.

Pattern Stitches

FRONT POST SC *(abbreviated FPsc):* Insert hook from **front to back to front** around post of sc in rnd below (**Fig 1**); hook yarn and draw lp through; complete st as a sc (YO and draw through 2 lps on hook).

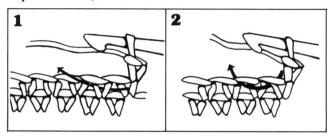

BACK POST SC *(abbreviated BPsc):* Same as FPsc, except insert hook from **back to front to back** around post of sc in rnd below (**Fig 2**).

SAGUARO CACTUS

Size

Approx 12″ tall

Materials

Rug yarn:
    70-yd skein emerald green
    2 yds bright yellow
Size I aluminum crochet hook (or size required for gauge)
Polyester fiber *(for stuffing)*
Flower pot *(size and shape of your choice)*
Sand or aquarium pebbles *(for potting)*
Cardboard piece *(to fit inside of pot, approx 1″ from top)*
White craft glue or toothpicks *(for securing base of cactus)*
Sewing thread in matching colors

Gauge

In sc, 3 sts = 1″

Instructions

BODY OF CACTUS: Beg at top, with green, ch 2.

Saguaro (center back)

Prickly Pear (left)   **Barrel (right)**

Rnd 1: Work 8 sc in 2nd ch from hook. (*NOTE: Do not join; work continuous rnds. Use a small safety pin or piece of yarn in contrasting color and mark first st of rnd; move marker at beg of each rnd.*)

Rnd 2: Work 2 sc in each sc around = 16 sc.

Rnd 3: * Work FPsc around post of next sc, work BPsc around post of next sc. Rep from * around. Rep Rnd 3 until piece measures approx 12″ long. (*NOTE: You will be working each FPsc around post of prev FPsc and each BPsc around post of prev BPsc.*) At end of last rnd, join with a sl st in beg sc. Finish off; weave in ends. Stuff cactus firmly.

SHORT ARM: Beg at top, with green, ch 2.

Rnd 1: Work 6 sc in 2nd ch from hook. (*NOTE: Do not join; work continuous rnds. Mark first st of rnd as before.*)

Rnd 2: Work 2 sc in each sc around = 12 sc.

Rnd 3: * Work FPsc around post of next sc, work BPsc around post of next sc. Rep from * around. Rep Rnd 3 until piece measures approx 3″ long. Then work bottom shaping as follows.

    Rnd 1: Sl st in each of next 6 sts. * Work FPsc around post of next st, work BPsc around post of next st. Rep from * twice more.

Rnd 2: Sl st **in both lps** in each of next 6 sl sts. * Work FPsc around post of next st, work BPsc around post of next st. Rep from * twice more.

Rnd 3: Rep prev Rnd 2.

Rnd 4: * Work FPsc around post (*under 2 top threads*) of next sl st, work BPsc around post of next sl st. Rep from * twice more. Work (FPsc around post of next st, BPsc around post of next st) 3 times; join with a sl st in beg st.

Finish off; weave in ends. Stuff arm firmly. With matching sewing thread, sew arm to side of cactus, approx 4" from top.

LONG ARM: Work same as short arm until piece measures approx 4" long (instead of 3" long) before bottom shaping. Then work shaping in same manner. Stuff arm firmly. With matching sewing thread, sew arm to opposite side of cactus from other arm, approx 5" from top.

BLOSSOM: With yellow, ch 5, join with a sl st in beg ch to form a ring. Ch 4, sl st in same ch as joining. Work (sl st, ch 4, sl st) in each of next 4 chs (*5 petals made*). Finish off; weave in ends. With matching sewing thread, sew to top of body of cactus.

POTTING: Cut cardboard piece to fit inside pot, approx 1" below top edge. Cut a hole slightly smaller than the size of the cactus base in cardboard piece at desired position. Pull base of cactus through hole. Glue in place or secure by inserting toothpicks beneath cardboard into base of cactus. Place cardboard piece with cactus into pot (*if pot is deep, weight bottom—under cardboard piece—with small rocks or sand*). Secure cardboard to pot with glue; let dry. Cover top of cardboard with sand or aquarium pebbles.

BARREL CACTUS

Size

Approx 4" tall

Materials

Rug yarn:
    70-yd skein light lime green
    5 yds tangerine
Size I aluminum crochet hook (or size required for gauge)
Polyester fiber (*for stuffing*)
Flower pot (*size and shape of your choice*)
Sand or aquarium pebbles (*for potting*)
Cardboard piece (*to fit inside pot, approx 1" from top*)
White craft glue or toothpicks (*for securing base of cactus*)

Sewing thread in matching tangerine color

Gauge

In sc, 3 sts = 1"

Instructions

(*NOTE: All rnds are worked on right side.*) Beg at top, with green, ch 2.

BODY: Rnd 1: Work 8 sc in 2nd ch from hook. Join with a sl st in beg sc.

Rnd 2: Ch 1, 2 sc in same st as joining; work 2 sc in each rem sc around. Join with a sl st in beg sc = 16 sc.

Rnd 3: Pull up lp on hook to approx ½"; work 2 CL (cluster) in same st as joining. [**To work CL: * YO (yarn over) hook, insert hook in st and pull up a lp; rep from * 3 times more (9 lps now on hook); YO and draw through all 9 lps on hook (*Fig 3*) = CL made.**] * Sc in next sc, work 2 CL in next st. Rep from * around to last sc, sc in last sc. Ch 1, join with a sl st in sp between first 2 CL at beg of rnd = 8 2-CL groups.

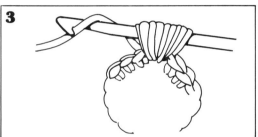

Rnd 4: Pull up lp on hook to approx ½"; work 2 CL in same sp as joining. * Work BPsc (back post sc) around post of next sc, work 2 CL in sp between CL of next 2-CL group. Rep from * around to last sc, work BPsc around post of last sc. Ch 1, join with a sl st in sp between first 2 CL at beg of rnd.

Rnds 5 through 10: Rep Rnd 4, 6 times.

Rnd 11 (dec rnd): Pull up lp on hook to approx ½"; work CL in same sp as joining. * Work BPsc around post of next sc, work CL in sp between CL of next 2-CL group. Rep from * around to last sc, work BPsc around post of last sc. Ch 1, join with a sl st in top of beg CL = 16 sts (8 CL + 8 BPsc).

Rnd 12: Ch 1, sc in same st as joining. * Sc in next sc, sc in top of next CL. Rep from * around to last sc, sc in last sc. Join with a sl st in beg sc = 16 sc.

Rnd 13: Ch 3, dc in next st and in each rem st around. Join with a sl st in top of beg ch-3.

Rnd 14: Rep Rnd 13. Finish off; weave in all ends. Stuff cactus firmly into a round shape.

BLOSSOM: With tangerine, ch 9; join with a sl st to form a ring. Work (ch 8, sl st in ring) 10 times. Finish off; weave in ends. With matching sewing thread, sew blossom to top of cactus.

POTTING: Same as saguaro cactus.

PRICKLY PEAR CACTUS

Size

Approx 13″ tall

Materials

Rug yarn:
     70-yd skein medium lime green
     2 yds bright yellow
     12 yds bright pink
Size G aluminum crochet hook (or size required for gauge)
Polyester fiber (for stuffing)
Flower pot (size and shape of your choice)
Sand or aquarium pebbles (for potting)
Cardboard piece (to fit inside of pot, approx 1″ from top)
White craft glue or toothpicks (for securing base of cactus)
Sewing thread in matching green and pink colors

Gauge

In sc, 4 sts = 1″

Instructions

BOTTOM BRANCH (make 2 pieces): Beg at base, with green, ch 4.

Row 1: Work (sc, dc) in 2nd ch from hook; sk next ch, work (sc, dc) in last ch.

Row 2: Ch 2, turn. Work (sc, dc) in 2nd ch from hook (increase made); sk first dc, work (sc dc) in next sc; sk next dc, work (sc dc) in last sc.

Row 3: Ch 2, turn. Work (sc, dc) in 2nd ch from hook (increase made); sk first dc, work (sc, dc) in next sc. * Sk next dc, work (sc, dc) in next sc. Rep from * across = 4 sc-dc groups.

Rows 4 through 7: Rep Row 3, 4 times. At end of Row 7, you should have 8 sc-dc groups.

Row 8: Ch 1, turn. Sk first dc, work (sc, dc) in next sc. * Sk next dc, work (sc, dc) in next sc. Rep from * across = 8 sc-dc groups.

Row 9: Rep Row 8.

Row 10: Ch 1, turn. Sk first dc. * Work (sc, dc) in next sc, sk next dc. Rep from * to last sc, sc in last sc = 7 sc-dc groups.

Row 11: Ch 1, turn. Sk first 2 sts (sc, dc). * Work (sc, dc) in next sc, sk next dc. Rep from * to last sc, sc in last sc = 6 sc-dc groups.

Rows 12 and 13: Rep Row 11, twice. At end of Row 13, you should have 4 sc-dc groups. Finish off; weave in ends.

MIDDLE BRANCH (make 2 pieces): Beg at base, with green, ch 4.

Rows 1 through 3: Rep Rows 1 through 3 of bottom branch.

Rows 4 and 5: Rep Row 3 of bottom branch, twice = 6 sc-dc groups.

Rows 6 through 9: Rep Rows 8 through 11 of bottom branch. At end of Row 9, you should have 4 sc-dc groups. Finish off; weave in ends.

TOP BRANCH (make 2 pieces): Beg at base, with green, ch 4.

Rows 1 through 3: Rep Rows 1 through 3 of bottom branch.

Row 4: Rep Row 8 of bottom branch = 4 sc-dc groups.

Row 5: Ch 1, turn. Sk first dc, sc in next sc. * Sk next dc, work (sc, dc) in next sc. Rep from * once more. Sk next dc, sc in last sc = 2 sc-dc groups.

Row 6: Ch 1, turn. Sc in first sc. * Sk next dc, work (sc, dc) in next sc. Rep from * once more. Sl st in last sc. Finish off; weave in ends.

ASSEMBLING: With matching sewing thread, sew 3 edges of corresponding pieces of bottom branch tog. Lightly stuff, retaining flatness; then sew rem side closed.

Sew and stuff corresponding pieces of middle branch in same manner. Then sew base of middle branch to top of bottom branch.

Sew and stuff corresponding pieces of top branch in same manner. Then sew base of top branch to top of middle branch toward one side.

BLOSSOMS (make 2): Beg at top, with yellow, ch 2.

Rnd 1: Work 6 sc in 2nd ch from hook, changing to pink in last sc. **(To change color: Work last sc until 2 lps rem on hook; finish off yellow; with pink, YO and draw through rem 2 lps on hook = color changed.)** (NOTE: Do not join; work continuous rnds. Mark first st of rnd.)

Rnd 2: Work 2 sc in each sc around = 12 sc.

Rnd 3: Rep Rnd 2 = 24 sc.

Rnd 4: * Sk one sc, sc in next sc. Rep from * around = 12 sc.

Rnd 5: Rep Rnd 4 = 6 sc. Before working next rnd, lightly stuff blossom.

Rnd 6: * Sk one sc, sl st in next sc. Rep from * around = 3 sl sts. Finish off; weave in ends. With matching sewing thread, sew one blossom to top of top branch and the other blossom to top of middle branch as shown in photo.

POTTING: Same as saguaro cactus.

MOUSE WEDDING PARTY

designed by Sue Penrod

You are cordially invited to attend the wedding of the season: Miss Mouse, a demure 8″-tall figure, dressed in her white lacy gown and veil, will be wed to Mr. Mouse, a charming gentlemouse complete with his formal morning coat. In attendance will be a bridesmouse, best mouse, a petite flower mouse and a darling ring bearer-mouse, proudly carrying two golden rings on a tiny pillow. The nuptials will be performed by the Reverend Mr. Mouse, complete with his wire glasses.

Size

Approx height: bride and bridesmaid—6″
                  groom and best man—7″
                  minister—7″
                  flower girl—5″
                  ring bearer—5½″

Materials

Worsted weight yarn:
    2 oz each of white, light gray and black

1 oz each of peach and yellow
6 yds pink

Size E aluminum crochet hook (or size required for gauge)

Styrofoam forms (*see Materials Note below*):
    2, 4" cones (*for bride and bridesmaid*)
    3" cone (*for flower girl*)
    2" egg (*for ring bearer*)
    2, 2½" eggs (*for groom and best man*)
    3" egg (*for minister*)

2 Jump rings (¼" diameter) for wedding rings

Artificial small flowers of your choice (*for bouquets and boutonnieres*)

5" Length of #20 wire (*for eyeglasses*)

Small felt pieces in light pink, medium gray, white and black

White craft glue

Small amount of polyester fiber (*for stuffing heads*)

Plastic head straight pins (*available in sewing stores*):
    14 white, 17 yellow and 18 black (*49 total—for buttons and trim*)

8 Metal washers (*available in hardware stores*), ¾" diameter with ¼" center hole diameter (*for feet*)

Common nails (*available in hardware stores*): six, 3" long and two, 2½" long (*8 total—for dowels inside of legs*)

Tracing paper and pencil

Size 16 tapestry needle or yarn needle

[*MATERIALS NOTE: If unable to find styrofoam cone sizes as specified, buy larger size and cut off excess at base (cuts easily with a sharp knife).*]

Gauge

In sc, worked in back lp of sts, 5 sts = 1";
9 rnds = 2"

General Instructions

Throughout each pattern, unless otherwise specified, work as follows.

1. **Work continuous rnds.** Do not join rnds; do not chain and turn. Use a small safety pin or piece of yarn in contrasting color and mark first st of rnd. Move marker at beg of each rnd.

2. Always work **in back lp** of each st (*lp away from you—**Fig 1***).

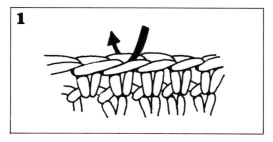

3. When instructions say to "**work even**", work sc in each st for specified number of rnds, without increasing or decreasing.

4. Be sure to achieve gauge as specified (5 sts = 1"; 9 rnds = 2"). If you do not have the correct number of sts and rnds per inch, your work will not fit over the styrofoam forms and will not look exactly as shown in photo.

BRIDE AND BRIDESMAID

Before proceeding, read General Instructions. Bride and bridesmaid are worked in same manner; color changes for bridesmaid are written in parentheses.

HEAD: Beg at top, with gray, ch 4; join with a sl st to form a ring.

Rnd 1: Work 2 sc in each ch around = 8 sc. (*NOTE: Mark first st of rnd; do not join rnds. Continue by working in back lp of sts.*)

Rnd 2: Work 2 sc in each sc around = 16 sc.

Rnds 3 and 4: Work 2 rnds even.

Rnd 5: Sc in next sc, * 2 sc in next sc, sc in each of next 2 sc; rep from * around = 21 sc.

Rnd 6: Work even.

Rnd 7: Sc in next sc, * 2 sc in next sc, sc in next sc; rep from * around = 31 sc.

Rnds 8 and 9: Work 2 rnds even.

Rnd 10: Sc in next sc, * sk one sc, sc in each of next 2 sc; rep from * around = 21 sc.

Rnd 11: * Sc in next sc, sk one sc; rep from * to last sc; sc in last sc, changing to white (peach) for dress. **(To change colors: Work sc until 2 lps rem on hook; finish off color being used. Tie in new**

color, YO and draw through 2 lps on hook = color changed.) You should now have 11 sc. Lightly stuff and shape head (*stuffing should not be visible through sts*). Continue with white (peach) and work bodice of dress as follows.

BODICE: Rnd 1: Work even = 11 sc. (*NOTE: Remember to work in back lp of sts.*)

Rnd 2: Sc in next sc, * 2 sc in next sc, sc in next sc; rep from * around = 16 sc.

Rnd 3 (marking rnd): (*NOTE: In this rnd, 2 sts are marked for sewing sleeves to dress later.*) Work 2 sc in next sc, sc in next sc, 2 sc in next sc. In next sc, work sc **in back lp** and mark front lp (*use marker different from beg of rnd*). * Work 2 sc in next sc, sc in next sc; rep from * 3 times more. In next sc, work 2 sc **in back lp** and mark front lp. Sc in next sc, 2 sc in next sc, sc in last sc = 24 sc.

Rnds 4 through 7: Work 4 rnds even. At end of last rnd, do not finish off. Continue with white (peach) and work skirt as follows.

SKIRT: Before beginning next rnd, mark front lp of first sc (*use marker different from beg of rnd*) for working bodice edging later.

Rnd 1: Work (sc, ch 2) for bride or (sc, ch 1) for bridesmaid in marked lp and **in front lp** of each rem sc around (*back lps are used later for underskirt*).

Rnd 2: * Sc in next ch-sp, ch 2 for bride or ch 1 for bridesmaid; rep from * around.

Rep Rnd 2, ten times for bride or six times for bridesmaid.

For bridesmaid only: Rep Rnd 2, twice more, substituting ch 2 for ch 1 (10 rnds total).

Edging: Work (sc, ch 3) twice in each ch-sp around; join with a sl st **in both lps** of beg sc. Finish off; weave in end.

BODICE EDGING: Hold work with head to your left and skirt to your right. With white (peach), make a slip knot on hook. Join with a sc in marked lp at waist (*insert hook under lp from right to left*). Working directly to the left of last st worked in unused (*front*) lp of sts, work (ch 4, sc) in each rnd across center front to last white (peach) rnd at neck. Continue edging around neck. With head away from you, work (ch 4, sc) in front (*unused*) lp of each st around last rnd of white (peach) at neck. Finish off; weave end into front edging. Weave in other end of edging at waist.

UNDERSKIRT: Hold work with head toward you; fold skirt over at waist, bringing skirt back toward you. With white (peach), make a slip knot on hook.

Rnd 1: Join with a sc at center back in unused (*back*) lp of st. You will be working in last rnd of bodice (*front lps were used for skirt*). Sc in unused lp of each rem st around = 24 sc. (*NOTE: Mark first st of rnd; do not join rnds. Continue to work in back lp of sts.*)

Rnd 2: * Sc in each of next 3 sc, 2 sc in next sc; rep from * around = 30 sc.

Rnd 3: Work even.

Rnd 4: * Sc in each of next 4 sc, 2 sc in next sc; rep from * around = 36 sc.

Rnds 5 and 6: Work 2 rnds even.

Rnd 7: * Sc in each of next 5 sc, 2 sc in next sc; rep from * around = 42 sc.

Rnds 8 through 12: Work 5 rnds even.

Rnd 13 (edging): Work (ch 2, sc) **in front lp** of each sc around (*back lps will be used to work base*). Do not finish off; continue as follows.

BASE: Rnd 1: Hold bottom edging just worked back toward you. Work sc in unused (*back*) lp of each st around = 42 sc. (*NOTE: Mark first st of rnd; do not join rnds. Continue by working in back lp of sts.*) Insert 4″ styrofoam cone inside of dress, having tip of cone at neck.

Rnd 2: Sc in each of next 2 sc, * sk one sc, sc in each of next 3 sc; rep from * around = 32 sc.

Rnd 3: * Sk one sc, sc in each of next 3 sc; rep from * around = 24 sc.

Rnd 4: * Sk one sc, sc in each of next 2 sc; rep from * around = 16 sc.

Rnd 5: * Sk one sc, sc in next sc; rep from * around = 8 sc.

Rnd 6: * Sk one sc, sl st in next sc; rep from * around = 4 sl sts. Finish off, leaving approx 4″ end. Thread into tapestry needle; weave through sts of last rnd. Draw up tightly and fasten securely.

SLEEVES (*make 2*): With white (peach), leave approx 12″ end for sewing sleeve to dress later, ch 10; join with a sl st to form a ring.

Rnd 1: Sc in each ch around = 10 sc. (*NOTE: Mark first st of rnd; do not join rnds.*)

Rnd 2: Sc **in both lps** of each sc around.

Rnds 3 through 9: Rep Rnd 2, 7 times.

Rnd 10 (edging): Work (sc, ch 4) **in front lp** of each sc around (*back lps will be used to work hand*). Join with a sl st **in both lps** of beg sc. Finish off; weave in end.

HANDS (*make 2*): Hold sleeve edging just worked back toward you. With gray, make a slip knot on hook.

Rnd 1: Join with a sc **in unused (back) lp** of any sc *(behind edging).* Sc in unused lp of each rem sc around = 10 sc.

Rnd 2: Sc **in both lps** of each sc around.

Rnd 3: * Sk one sc, sc **in both lps** of next sc; rep from * around = 5 sc. Finish off in same manner as base. *(NOTE: At end of 2nd sleeve and hand, tack end of both hands tog before finishing off.)*

Attach each sleeve to dress as follows. Thread beg sewing length into tapestry needle. Sew beg edge of sleeve closed *(do not stuff sleeve).* Then sew this edge to side of dress, having top edge of sleeve at marker.

TAIL: With gray, ch 24. Work sc in 2nd ch from hook and in each rem ch across. Finish off, leaving approx 14″ sewing length. Thread into tapestry needle; sew length of tail closed, having wrong side of sts to outside of tail. Continue with same sewing length and attach tail to underskirt at center back, approx 5 rnds down from waist.

LEFT EAR: With gray, ch 6. Work sc in 2nd ch from hook *(bottom of ear)*; work (hdc, dc) in next ch, 2 tr in next ch; work (2 tr, dc) in next ch, work (hdc, sc) in last ch *(top of ear).* Finish off, leaving approx 8″ sewing length. Thread into tapestry needle and sew ear to left side of head as shown in photo, slightly cupping ear toward front of mouse.

RIGHT EAR: With gray, ch 6. Work (sc, hdc) in 2nd ch from hook *(top of ear)*; work (dc, 2 tr) in next ch, 2 tr in next ch; work (dc, hdc) in next ch, sc in last ch *(bottom of ear).* Finish off and sew to right side of head in same manner as other ear.

MUZZLE: With gray, make two ½″ diameter pompons. [*NOTE: To make small pompon: Wrap yarn around finger (index or middle) approx 18 times. Slip yarn off finger, holding strands tog. With single strand of yarn (approx 10″ long), tie strands tog at center. Cut looped ends and trim to desired size.*] Attach pompons side by side to lower center front of head, approx 3 to 4 rnds above neck.

NOSE: With pink, ch 3, sl st in 3rd ch from hook. Finish off, leaving approx 4″ end. Push wrong side of chs to outside of nose, making a small puff. Attach to head between and at top of pompons.

WHISKERS: Cut 3 strands of white, each 2″ long. With crochet hook, pull each strand through front of face, under nose. Trim ends to desired equal lengths on each side of nose.

EYES AND EAR LININGS: Trace outlines in *Fig 2* on paper. Cut outlines and use as patterns on felt. (*NOTE: To prevent pattern piece from slipping on felt, tape piece on felt with cellophane tape. Cut*

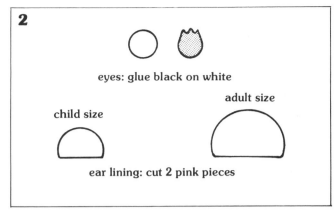

2

eyes: glue black on white

adult size

child size

ear lining: cut 2 pink pieces

felt piece through tape; then discard tape.) With glue, attach felt pieces as shown in photo.

BUTTONS: Insert straight pins, 6 white-head for bride or 4 yellow-head for bridesmaid, evenly spaced down front center edging of bodice.

VEIL: Beg at top, with white (peach), ch 16; join with a sl st to form a ring, being careful not to twist sts.

Rnd 1 (right side): Work (ch 2, sc) in each ch around, join with a sl st in beg ch-2 sp. Continue veil by working back and forth in rows as follows.

Row 1: Ch 3, turn; work (sc, ch 2) in each of first 6 ch-sps, sc in next ch-sp. Leave rem ch-sps unworked for front of crown.

Row 2: Ch 3, turn; work (sc, ch 2) in each of 6 ch-sps across, sc in sp under turning ch.

Rep Row 2, 7 times for bride or once more for bridesmaid.

Edging: Ch 1, turn; work (sc, ch 3) twice in each of 6 ch-sps across, work (sc, ch 3, sc) in sp under turning ch. Finish off; weave in ends. Place veil on head, having crown on top of head slightly overlapping top edge of ears. Insert 5 white (yellow) head straight pins evenly spaced across front of crown.

BOUQUET DOILY: With white, ch 6, join with a sl st to form a ring.

Rnd 1: Ch 1, work 10 sc in ring; join with a sl st **in both lps** of beg sc. Continue by working **in both lps** of each sc as follows.

Rnd 2: Ch 1, sc in same st as joining, 2 sc in next sc; * sc in next sc, 2 sc in next sc; rep from * around, join with a sl st **in both lps** of beg sc = 15 sc.

Rnd 3 (edging): Work (ch 4, sc) in each sc around, ch 4, join with a sl st in first ch of beg ch-4. Finish off; weave in ends. Place flower stems through center hole of doily, having right side of doily facing flowers. Twist stems and secure in place. Place bouquet in hands of mouse and secure with thread or straight pin.

FLOWER GIRL

Before proceeding, read General Instructions.

HEAD: Beg at top, with gray, ch 4; join with a sl st to form a ring.

Rnd 1: Work 2 sc in each ch around = 8 sc. (*NOTE: Mark first st of rnd; do not join rnds. Continue by working in back lp of sts.*)

Rnd 2: Work 2 sc in each sc around = 16 sc.

Rnds 3 through 5: Work 3 rnds even.

Rnd 6: * Sc in next sc, 2 sc in next sc; rep from * around = 24 sc.

Rnds 7 through 9: Work 3 rnds even.

Rnd 10: * Sk one sc, sc in next sc; rep from * around, changing to yellow in last sc = 12 sc. Lightly stuff and shape head. Continue with yellow and work dress as follows.

BODICE: Rnd 1: Work even **in back lp** of sts = 12 sc.

Rnd 2: * Sc in next sc, 2 sc in next sc; rep from * around = 18 sc.

Rnd 3 (marking rnd): (*NOTE: In this rnd, 2 sts are marked for sewing sleeves to dress later.*) Sc in each of next 4 sc. In next sc, sc **in back lp** and mark front lp (*use marker different from beg of rnd*). Sc in each of next 8 sc. In next sc, sc **in back lp** and mark front lp. Sc in each of rem 4 sc.

Rnd 4: Sc in each of next 2 sc, * 2 sc in next sc, sc in each of next 3 sc; rep from * around = 22 sc.

Rnd 5: Work even. Do not finish off; continue as follows.

SKIRT: Before beginning next rnd, mark front lp of first sc (*use marker different from beg of rnd*) for working bodice edging later.

Rnd 1: Work (sc, ch 1) in marked lp and **in front lp** of each rem sc around (*back lps are used later for underskirt*).

Rnd 2: * Sc in next ch-sp, ch 1; rep from * around.

Rnds 3 through 6: Rep Rnd 2, 4 times.

Rnd 7: * Sc in next ch-sp, ch 2; rep from * around.

Rnd 8: Rep Rnd 7 to last ch-sp; sc in last ch-sp, changing to peach. Join with a sl st **in both lps** of beg sc.

Rnd 9 (edging): Continuing with peach, work (sc, ch 2) twice in each ch-sp around, join with a sl st **in both lps** of beg sc. Finish off; weave in end.

BODICE EDGING: With peach, work in same manner as bride and bridesmaid, substituting ch 3 for each ch 4.

UNDERSKIRT: Hold work with head toward you; fold skirt over at waist, bringing skirt back toward you. With yellow, make a slip knot on hook.

Rnd 1: Join with a sc at center back in unused (*back*) lp of st. You will be working in last rnd of bodice (*front lps were used for skirt*). Sc in unused lp of each rem st around = 22 sc. (*NOTE: Remember to mark first st of rnd; do not join rnds. Continue by working in back lp of sts.*)

Rnds 2 and 3: Work 2 rnds even.

Rnd 4: Sc in each of next 2 sc, * 2 sc in next sc, sc in each of next 3 sc; rep from * around = 27 sc.

Rnds 5 through 9: Work 5 rnds even. At end of last rnd, change to peach in last sc. (*Drop yellow; do not cut—will be used later for base.*)

Rnd 10 (edging): Work (sc, ch 2) **in front lp** of each sc around to last sc; sc **in front lp** of last sc, join with a sl st **in both lps** of beg sc. Finish off peach; weave in end.

BASE: Rnd 1: Hold bottom edging just worked back toward you. Continuing with yellow, work sc in unused (back) lp of each st around = 27 sc. (*NOTE: Mark first st of rnd; do not join rnds. Continue by working in back lp of sts.*) Insert 3″ styrofoam cone inside of dress, having tip of cone at neck.

Rnd 2: * Sk one sc, sc in each of next 2 sc; rep from * around = 18 sc.

Rnd 3: * Sk one sc, sc in next sc; rep from * around = 9 sc.

Rnd 4: Sl st in next sc, * sk one sc, sl st in next sc;

rep from * around = 5 sl sts. Finish off in same manner as bride.

SLEEVES (make 2): With yellow, leave approx 10″ end for sewing sleeve to dress later, ch 8; join with a sl st to form a ring.

Rnd 1: Sc in each ch around = 8 sc. (*NOTE: Mark first st of rnd; do not join rnds.*)

Rnd 2: Sc **in both lps** of each sc around.

Rnds 3 through 7: Rep Rnd 2, 5 times. At end of last rnd, change to peach in last sc for edging.

Rnd 8 (edging): Work (sc, ch 2) **in front lp** of each sc around (*back lps will be used to work hand*). Join with a sl st **in both lps** of beg sc. Finish off; weave in end.

HANDS (make 2): Work same as bride and bridesmaid, having 8 sc in Rnds 1 and 2 and 4 sc at end of Rnd 3. (*NOTE: At end of 2nd sleeve and hand, do not tack end of both hands tog.*) Attach sleeves to dress in same manner as bride and bridesmaid.

TAIL: With gray, ch 18. Work sc in 2nd ch from hook and in each rem ch across. Finish off, sew length of tail closed and then sew to underskirt at center back, approx 4 rnds down from waist, in same manner as bride and bridesmaid.

LEFT EAR: With gray, ch 5. Work sc in 2nd ch from hook (*bottom of ear*); work (hdc, dc) in next ch, 2 tr in next ch; work (dc, hdc, sc) in last ch (*top of ear*). Finish off and sew to left side of head in same manner as bride and bridesmaid.

RIGHT EAR: With gray, ch 5. Work (sc, hdc, dc) in 2nd ch from hook (*top of ear*); work 2 tr in next ch, work (dc hdc) in next ch, sc in last ch (*bottom of ear*). Finish off and sew to right side of head in same manner as other ear.

MUZZLE: With gray, make two ⅜″ diameter pompons and attach side by side to lower center front of head.

NOSE: Make and attach to head in same manner as bride and bridesmaid.

WHISKERS: Same as bride and bridesmaid.

EYES AND EAR LININGS: Work in same manner as bride and bridesmaid.

BUTTONS: Insert 3 yellow-head straight pins evenly spaced down front center edging of bodice.

BOW: Cut 6″ strand of yellow. Use crochet hook and pull through st at top of head. Tie into a bow; trim ends.

BASKET: With white, ch 4, join with a sl st to form a ring.

Rnd 1: Work 8 sc in ring. (*NOTE: Mark first st of rnd; do not join rnds.*)

Rnd 2: Work 2 sc **in both lps** of each sc around = 16 sc.

Rnd 3: Rep Rnd 2 = 32 sc.

Rnd 4: Work hdc **in both lps** of each sc around to last sc, sc **in both lps** of last sc. Join with a sl st **in both lps** of beg hdc. Do not finish off; ch 10 for handle, sk next 15 sts, sl st in next sc. Finish off; weave in ends. Place basket over right arm just above sleeve edging. Fill basket with flowers. Sew or pin basket in place. Place single flower in left hand by inserting stem of flower into hand.

GROOM AND BEST MAN

Before proceeding read General Instructions. Groom and best man are worked in same manner; color changes for best man are written in parentheses.

HEAD: Work same as bride and bridesmaid. At end of last rnd (*Rnd 11*), change to white (peach) in last sc for shirt collar. Lightly stuff and shape head.

SHIRT COLLAR: With white (peach), work as follows **in front lp** of each st (*back lps will be used to work jacket and shirt*). In first st, work (sl st, ch 2) **in front lp** and mark back lp (*use marker different from beg of rnd*) for working jacket later. Hdc in each of next 3 sts, work (2 dc, hdc) in next st, sl st in next st (*center front*); work (hdc, 2 dc, hdc) in next st, hdc in each of rem 4 sts. Join with a sl st in top of beg ch-2. Finish off; weave in end.

JACKET AND SHIRT: Hold shirt collar back toward you. With black, make a sl knot on hook.

Rnd 1: Working **in unused (back) lp** of each sc (*behind collar*), join with a sc in marked lp; * 2 sc in next sc, sc in next sc; rep from * around = 16 sc. (*NOTE: Mark first st of rnd; do not join rnds. Continue by working in back lp of sts.*)

Rnd 2: (*NOTE: Beginning on this rnd, you will be changing colors for shirt at front of mouse. Always change colors in st before new color begins. Do not finish off colors; bring color loosely across back of work.*) With black, work (sc in next sc, 2 sc in next sc) twice, sc in each of next 2 sc. With white (peach) (*remember to change colors in prev sc*), sc in same st (*where prev sc was just worked*); work (sc in next sc, 2 sc in next sc) twice. With black (*bring yarn loosely across back of work*), work (sc in next sc, 2 sc in next sc) 3 times = 24 sc.

Rnd 3 (marking rnd): (*NOTE: In this rnd, 2 sts are marked for sewing sleeves to jacket later.*) With black, sc in each of next 5 sc. In next sc, work sc **in back lp** and mark front lp. Sc in each of next 3 sc. With white (peach) [*bring yarn back toward you across back of work*], sc in each of next 5 sc. With black, sc in each of next 3 sc. In next sc, work sc **in back lp** and mark front lp. Sc in each of rem 6 sc.

Rnd 4: With black, sc in each of next 9 sc. With white (peach), sc in each of next 5 sc. With black, sc in each of rem 10 sc.

Rnd 5: With black, sc in each of next 10 sc. With white (peach), sc in each of next 3 sc. With black, sc in each of rem 11 sc.

Rnd 6: Rep Rnd 5.

Rnd 7: With black, work (sc in each of next 3 sc, 2 sc in next sc) twice; sc in each of next 3 sc. With white (peach), 2 sc in next sc. With black, work (sc in each of next 3 sc, 2 sc in next sc) 3 times = 30 sc.

Rnds 8 through 11: Continuing with black only [finish off white (peach)], work 4 rnds even. At end of last rnd, work sl st **in both lps** of last sc (instead of sc in back lp).

EDGING: Ch 4, turn. With head away from you, work **in back lp** (*lp away from you*) of sts (*front lps are used later for pants*) as follows. Sk sl st, 3 tr in next st, dc in each of next 15 sts; work (dc, hdc, sc) in next sc.

Continue edging up front center of jacket. Hold work with head to your left and last sts worked to your right. Working directly to the left of last sts worked in unused (*front*) lp of sts, work sl st in each of next 3 rnds. You should now be directly below right lower st of shirt (**Fig 3**).

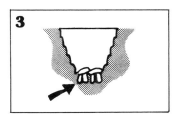

Continue edging for left lapel. Working in left end st of each rnd of shirt, beg in next st to the right (*above*) and work sc in each of next 3 rnds; hdc in next rnd, dc in next rnd, 2 dc in next rnd. Work 3 dc in next black rnd at neck.

Continue edging around neck for collar. With head toward you, work dc in unused (*front*) lp of each st around neck to st directly above right end st of shirt. (*NOTE: Be careful to work collar directly below shirt collar, especially where work jogs at end of rnd.*) Work 3 dc in next st.

Continue edging for right lapel. Working in right end st of each rnd of shirt, 2 dc in next rnd, dc in next rnd; hdc in next rnd, sc in each of next 3 rnds. Finish off; weave end into center edging.

Continue edging around bottom edge. Hold work with head away from you. Join black with a sl st in same lp where (dc, hdc, sc) were worked at lower edge of center front. Ch 2, hdc in same st as joining; dc **in back lp** of each rem st around to last st, work (3 tr, ch 3, sl st) all **in back lp** of last st. Finish off; weave end into other tail of jacket and secure tails to outside of jacket. Weave end at bottom edge of center front into edging, closing gap at bottom.

PANTS: Hold work with head toward you; fold bottom edging of jacket back toward you. With gray, make a slip knot on hook.

Rnd 1: Join with a sc in unused lp of any st behind edging. Sc in unused lp of each rem st around = 30 sc. (*NOTE: Mark first st of rnd; do not join rnds. Continue by working in back lp of sts.*) Insert 2½" styrofoam egg inside of jacket, having smaller end at neck.

Rnd 2: * Sk one sc, sc in each of next 2 sc; rep from * around = 20 sc.

Rnd 3: Work even.

Rnd 4: * Sk one sc, sc in next sc; rep from * around = 10 sc.

Rnd 5: * Sk one sc, sl st in next sc; rep from * around = 5 sl sts. Finish off in same manner as base of bride and bridesmaid. Push up shirt and jacket collars at back of neck.

PANTS LEGS (make 2): With gray, leave approx 12" sewing length, ch 10; join with sl st to form a ring.

Rnd 1: Sc in each ch around = 10 sc. *(NOTE: Do not join rnds; mark first st of rnd and move marker at beg of each rnd.)*

Rnd 2: Sc **in both lps** of each sc around.

Rnds 3 through 8: Rep Rnd 2, 6 times.

Rnd 9 (edging): Sc **in front lp** of each sc around *(back lps will be used for foot)*. Join with a sl st **in both lps** of beg sc. Finish off; weave in end.

FEET *(make 2):* Fold bottom edging just worked back toward you. With gray, make a sl knot on hook.

Rnd 1: Join with a sc in unused lp of any st *(behind edging)*. Sc in unused lp of each rem st around = 10 sc. *(Do not join rnds.)*

Rnd 2: * Sk one sc, sc **in both lps** of next sc; rep from * 3 times, sc **in both lps** in each of rem 2 sc = 6 sc.

Rnd 3: Hold metal washer at top of rnd and work the following sts over outside ring of washer as follows. Work 2 sc **in both lps** of each sc around = 12 sc. Join with a sl st **in both lps** of beg sc. Finish off; weave in end.

Attach to body as follows. Insert 3″ nail into bottom of each foot and up through center of leg. Then insert tip of nail into bottom of mouse, positioning for best balance. Sew top edge of pants legs to bottom of mouse.

TRIM *(make 2):* With black, ch 10. Finish off, leaving approx 6″ sewing length. Sew to length of pant leg, at outer side, having wrong side of chain facing you.

SLEEVES *(make 2):* With black, work same as bride and bridesmaid through Rnd 9.

Rnd 10 (edging): Sc **in front lp** of each sc around *(back lps will be used for hand)*. Join with a sl st **in both lps** of beg sc. Finish off; weave in end.

HANDS *(make 2):* Work same as bride and bridesmaid. *(NOTE: At end of 2nd sleeve and hand, do not tack end of both hands tog.)* Attach to jacket in same manner as bride and bridesmaid.

TAIL AND EARS: Work same as bride and bridesmaid.

MUZZLE, NOSE AND WHISKERS: Work same as bride and bridesmaid, substituting black *(instead of pink)* for nose.

EYES, EYEBROWS AND EAR LININGS: Using outlines in *Fig 4*, work in same manner as bride and bridesmaid. Attach eyebrows only on groom.

BUTTONS: Insert 3 white-(yellow-) head straight

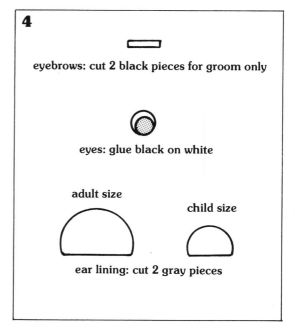

4

eyebrows: cut 2 black pieces for groom only

eyes: glue black on white

adult size

child size

ear lining: cut 2 gray pieces

pins evenly spaced down center front of shirt. Insert 2 black-head straight pins evenly spaced down lower center front of jacket. Insert black-head straight pin through end of each sleeve at lower outside edge above sleeve edging and then into jacket.

BOW TIE: Cut 6″ strand of black. With crochet hook, pull strand through front center black st below shirt collar and tie into a small bow. Trim ends to approx ¼″ in length.

BOUTONNIERE: Attach a single flower to left lapel, securing with thread or straight pin *(insert through center of flower and then into jacket)*.

MINISTER

Before proceeding, read General Instructions.

HEAD: Work same as bride and bridesmaid. At end of last rnd *(Rnd 11)*, change to white in last sc for collar. Lightly stuff and shape head.

COLLAR: Continuing with white, work 2 rnds even *(11 sc in each rnd)*. At end of last rnd, change to black in last sc for jacket.

JACKET: Rnd 1: Sc in next sc, * 2 sc in next sc, sc in each of next 2 sc; rep from * to last sc, 2 sc in last sc = 15 sc.

Rnd 2: * Sc in each of next 2 sc, 2 sc in next sc; rep from * around = 20 sc.

Rnd 3 (marking rnd): *(NOTE: In this rnd, 2 sts are marked for sewing sleeves to jacket later.)* Sc in each of next 3 sc, 2 sc in next sc, sc in each of next 2 sc. In

next sc, sc **in back lp** and mark front lp. * Work 2 sc in next sc, sc in each of next 3 sc; rep from * once more. Work 2 sc in next sc, sc in next sc. In next sc, work sc **in back lp** and mark front lp. Sc in next sc, 2 sc in last sc = 25 sc.

Rnd 4: * Sc in each of next 4 sc, 2 sc in next sc; rep from * around = 30 sc.

Rnds 5 through 9: Work 5 rnds even.

Rnd 10: * Sc in each of next 5 sc, 2 sc in next sc; rep from * around = 35 sc.

Rnds 11 through 13: Work 3 rnds even. At end of last rnd, work sl st in last sc (instead of sc).

EDGING: Ch 4, turn. With head away from you, work **in back lp** of sts (*front lps are used later for pants*) as follows. Work 3 tr in next st, dc in each of next 15 sts, work (dc, hdc, sc) in next st.

Continue edging up front center of jacket. Hold work with head to your left and last sts worked to your right. Working directly to the left of last sts worked in unused (*front*) lp of sts, work sl st in each of next 9 rnds.

Continue edging for left lapel. Work (sc, hdc, dc) in next rnd one st to the right (*above*). Dc in next rnd above. Work 3 dc in next rnd, one st to the right (*above*).

Continue edging around neck for collar. With head toward you, work dc in unused (*front*) lp of each st around neck to within 4 sts of left lapel. Work 3 dc in next st. (*Leave 3 sts at front of neck unworked.*)

Continue edging for right lapel. Having one st between lapels, work dc in next rnd. Working in st next to other lapel, work (dc, hdc, sc) in next rnd. Finish off; weave end into front edging.

Continue edging around bottom edge. Hold work with head away from you. Join black with a sl st in same lp where (dc, hdc, sc) were worked at lower edge of center front. Ch 2, hdc in same lp; dc **in back lp** of each rem st around to last st; work (3 tr, ch 3, sl st) **in back lp** of last st. Finish off; weave end into other tail and secure tails to outside of jacket.

Weave end at bottom edge of center front into edging, closing gap at bottom.

PANTS: Hold work with head toward you; fold bottom edging of jacket back toward you. With black, make a slip knot on hook.

Rnd 1: Join with a sc in unused lp of any st behind edging. Sc in unused lp of each rem st around = 35 sc. (*NOTE: Mark first st of rnd; do not join rnds. Continue by working in back lp of sts.*) Insert 3" styrofoam egg inside of jacket, having smaller end at neck.

Rnd 2: Sk one sc, sc in next sc; * sk one sc, sc in each of next 2 sc; rep from * around = 23 sc.

Rnd 3: Work even.

Rnd 4: Sc in next sc * sk one sc, sc in next sc; rep from * around = 12 sc.

Rnd 5: * Sk one sc, sl st in next sc; rep from * around = 6 sl sts. Finish off in same manner as base of bride and bridesmaid. Push up jacket collar at back of neck.

PANTS LEGS AND FEET (*make 2*): Work same as groom and best man, excluding side trim on pants legs.

SLEEVES AND HANDS (*make 2*): Work same as groom and best man. At end of 2nd sleeve and hand, tack end of both hands tog. Sew to jacket in same manner as groom and best man.

TAIL AND EARS: Work same as bride and bridesmaid.

MUZZLE, NOSE AND WHISKERS: Work same as groom and best man.

EYES AND EAR LININGS: Work same as groom and best man.

EYEGLASSES: Following diagram in **Fig 5**, bend wire around pencil to form the loops of the glasses. Place glasses on head, slightly below eyes; insert ends of wire into head to secure.

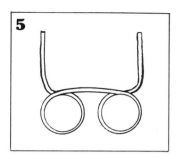

5

BUTTONS: Insert 2 rows each of 5 black-head straight pins evenly spaced down front center of jacket (one on each side of center edging).

THE GOOD BOOK: For cover, cut a piece of black felt, 1¾" × 1½". Fold in half the long way. Then cut a piece of white paper just slightly smaller; fold in half in same manner and glue to inside of cover. Place book in minister's joined hands.

RING BEARER

Before proceeding, read General Instructions.

HEAD: Work same as flower girl, changing to yellow in last sc of Rnd 10 for shirt collar. Lightly stuff and shape head.

SHIRT COLLAR: With yellow, work as follows **in front lp** of each st (*back lps will be used to work jacket and shirt*). In first st, work (sl st, ch 1, sc) **in front lp** and mark back lp (*use marker different from beg of rnd*) for working jacket later. Sc in each of next 3 sts, work (2 hdc, sc) in next st; sl st in next st (*center front*); work (sc, 2 hdc, sc) in next st, sc in each of rem 5 sts; join with a sl st **in both lps** of beg sc. Finish off; weave in end.

JACKET AND SHIRT: Hold shirt collar back toward you. With black, make a sl knot on hook.

Rnd 1: Working **in unused (back) lp** of each sc (*behind collar*), join with a sc in marked lp, sc in unused lp of each rem st around = 12 sc. (*NOTE: Mark first st of rnd; do not join rnds. Continue by working in back lp of sts.*)

Rnd 2: (*NOTE: Beginning on this rnd, you will be changing colors for shirt at front of mouse. Always change colors in st before new color begins. Do not finish off colors; bring color loosely across back of work.*) With black, sc in next sc, 2 sc in next sc, sc in each of next 2 sc. With yellow (*remember to change colors in prev sc*), sc in same st (*where prev sc was just worked*); sc in next sc, 2 sc in next sc, sc in next sc. With black, 2 sc in next sc, work (sc in next sc, 2 sc in next sc) twice = 18 sc.

Rnd 3 (marking rnd): (*NOTE: In this rnd, 2 sts are marked for sewing sleeves to jacket later.*) With black, sc in each of next 3 sc. In next sc, work sc **in back lp** and mark front lp. Sc in each of next 2 sc. With yellow, sc in each of next 3 sc. With black, sc in each of next 2 sc. In next sc, work sc **in back lp** and mark front lp. Sc in each of rem 6 sc.

Rnd 4: With black, sc in each of next 6 sc. With yellow, sc in each of next 3 sc. With black, sc in each of rem 9 sc.

Rnd 5: With black, sc in each of next 2 sc, 2 sc in next sc; sc in each of next 2 sc, sc in next sc. With yellow, sc in same st (*where prev sc was just worked*), sc in next sc. With black, sc in next sc, 2 sc in next sc; work (sc in each of next 2 sc, 2 sc in next sc) 3 times = 24 sc.

Rnd 6: With black, sc in each of next 7 sc. With yellow, sc in each of next 2 sc. With black, sc in each of rem 15 sc.

Rnd 7: Continuing with black only (*finish off yellow*), work 2 rnds even.

EDGING: Sl st **in front lp** of next sc; ch 2, turn. With head away from you, work **in back lp** of sts (*front lps are used later for pants*) as follows. Hdc in each of next 3 sts, work (3 dc, ch 2, sl st) in next st; work (sl st, ch 2, 3 dc) in next st, hdc in each of next 12 sts; work (2 hdc, sc) in next st.

Continue edging up front center for jacket. Hold work with head to your left and last sts worked to your right. Work sl st in unused lp of st in next rnd directly to the left of last sts worked. You should now be directly below right lower st of shirt.

Continue edging for left lapel. Working in left end st of each rnd of shirt, beg in next st to the right (*above*) and work sc in each of next 2 rnds, hdc in each of next 2 rnds, 2 hdc in next rnd. Work 3 hdc in next black rnd.

Continue edging around neck for collar. With head toward you, work hdc in unused (*front*) lp of each st around neck to st directly above right end st of shirt. (*NOTE: Be careful to work collar directly below shirt collar, especially where work jogs at end of rnd.*) Work 3 hdc in next st.

Continue edging for right lapel. Working in right end st of each rnd of shirt, 2 hdc in next rnd, hdc in each of next 2 rnds, sc in each of next 2 rnds. Finish off; weave end into center edging.

Continue edging around bottom edge. Hold work with head away from you. Join black with a sl st in same lp where (2 hdc, sc) were worked at lower edge of center front. Ch 1, hdc in back lp of each rem st around; hdc in next st at base of beg ch-2. Join with a sl st in top of beg ch-2. Finish off; weave in end and tack tails to outside of jacket. Weave end at bottom edge of center front into edging, closing gap at bottom.

PANTS: Hold work with head toward you; fold bottom edging of jacket back toward you. With gray, make a slip knot on hook.

Rnd 1: Join with a sc in unused lp of any st (*behind edging*). Sc in unused lp of each rem st around = 24 sc. (*NOTE: Mark first st of rnd; do not join rnds. Continue by working in back lp of sts.*) Insert 2″ styrofoam egg inside of jacket, having smaller end at neck.

Rnd 2: * Sk one sc, sc in each of next 2 sc; rep from * around = 16 sc.

Rnd 3: * Sk one sc, sc in next sc; rep from * around = 8 sc.

Rnd 4: * Sk one sc, sl st in next sc; rep from * around = 4 sl sts. Finish off in same manner as base of bride and bridesmaid. Push up shirt and jacket collars at back of neck.

PANTS LEGS: (*make 2*): With gray, leave approx 12″ sewing length, ch 8; join with a sl st to form a ring.

Rnd 1: Sc in each ch around = 8 sc. (*NOTE: Mark first st of rnd; do not join rnds.*)

Rnd 2: Sc **in both lps** of each sc around.

Rnds 3 through 6: Rep Rnd 2, 4 times.

Rnd 7 (edging): Sc **in front lp** of each sc around (*back lps will be used for foot*). Join with a sl st **in both lps** of beg sc. Finish off; weave in end.

FEET (*make 2*): Fold bottom edging just worked back toward you. With gray, make a slip knot on hook.

Rnd 1: Join with a sc in unused lp of any st (*behind edging*). Sc in unused lp of each rem st around = 8 sc. (*Do not join rnds.*)

Rnd 2: Hold metal washer at top of rnd and work the following sts over outside ring of washer as follows. Ch 1, * 2 sc in next sc, sc in next sc; rep from * around = 12 sc. Join with a sl st **in both lps** of beg sc. Finish off; weave in end. Attach to bottom of mouse in same manner as groom and best man, substituting 2½″ nails for 3″ nails.

SLEEVES (*make 2*): With black, work same as flower girl through Rnd 7.

Rnd 8 (edging): Continuing with black, work sc in **in front lp** of each sc around (*back lps will be used for hand*). Join with a sl st **in both lps** of beg sc. Finish off; weave in end.

HANDS (*make 2*): Work same as flower girl. At end of 2nd sleeve and hand, sew end of both hands tog. Attach to jacket in same manner as bride and bridesmaid.

TAIL, EARS, MUZZLE, NOSE AND WHISKERS: Work same as flower girl, substituting black (*instead of pink*) for nose.

EYES AND EAR LININGS: Work same as groom and best man (*do not attach eyebrows*).

BOW TIE AND BOUTONNIERE: Work same as groom and best man.

BUTTONS: Insert 2 yellow-head straight pins evenly spaced down front center of shirt.

RING PILLOW: Beg at center front, with white, ch 4; join with a sl st to form a ring.

Rnd 1: Work 2 sc in each ch around = 8 sc. (*Do not join rnds.*)

Rnd 2: * Work 2 sc **in back lp** of next sc, sc **in back lp** of next sc; rep from * around = 12 sc.

Rnd 3 (edging): Work (sc, ch 2) **in front lp** of each sc around (*back lps are used on next rnd for back of pillow*).

Rnd 4: Sc **in back lp** of each st around (*behind edging*) = 12 sc.

Rnd 5: * Sk one sc, sc **in both lps** of next sc; rep from * around = 6 sc. Finish off in same manner as base of bride and bridesmaid.

RIBBON: Cut 8″ strand of peach. Weave strand through ch-2 sps of edging rnd, beg and ending at end of rnd. Tie into a bow and trim ends evenly. Attach 2 jump rings to top of pillow for wedding rings. Place pillow on top of ring bearer's hands; sew or pin pillow in place.

GOLDFISH MOBILE

This delightful project is fun to make and even more fun to watch as it moves in the wind. Just be sure to keep the family cat away!

Size

Each fish measures approx 4″ long

Materials:

American Thread Dawn Sayelle Knitting Worsted Size Yarn:

> 1½ oz each of lemon, orange, copper, hot orange and shaded oranges

Size G aluminum crochet hook (or size required for gauge)
Polyester fiber (*for stuffing*)
Two 18″ Dowels (¼″ diameter), painted bright yellow or in color of your choice
42 gold sequins (8 mm diameter) for eyes
42 orange facet beads (6 mm diameter) for eyes
Orange sewing thread (*for attaching sequins and beads*)
Nylon translucent thread or fishing line (*for stringing*)
Plastic ring (1″ diameter)

Gauge

In sc, 4 sts = 1″; 4 rows = 1″

Instructions

Make 5 fish with orange; then make 4 fish in each of the following colors: hot orange, shaded oranges, lemon and copper (21 fish total).

Beg at tail, ch 4.

Row 1: Sc in 2nd ch from hook and in each of next 2 chs = 3 sc.

Row 2: Ch 1, turn; work double loop st in first sc. **[To work double loop st: Insert hook in first sc and draw up a lp (2 lps now on hook); wrap yarn 3 times around tip of left index finger, insert hook in front of yarn and through first 2 lps on finger (*Fig 1*); keeping lps on finger, draw both lps through one lp on hook; bring left index finger down in front of work, sk first 2 lps on finger and insert hook through 3rd lp on finger (*Fig 2*), draw lp through all lps on hook; drop both lps off finger = double loop st made.]** Work another double loop st in same sc; then work 2 double loop sts in each of rem 2 sc = 6 double loop sts.

Row 3: Ch 1, turn; dec over first 2 sts. **[To make**

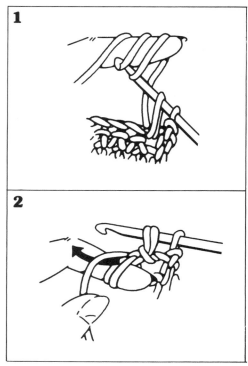

142

dec: Draw up a lp in each of first 2 sts, YO and draw through all 3 lps on hook = dec made.]
* Dec over next 2 sts; rep from * once more = 3 sts.

Row 4: Ch 1, turn; sc in each sc across.

Row 5: Rep Row 4.

Row 6: Ch 1, turn; 2 sc in first sc, sc in next sc, 2 sc in last sc = 5 sc.

Row 7: Rep Row 4.

Row 8: Ch 1, turn; 2 sc in first sc, sc in each of next 3 sc, 2 sc in last sc = 7 sc.

Rows 9 through 11: Rep Row 4, 3 times.

Row 12: Ch 1, turn; dec over first 2 sc, sc in each of next 3 sc, dec over last 2 sc = 5 sc.

Row 13: Ch 1, turn; dec over first 2 sc, sc in next sc, dec over last 2 sc = 3 sc.

Row 14: Ch 1, turn; sk first sc, dec over last 2 sc. Finish off; weave in ends.

Make another piece in same manner. Finish off, leaving approx 20″ sewing length. Thread into tapestry or yarn needle; sew matching edges of both pieces tog with overcast st, leaving a small opening for stuffing. Lightly stuff fish; then sew small opening closed. Weave in ends.

EYES: With orange sewing thread, sew one sequin and one bead (**Fig 3**) on each side of fish as shown in photo.

ASSEMBLING: With lemon, leave approx 10″

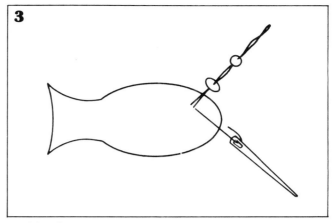

end for fastening center of dowels later, make a slip knot on hook; then work scs around plastic ring to cover. Finish off, leaving approx 10″ end; tie this end and beg end tog. Cross dowels; tie ring securely to crossed dowels at top. Weave ends into sts around ring.

Cut five, 42″ lengths of nylon translucent thread (or fishing line). First, string 4 fish (thread length into sewing needle), 4″ apart on 4 lengths, securing thread at top of each fish with several overcast sts and arranging colors as desired. Then tie end of each stringing length to each end of dowels (approx 1″ from end), having top fish of one length 8″ from dowel, next 4″, next 6″ and next 2″. Last, string 5 fish, 4″ apart on remaining length and attach to center of dowels, having top fish 1″ from dowels.

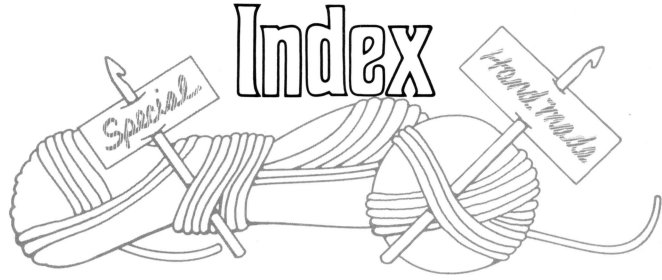

Index